HOPPIN' JOHN'S
LOWCOUNTRY
COOKING

HOPPIN' JOHN'S LOWCOUNTRY COOKING

Recipes and Ruminations from Charleston & the Carolina Coastal Plain

—

John Martin Taylor

BANTAM BOOKS
NEW YORK · TORONTO · LONDON · SYDNEY · AUCKLAND

HOPPIN' JOHN'S LOWCOUNTRY COOKING
A Bantam Book / May 1992

Permissions to quote from copyrighted work may be found on page 333.

BOOK DESIGN BY JOEL AVIROM

PATTERN DESIGN BY BETH KROMMES

Map on p. xiii designed by GDS/Jeffrey L. Ward.

For information address: Bantam Books.

The words "Hoppin' John's" and the portrayal of a chef carrying a tray
of books are the trademark of John Martin Taylor. It is Registered in
U.S. Patent and Trademark Office.

Library of Congress Cataloging-in-Publication Data
Taylor, John Martin, 1949–
    Hoppin' John's lowcountry cooking : recipes and ruminations from
Charleston & the Carolina coastal plain / John Martin Taylor.
        p.   cm.
    Includes bibliographical references and index.
    ISBN 0-553-08231-0
    1. Cookery, American—Southern style.   2. Cookery—South Caro-
lina—Charleston.   3. Charleston (S.C.)—Social life and customs.
I. Title.
TX715.2.S68T39   1992
641.59757—dc20   91-42532
                                                                              CIP

Published simultaneously in the United States and Canada

Bantam Books are published by Bantam Books, a division of Bantam Doubleday Dell Publishing Group, Inc. Its trademark, con-
sisting of the words "Bantam Books" and the portrayal of a rooster,
is Registered in U.S. Patent and Trademark Office and in other
countries. Marca Registrada. Bantam Books, 666 Fifth Avenue,
New York, New York 10103.

PRINTED IN THE UNITED STATES OF AMERICA

RRH   0   9   8   7   6   5   4   3   2   1

For my father

CONTENTS

ACKNOWLEDGMENTS

I am indebted most of all to the good cooks who have influenced me through the years, some of whom I know only through their writings and recipes. My parents and my grandmothers always shared kitchen wisdom with me. My mother was a great cook; I inherited hundreds of cookbooks from her. What I learned from Thom Tillman and Jane Grigson continues to inspire me. I refer to the books of Elizabeth David, Paula Wolfert, and Bill Neal almost daily.

Karen Hess has set the standard for culinary historians; she has forever been generous, sharing her time and sending me photocopies of rare works and her works in progress, often with discoveries that relate directly to my work.

The University of South Carolina Press has republished several old Lowcountry cookbooks. Without them, this work would not exist.

Material for this book came in many forms. It was Verta Grosvenor's *Vibration Cooking, or the Travel Notes of a Geechee Girl,* that first made me aware of the power of the Lowcountry's food and language. She has become a friend and a source of inspiration. Mary Clare Ulmer in Hell Hole Community has shared pickling and cake-making tips; Erlene Davis and Ruth Wooten in Walterboro have taught me about greens and biscuits. Several Lowcountry butchers prepare traditional recipes and have been supportive: thanks to Frank Marvin in Hollywood, Frank McCormack in Ehrhardt, and Foots Brodie in Orangeburg. What I know of rice culture I learned from Dick and Tricia Schulze. Macky Hill knows Berkeley County and the Cooper River plantations like the back of his hand; his family has welcomed me at its Middleburg Plantation many times. Mary Huguenin and I have picked chanterelles at Halidon Hill; she was instrumental in assembling my workhorse, *Charleston Receipts.* I have been greeted warmly in gardens and farms throughout the Lowcountry; Skip and Margaret Madsen have taught me about herbs, and the Limehouses—both the farmers and the food distributors—have helped me find the finest produce. Pink Brown grows the most beautiful and delicious melons and vegetables; the photographer did not doctor them. Vernon Skill has brought me pounds of venison. My friends Debbie Marlowe and Lee Ivey always know the perfect wine to accompany a meal; Debbie has often cooked for me, providing me a break from the kitchen. Marcella Giannasio and Alva Alsbrooks have been wonderful neighbors. And George and Cecilia Holland of Logan Turnpike Farm mill the best grits I know and allow me to call them my own.

Several Charlestonians have given me generous access to their families' manuscript receipt books; Bob Simons and Henrietta Evatt let me keep the yellowed old books for extended periods. Harriet McDougal offered sound advice from early on, then presented me with a gift of a fine rare copy of her grandmother's *Carolina Rice Cook Book* even as she was still digging out from the rubble of the hurricane. Bless her.

The staff of the South Carolina Wildlife and Marine Resources Department has fielded many of my questions relating to salt marshes and seafood. Donna Florio always has a smile and an answer for me. Both Crosby's and Doug's Seafood markets have been helpful. And Allan Raisman of the Waxler Company in Chicago taught me, over the phone, about the many types of herring and how they are cured.

My Yankee girlfriends have been my biggest cheerleaders. Veterans in the publishing industry, they have led this reluctant southerner down all the right paths. Elizabeth (Susie) Schneider; Nancy Harmon Jenkins; my agent, Doe Coover; and my editor, Fran McCullough, are all due my humble thanks. Without them I never would have found a home at Bantam, where Coleen O'Shea believed in my work, even as deadlines passed. Bantam has been wonderful to work with. Special thanks to Chris Benton and Chris Fortunato, and to the photographer Stewart O'Shields and his colleague David Norton.

Much of this material has appeared before in *Omnibus*, Charleston's "alternative" newspaper. Hats off to Pete Wyrick for continuing the paper begun by William van Hettinga.

Nach Waxman gave me his cookbook store idea; he walked me through the literature of food and showed me how to be a businessman, which allowed me to come home to my beloved Lowcountry. I am grateful. Jean-Sébastien Stehli and Laure Olive patronized my art while making me write about food; they are partly responsible for my success.

Alice Marks has been a wonderful friend, bringing me lunch innumerable times. Her generosity of spirit, her laughter, her recipes, and her stamina make her my idea of the quintessential southern woman.

Philip Bardin, Richard Perry, Bill Hughes, Donna Skill, and Sunny Davis are all great cooks and dear friends. They have shared their ideas and their time; they have watched the store while I was writing, and they have helped me check recipes. I could not have written the book without them. Nor without Joann Yaeger, the best cook I know.

Mary Fanning Taylor is due thanks for thirty years of cocktails, laughter, tomato sandwiches, and unconditional love—not to mention the sense she makes out of my hundreds of grocery receipts marked "ingredients."

Kelly Bugden's sweet tooth and friendship are exemplary. A brilliant pastry chef, he patiently taught me his superior technique for making pie-crust. Mark Gray may well be the best confectioner in this country. He has been a good friend and teacher, always kind and generous with his time and recipes.

The McGees, the Earlys, the Foys, and Michael Jordan have shared beachhouses at Edisto with me. They know the relaxation and inspiration that time there provides. The book evolved in their kitchens.

The staffs of the South Carolina Historical Society, the Charleston Museum, and the Charleston County Library have endured me at length. Steve Hoffius of the Historical Society has been exceptionally generous.

Lucille Grant is always willing to share her cooking knowledge with me. In a Lowcountry rampant with shortcuts, canned soups, and micro-waves, she remains a real Lowcountry cook, and I am thankful to have her as a friend.

Finally, I must acknowledge all of my family and friends who have remained supportive and loving in the face of dozens of "regrets"—among them, Adrianne Massey, Mary Edna Fraser, Sally Stafford, Linda Clifford, Scot Hinson, Brigitte Arndt, Bob and Julia Christian, and Douglas and Julia Hunter. My sister Sue has shown an increased interest in cooking, at least partially to show me support; I am tickled. Bessie Hanahan and Libby Demetree would much rather have been partying with me than listening to me call out pounds, cups, and teaspoons. They have been particularly thoughtful. And the B-52's continue to provide a musical background to all I do in the kitchen; my nods to vegetarianism come at the request of Kate Pierson, who has often inspired me to cook meatless versions of many of these dishes. Thank you all.

I worked on this book for several years. In 1989, South Carolina was struck by a disastrous hurricane. Sandlappers—residents of the Lowcoun-try—showed an indomitable spirit, without losing their sense of humor or faith. I am proud of us all.

John Martin Taylor
Charleston, 1991

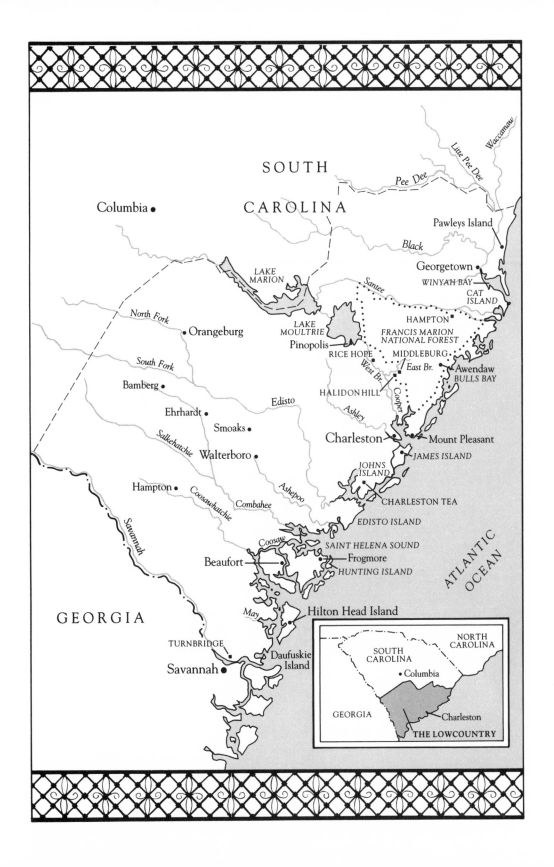

SOUTH

CAROLINA

Columbia •

Pawleys Island

Pee Dee

Little Pee Dee

Waccamaw

Black

Georgetown •

LAKE MARION

WINYAH BAY

CAT ISLAND

North Fork

Orangeburg •

LAKE MOULTRIE

HAMPTON

Pinopolis •

Santee

FRANCIS MARION NATIONAL FOREST

RICE HOPE

MIDDLEBURG

South Fork

Bamberg •

West Br.

• *East Br.*

Awendaw

BULLS BAY

Ehrhardt •

Edisto

HALIDON HILL

Cooper

Smoaks •

Salkehatchie

Ashley

Walterboro •

Charleston

Mount Pleasant •

JAMES ISLAND

Hampton •

Ashepoo

JOHNS ISLAND

Coosawhatchie

Combahee

CHARLESTON TEA

Savannah

EDISTO ISLAND

Coosaw

SAINT HELENA SOUND

Beaufort •

Frogmore

HUNTING ISLAND

ATLANTIC

OCEAN

GEORGIA

May

Hilton Head Island

TURNBRIDGE

Daufuskie Island

Savannah •

NORTH CAROLINA

SOUTH CAROLINA

• Columbia

GEORGIA

Charleston

THE LOWCOUNTRY

HOPPIN' JOHN'S
LOWCOUNTRY COOKING

1

ABOUT THE LOWCOUNTRY

To describe our growing up in the lowcountry of South Carolina, I would have to take you to the marsh on a spring day, flush the great blue heron from its silent oc-cupation, scatter marsh hens as we sink to our knees in mud, open an oyster with a pocketknife and feed it to you from the shell and say, "There. That taste. That's the taste of my childhood."

Pat Conroy, *The Prince of Tides*

For years, my family's was one of three sailboats on Hilton Head Island, now nine marinas and twenty-five golf courses strong. My mother would send me off in the dinghy with a bucket, at low tide if possible, to bring back our lunch. In the summertime I might simply empty the crab trap, but I always cleaned the crabs live before cooking them, still my preferred method, which saved space and time in the galley. In the fall I would cast the shrimp net until I had a pound or two, filling the bucket with clean creek water in which Mother would cook them, with no other seasoning. Once the water came to a boil, she threw in the shrimp for just a moment, until they began to blush, then drained them into a colander. Under the colander was a folded towel that she would then wring out, lay steaming on the counter, sprinkle lavishly with salt and then the shrimp, and roll up for ten minutes or so while we munched on "relish" of raw carrots, radishes, and celery. The shrimp would finish cooking in the steaming towel, and the salt would melt and magically recrystallize on the inside of the shrimp shells, popping them away from their sweet flesh, the shrimp never having left their environment and literally moments out of the water.

The colder "r" months saw me on the salt-marsh banks of pluff mud (so called for the sound that it makes as you sink into it), choosing eight-

and ten-inch oysters—all "singles." Mother would toss back any clusters or smaller ones. Garnished only by the glint of a January sun, May River oysters were then close to perfection—and better than any I've had since. Yankees talk about cold-water oysters being the best, but I have eaten American oysters in Rhode Island, New York, Massachusetts, and Washington state; abroad, I've eaten oysters in England, France, Portugal, and Spain. And nowhere have I tasted a meaty, juicy, salty oyster to compare with our uncultivated varieties here in the South Carolina Lowcountry, where they are continually washed by the incredible flow of our eight-foot tide, one of the largest on the East Coast of America.

That tide flows in and out of our vast marshlands, which sit up behind the barrier islands that run down the coasts of South Carolina, Georgia, and northern Florida. The South Carolina Lowcountry is unique among these Atlantic coastal regions. Settled in the late seventeenth century, when all of the land south of Virginia was granted to a handful of Barbadian planters who had restored Charles II to the throne, the Lowcountry is an area as rich in history and culture as the land is lush.

Geographically it includes the coastal plain of the state from Pawleys Island, near the North Carolina border, southward to the Savannah River, which is the Georgia state line. The Lowcountry extends inland about eighty miles to the Fall Line, a geographical divide not unlike the Mississippi River, which when crossed reveals a dramatic change in flora and fauna.

The Fall Line, where rivers falling to the sea make their last dive, is the first appearance of hills as you move inland from shore. It's easy to imagine those hills as sand dunes on the ancient shore; our soil, very sandy, was once ocean floor. We have palmettos and live oaks dripping Spanish moss, but they won't grow north of the Fall Line. Beavers won't come down across it into the Lowcountry, and water moccasins and gators won't go up above it. The area is at once tropical and not, with backyard banana trees sometimes bearing fruit and winter frosts sometimes killing them to the ground.

As the watershed of the entire eastern half of the Blue Ridge Mountains, which have the heaviest rainfall in the country, the subtropical Lowcountry has a growing season three-and-a-half months longer than the region of its water source. This climatic contrast is sufficient to account for its vast array of plant life. Indeed the South Carolina Lowcountry in its ten thousand square miles has more species of plants than all of Europe in its 10 million. Among the early settlers here were many planters who manipulated this land, took advantage of its waters and tides, and produced rice, indigo, and cotton on a scale unequaled today.

In the three counties into which modern Charleston, the capital of the Lowcountry, sprawls, there are more than five hundred thousand acres of wetlands—salt marsh, rivers, swamps, ponds, creeks, lakes, and former rice fields. That's an acre per resident! The people of the Lowcountry—Sandlappers—have lived off those waters, played on them, and made them their lives for three hundred years. For two hundred years the economy was based largely on rice: to know Charleston was to know rice and rice culture. When early colonists arrived, they found a low, flat coastal plain dotted here and there with pine thickets and hardwood forests, sinuous black rivers banked with acres of marshland, now full, now empty, then full again, and the great flow of that tide bringing into its grasses to feed and spawn the crabs, shrimp, oysters, shad, and sturgeon that entered the cuisine early on.

Politically and culturally the Carolina Lowcountry was different from other colonies from the start. Even neighboring Georgia, geographically similar, shared little history with South Carolina. Samuel Gaillard Stoney wrote, "Charleston was not only the capital of the Province of Carolina, but also its 'mother-settlement,' its seaport and town of trade, the heart and soul of the pioneer settlement of all the Southeast. Charleston has more historic architecture now than Williamsburg ever had even when it was truly new."

The English philosopher John Locke had written for the Carolina colonists a constitution that established a proprietary government based on an aristocracy of landgraves, caciques, and lesser nobility. But land ownership proved to be the basis of the real Lowcountry aristocracy, and landowners continued to make law and shape the culture long after the Revolution. American plantation society was born to the Lowcountry, where it flourished.

The colonists' knowledge of plantation life had been garnered in sugar production in the West Indies. Lowcountry planters relied on native American corn as a staple crop for both master and slave, but it was rice, then indigo and cotton, that built Charleston mansions and Lowcountry plantations and necessitated cheap labor. Slaves were brought into the area by the tens of thousands, and with them came plants from West Africa and knowledge of marsh cultivation of rice.

Early colonists found the woods full of peaches, pomegranates, and figs, all brought a hundred years earlier by Spanish settlers who left them abandoned to naturalize into the environment on their own. It was a land of panthers and bison and wolves, now almost completely gone. And it was a land of alligators, bears, deer, and huge snakes and birds, all very much still here.

Out of that subtropical jungle the slaves carved the vast rice plantations along the banks of the Lowcountry's many rivers, named for the native Americans who at first welcomed the white man. Eventually the Indians of the area would all but die out in their fights against enslavement, loss of land, and newly introduced Old World diseases. Their trade routes to the interior were taken over by white men financed by Charleston merchants, so that even the wild hinterlands became the domain of the Lowcountry aristocracy. Virtually owned and operated by the plantation system, the Lowcountry was different not only from the South Carolina Upcountry but from the rest of the nation as well. Charleston's archivist and novelist Harlan Greene wrote, "By 1708, so many African slaves had been brought into Charles Towne and the surrounding lowcountry that they had already achieved a black majority. The delicate interplay of black and white that would write Charleston's history began quite early. The overlapping chronicles are as connected and fretted as the coils in the sweetgrass Gullah baskets sold in the city Market."

Gullah is the language of the descendants of slaves in the area. Often mistakenly called a pidgin English, Gullah is filled with Africanisms from several West African languages. It was the spoken language between master and slave and among slaves themselves on the plantations, where they were not allowed to learn to read or write. The language lingered the way the art of sweetgrass weaving has; neither exists in America outside the Lowcountry.

Lowcountry blacks, also called Geechees, clung to their patois long after the abolition of slavery, well into the twentieth century. Isolated as they often were on the Sea Islands south of Charleston, where their forebears had slaved on cotton plantations, their culture remained little changed until bridges to those islands began with midcentury development. Just north of Charleston, near Mount Pleasant, a community of basket weavers still makes the sweetgrass fanner baskets that were used to separate the rice from the chaff on the rice plantations. Most of the traces of Africanisms in their language are gone; they no longer speak pure Gullah. But the baskets that they weave are identical to ones woven in the rice-growing regions of West Africa, and if you buy one along U.S. Highway 17—the Ocean Highway—you are likely to be given some "broadus," Gullah for something extra, at no charge.

Nowhere in America did the cooking of master and slave combine so gracefully as it did in the Lowcountry kitchen. You will see decidedly English and French recipes in this collection, but they will have been seasoned through the years by black hands. Hoppin' john, our bean and rice pilau, which we eat on New Year's Day, is daily fare in the rice lands of West Africa. Black cooks in plantation kitchens taught their mistresses about the dish, in much the same language as that of Verta Grosvenor, who began her *Vibration Cooking, or the Travel Notes of a Geechee Girl,* with the following recipe for the dish:

> *Cook black-eyed peas.*
> *When they are almost done add rice.*
> *Mix rice and peas together.*
> *Season and—voilà!—you got it.*

It is not European, African, or West Indian dishes specifically that characterize Lowcountry cooking; rather, it is the nuances of combination and a respect for the past that make the cuisine unique. Sweeping generalizations about the South and southern food simply don't apply to this distinctive area. Lowcountry food is Creole cooking, but it is more heavily influenced by Africans than is the cuisine of Louisiana. Country French traditions abound, reflecting the heavy populations of Huguenots here, but soups in the Lowcountry might contain okra or the water in which rice is cooked as thickeners rather than a roux. The cooking is often more closely akin to the stewpot cooking of West Africa, with its benne (sesame seeds), okra, and eggplant. Sephardic Jews from Portugal and Spain brought tomatoes to Charleston years before they were accepted elsewhere in the colonies, and Mediterranean traditions such as sun-drying tomatoes and making pasta appear in early Charleston cookbooks.

Anna Pinckney, the granddaughter of a slave and an accomplished cook, has pointed out some of the things that define Lowcountry food: "Yard eggs. Pure vanilla. Coconut juice. Grated nutmeg. Clabber. Cooking longer on a wood stove. Bringing some broadus. Sorghum. Rice." Philip Simmons, Charleston's octogenarian blacksmith famous for his wrought-iron gates and fences, grew up on Daniel Island, just across the river from Charleston; he has said that Sea Islanders can be identified by what they eat: "Well, Geechee [people] mostly like rice and most of the people come in see you eating a lot of rice, they call you Geechee. So I'm a colored, black Geechee." He fondly recalls his favorite dish, his grandmother's okra soup with dried shrimp served over rice, "Geechee style, so dry that each grain fall apart."

But Mary Ann Foy, who grew up white and middle-class in Hampton, near the Savannah River, thought everyone ate rice with every meal. She remembers calling home crying as a young child because no rice was served with lunch at the home of the friend she was visiting. Lucille Grant, Anna Pinckney's catering partner, says Lowcountry blacks and whites "eat the same thing. . . . You see, it's all boiled down. You eat butter beans, you eat okra, you eat tomato . . . you eat greens."

An area that has seen its population increase by a third in the past ten years, the Lowcountry is a haven for fishermen, sailors, hunters, farmers, and outdoorsmen of all sorts. When the shrimp are up in the creeks, I will stay up half the night pulling them in off the Battery in downtown Charleston, even when I have to go to work in the morning. And while some families have been worshiping in the same churches since their foundings, the men are likely to arrive on Sunday in their deck shoes and khakis, either on their way to or from a hunting or fishing expedition.

The Lowcountry is a land where the women have two first names. Like the early Charlestonians who first built vacation cottages there, Mary Edna Fraser takes off for the mountains at the first hint of fall to stock her larder with crisp apples and sourwood honey. There's Mary Clare Ulmer of Hell Hole Community, whose pantry skills could fill an entire volume and whose caramel cake was one of the very few foods allowed in our house that was not prepared by my mother. These women are as likely as the men to be involved in the hunting, fishing, and crabbing parties that often feed us in the Lowcountry; and they are more likely to maintain the kitchen and herb gardens reminiscent of those of eighteenth-century Charleston, only recently revived here.

Here in the Lowcountry one can meet many a grown man—black, white, rich, or poor—whose name or nickname is Bubba (even my family calls me that), and many of them have what we call jonboats, the preferred flatbottom boat used both on our lazy rivers up near the cypress swamps and in the marshlands in search of oysters, clams, marsh hens, and shrimp. Or they might own a sailboat and stock an expensive wine cellar, like early plantation owners and Charleston merchants.

At oyster roasts and Frogmore stews and barbecues and cotillions, at Hibernian Hall and museums and fish camps and plantations, and in fine old Charleston town houses, in suburbs, beachhouses, and condos, the Bubbas and the Mary Catherines meet to eat and drink. For three hundred years we have absorbed the rich cultural heritage of the Lowcountry, with great respect for all things historical and truly Charleston. It is a sort of wacky sense of pride that we have, and it often surfaces at these social gatherings that have always been an important part of Charleston's heritage. Few of us today are "bon yeuh" (born here) Charlestonians, but most of us live here by choice and are passionate about our region.

It can be argued that we are excessively proud here and that there is much in our history that warrants remorse. When I lived in Italy among Roman Catholics, I was often reminded that pride is, to them, a mortal sin. It is a horrible truth that the sophistication and wealth of Charleston were built at the expense of human dignity. Slavery and its crippling, long-standing effects should always be remembered as the evils that they are. Indeed one of the reasons that the great antebellum food of the Lowcountry has yet to be fully realized again is that we simply do not talk about things the way they were back then, when that great "civilization" was begot through slavery. The first study of slaves' diets has only recently been completed at a Lowcountry plantation site. By the same token, when Sherman set out on his march to destroy the South, his real goal was the sumptuous Ashley River plantations of Charleston. Some of the buildings were spared and are studied as great works of architecture. But the cuisine is only now being unearthed and restored to life.

Charlestonians have a long history of wars, floods, earthquakes, tornadoes, and hurricanes. The city has been very nearly destroyed several times and has always been rebuilt. But the Civil War threw the area into such poverty that former master and slave alike ate poorly, and the cuisine was nearly lost. Overcooked vegetables, oversalting, and fatty stews, often mistakenly identified as southern cooking, may have come to the Lowcountry in the stark poverty after the Civil War, when farms and rural traditions were lost here, but they are a reflection of that poverty, not the culinary heritage.

In the fall of 1989 a hurricane of unprecedented might fell on the land, with Charleston as ground zero. Eighty percent of the trees in the neighboring national forest were destroyed. Seventy-five percent of all roofs in the area were damaged. Pluff mud, the black, living slime from the marshes, poured into all areas that were landfill and many places where water had never gone before. Church steeples collapsed. Deer were blinded by flying pine needles. Sixty thousand of us were put out of our homes. Hundreds of businesses were destroyed, some never to be revived.

But a year after the storm the city almost appeared, at least to the newcomer, to be none the worse for the damage. And, like the horrible specter of slavery, none dare mention its name: we mostly refer to "the storm," or even "the recent unpleasantness." If we are too proud, then we deserve to be proud even of that, for to have witnessed the soaring communal spirit in the aftermath of the hurricane is to know that this part of the country has long ago overcome the racist brand we are often given by outsiders. Visitors to the city often comment on the lack of racial tension here. In spite of social segregation, blacks and whites are culturally bound in the Lowcountry. Nowhere is it more evident than in the kitchen.

The Lowcountry is people like Skip and Margaret Madsen of Johns Island, who are growing as extensive an herb garden as Martha Logan, who wrote her *Gardener's Kalendar* in 1751 in Charleston. And Dick and Tricia Schulze, who are growing the first Carolina Gold rice since flooding, storms, and out-of-state, mechanized competition finally killed rice in the Lowcountry at the outset of World War I.

The Lowcountry is Middleburg Plantation, the oldest house in South Carolina, which sits on the east branch of the Cooper River, where former rice fields brim with alligators and turtles for stews, prepared in time-honored Creole fashion at neighboring Rice Hope Plantation, much the same as when the area was first settled in the early eighteenth century. The Lowcountry is also the Barnes sisters of Smoaks, a railroad hamlet fifty miles west of Charleston where trains no longer go. They grow much of their food—butter beans and field peas and corn and peanuts—and their backyards are full of figs and pears and scuppernongs. Their brother Russell stirs the big iron kettle of pig fat with his oarlike lard paddle all day during butchering, bringing each of his sisters—mostly in their seventies—a bucket of the whitest lard to use in RuRu's angel biscuits, Lessie Rae's fried chicken, and Erlene's piecrust.

The Lowcountry is also the other side of the coin—the music crowd and the art matrons, Charleston's Old Guard and very wealthy new property owners downtown. They are often the very crabbers and hunters at church in deck shoes, but they might well spend the evening in tuxedo and patent pumps, raising money for wildlife or the arts or celebrating their heritage at a society ball. Much of the economic revival in Charleston has centered around the critically acclaimed Spoleto Festival USA, and once again Charleston's homes are resplendent and her halls full of music and drama. There is a healthy community of writers, and, like the Bubbas and Deborah Annes, all these Sandlappers share an unparalleled sense of place. You might overhear a Geechee and a Brooklynite exchange she-crab soup recipes at the grocery store. A good ol' boy will identify a pre-Columbian pottery shard from his backyard. We all partake of a ritual julep once a year and go crabbing with a child. And we love this place we call home.

Charleston, South Carolina, is a city of many firsts, and it may well be the first place in America to have developed a distinctive regional cuisine, however elusive that cooking might be today. Founded in 1670, it entered the world at a very exciting time, culinarily speaking: Dom Pérignon had just become cellarmaster at Hautvillers where Champagne was first bottled; French bread as we know it today was allowed on the market; and pineapples were first successfully grown in England that year. And though restaurants would not appear for another hundred years, coffeehouses, all the rage, had been around for about twenty years. It was the hedonistic time of good King Charles, restored to the throne by the planters he made lords and to whom he granted a territory as large as what was already settled in America by the English. Charleston, his namesake, was founded to re-create a miniature aristocratic London in the subtropical world that is the Lowcountry.

And so they came from upper-crust England, second sons of the aristocracy who settled along the Ashley River; and from overcrowded Barbados, with their plantation knowledge. Later, because there was so much land, it was offered to the religious fugitives of Europe; by the mid–eighteenth century 45 percent of the white settlers were French Huguenot and Charleston had the largest Jewish population in the New World. (Charleston is often called the "Holy City" because of its many denominations.) The heaviest influences would come from the tropics, where so many had lived before coming to Charleston, and from West Africa, the homeland of the tens of thousands of slaves who outnumbered the white people two to one and ran the rice plantations that were synonymous with the Lowcountry.

Modern Charleston affords us once again the opportunity to demand, as did its once grand and aristocratic society, the finest the culinary world has to offer. Charleston has always had the port necessary to support those demands. During the Republican period (between the Revolutionary and Civil wars), Charleston was sophisticated in its imitation of British royalty, well traveled and educated, a shopper's paradise, and, off and on, the richest city in America.

Not unlike today's "gourmets," Charlestonians imported the finest olive oils and wines, exotic fruits picked a few days before at the height of ripeness in Cuba, and pickles and plants from the Orient. Salsify and scorzonera and hyssop and sorrel were common garden plants. Many plantation owners grew oranges and lemons, some even building orangeries to house them in winter rather than risk losing them to our occasional hard freezes.

When Sarah Rutledge wrote *The Carolina Housewife* in 1847, she included German egg dishes, Italian pasta dishes, and fancy French fare in her collection of Carolina foods to be made by the black cooks in the open hearths and brick ovens of the plantations and town houses of the Low-country. But she also included the dishes that the black cooks had taught the mistresses of those houses, such as "hopping john" and "bennie soup," which they probably took for granted. *The Carolina Housewife* is really a preserving guide aimed at economizing on the bountiful foods of the region. But here we see coconuts, fresh from·the West Indies, entering the ver-nacular and pickles spiced with Southeast Asian flavors being made from melons, cauliflower, green beans, and peaches. Inventories of the extensive personal libraries kept by Charlestonians at the time reveal many contem-porary cooking and gardening titles. By the mid–nineteenth century, when the city was at a building peak rivaled only by that of today's developers, Charleston had had well over a hundred years of sophistication: by 1754 it boasted the best bookstore in America, with more than fifty thousand volumes (enormous even by today's standards).

In her classic book on the food of Morocco, Paula Wolfert gives four prerequisites for a great cuisine: a rich land with an abundance of ingre-dients, a variety of cultural influences, a great civilization, and a refined palace life, where royal kitchens challenge the imagination of cooks. Charleston, as the capital of the Lowcountry, developed a cuisine that would match its grandeur in architecture. That cuisine, possibly alone in America, passes Wolfert's test. Lowcountry cuisine is inventive and ex-travagant, and it plays on the incredibly rich bounty of the lush natural surroundings. The cuisine can be seen as a forerunner to many of today's most popular culinary ideas, with its unprecedented combinations of flavors and ingredients afforded by the spice and slave trade. West Africans in the kitchens threw hot peppers into otherwise bland Scottish soups. Peanuts were combined with shellfish. English preserves took on Caribbean influ-ences, and chutneys were made from all sorts of previously unknown fruits and vegetables here in our subtropical world.

It is a cuisine of the water—of the ocean and marshes and ponds and swamps: delicately smoked mullet and eel; heavenly light crab cakes that are practically all crab, ringed with a sauce reduced from the whole crabs themselves or served with a port-scented tomato catsup from a recipe that is as old as Charleston itself. And it is a cuisine of the Sea Islands, separated for centuries from mainland culture by the salt marshes and rivers, where the fertile former cotton fields now support truck farms of greens, corn, melons, peppers, potatoes, tomatoes, and onions.

It is the food of gardeners who were pioneers of good cooking here and who were growing many items in their Charleston kitchen gardens before Thomas Jefferson is credited with importing them for the first time, years later. And plants that wouldn't grow north of here, like pomegranates and loquats. And plants that came from here, like Sieva beans (pronounced "sivvy"—the tiniest, most delicious of the butter beans and quite unlike any lima grown elsewhere). It is a cuisine that reflects the many nationalities of settlers who came here seeking religious freedom when Carolina was the most religiously free place in the world (for a white man), and it is a cuisine that draws from the nations visited by the ever-traveling Charleston elite, many of whom were not only friends of Jefferson but also avid gardeners, amateur botanists, and often themselves foreign ministers.

Charles Cotesworth Pinckney, for example, was appointed minister to France in 1796, the year after Monroe. His brother Thomas was minister to England; his wife sent melon seeds to Martha Washington in 1799. El Dorado, his Santee River plantation house north of Charleston, was designed after a French château of the period and was surrounded by orange trees, whose fruits figure heavily in Lowcountry condiments, sauces, and desserts. And many other wealthy and curious Charlestonians such as the Manigaults, the Rhetts, and the Alstons spent years abroad, especially in Italy and France, and their letterbooks are spiced with culinary anecdotes.

The oft-quoted list of supplies for Mrs. Charles Alston's ball in Charleston in 1851 indicates both the decadent grandeur of the society and the culinary skills of the Lowcountry:

> *18 dozn plates—14 dozn knives—28 dozn spoons—6 dozn Wineglasses—*
> *As many Champaigne glasses as could be collected—4 wild Turkeys—4*
> *hams 2 for sandwiches & 2 for the supper tables, 8 patés—60 partridges—*
> *6 pr of Pheasants—6 pr Canvassback Ducks—5 pr of our wild ducks—8*
> *Charlotte Russes—4 Pyramids 2 of crystalized fruit & 2 of Cocoanut—4*
> *Orange-baskets—4 Italian Creams—an immense quantity of bonbons—7*
> *dozn Cocoanut rings—7 dozn Kiss cakes—7 dozn Macaroons—4 moulds of*
> *Jelly 4 of Bavarian cream—3 dollarsworth of Celery & lettuce—10 quarts*
> *of Oysters—4 cakes of chocolate—Coffee—4 small black cakes—*

This was fancy party fare that was also served at the many hotels that appeared in the city until the eve of the Civil War. Charleston's many social, religious, and ethnic organizations—as often as not mere ancestor worship groups—frequently held their banquets and balls in the grand public buildings that had been built after the great fire of 1838. Consider the menu (given verbatim here) offered at the Thirty-Seventh Anniversary

Dinner of the New England Society given at the Mills House on December 22, 1856 (see pages 14 and 15).

The grandiose lifestyle of the Lowcountry aristocracy, however, would not last. Harlan Greene has written that "in the twilight of the antebellum era, the city was beginning to resemble the Greek City State, whose role she was fulfilling. She would, with her fall, lead the Carolina Lowcountry and the whole South on to doom, like a heroine in Greek tragedy." Where there had been this vast wealth and decadence, there was absolute poverty after the Civil War. Nearly everything about Charleston changed, except the ancestor worship and the magnificent buildings that managed to survive. The Lowcountry stayed poor for the better part of a century. After the war and the subsequent abolition of slavery, rice cultivation was gradually eliminated by storms, floods, the silting caused by upriver cotton farming, and the introduction of the grain into other states where rice-harvesting machines too heavy for our soil proved too competitive for our hand labor. Salt marshes reclaimed much of the land. Ricebirds (bobolinks), once common fare on every Charleston table, left the state, seldom to be seen again. And many people as well left the state after the Civil War, seeking opportunities elsewhere. In 1880 Charleston County was 30 percent white. In 1930 it was half white. And by 1970, only 30 percent of the population was black—a total reversal of the former ratio.

We sacrificed our agrarian roots and rural values to the twentieth century, modernization coincidentally appearing as we lost our farms and wealth. We lost the craftsmanship of the kitchen and pantry, along with techniques of smoke-curing and pickling and cow milking. And since printed recipes follow only many years after popular usage—if at all—many of the great antebellum Creole recipes have quite possibly been lost forever. When the Writers' Project of the Work Projects Administration published its book on South Carolina in 1940, the chapter on cooking began: "Though South Carolina is widely noted for good food, and pride in old recipes is traditional, unfortunately it is hard to find many dishes of local renown on the menus of public eating-places. Only in private homes and at barbecues, turtle suppers, catfish stews, and oyster roasts can one, as a rule, sample the distinctive cookery of the affluent past."

Nowadays even the turtle suppers have disappeared. To find real Lowcountry food the tourist in Charleston would have to know a hunter or farmer or fisherman or someone here whose family has had a plantation in the area and still does. In other words, only where there has been no break with the past—with the land or the water—do the culinary traditions

Oysters on Shell

———

SOUP

Green Turtle　　　　　*Codfish Chowder*　　　　　*Julien*

———

Baked Rock Fish, à la Chambord

Salmon, Anchovy Sauce

———

Leg of Mutton, Caper Sauce
Turkey, Celery Sauce
Chickens and Pork, Tongue
Tenderloin Beef, with Mushrooms
Ham, St. James Style
Green Turtle Steak, Madeira Sauce
Capon, with Truffles
Boned Turkey, with Jelly, in form
Pheasants, en Belle Vue
Chicken, French Style
Patti de Volaile, Decorated
Bastelleon, à la Moderne
Cold Game Pie, Lobster Salad
Westphalia Ham, with Jelly
Chicken Salad
Patties, en Financiere
Fried Oysters, Chicken Croquettes
Pork and Beans, Old Style

———

Olives, Anchovies, Celery, Sardines, Currant Jelly
Cranberry Jelly, Lettuce, etc.

———

Baked, Mashed, and Fried Potatoes
Sweet Potatoes, Asparagus
Tomatoes, Spinach, Rice
Onions, Beets, Turnips

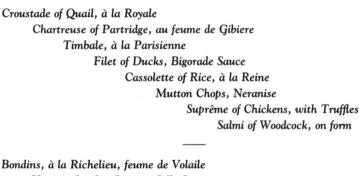

Croustade of Quail, à la Royale
    Chartreuse of Partridge, au feume de Gibiere
        Timbale, à la Parisienne
            Filet of Ducks, Bigorade Sauce
                Cassolette of Rice, à la Reine
                    Mutton Chops, Neranise
                        Suprême of Chickens, with Truffles
                            Salmi of Woodcock, on form

Bondins, à la Richelieu, feume de Volaile
    Venison Steaks, Currant Jelly Sauce
        Oyster Patties
            Beef, Turkey stuffed with oysters
                Saddle of Venison, Jelly Sauce
                    Capons, Saddle of Mutton, Cranberry Sauce
                        Canvasback Ducks, English Wild Ducks,
                            Grouse, Wild Turkeys, Pheasants

Pyramids of Crystallized Fruits
    Plum Pudding, Pumpkin Pies
        Mince Pies, Apple Pies
            Macaroons, Mainges
                French Cakes, Fancy Plates
                    Madeira Jelly, Maraschino Jelly
                        Omelet Soufflé, Charlotte Russe
                            Vanilla Ice Cream

Oranges, Bananas, Apples, Prunes
    Almonds, Walnuts, Pecan Nuts, Filberts
        Raisins, Coffee, and Liquors

Cigars   Cigarettes

continue. As I have worked to revive the great food of the Lowcountry, I have often been dismayed by octogenarians who have given me recipes that "have been in the family for generations" and that include such modern bastardizations as margarine—even as they hand me eighteenth-century manuscripts of pudding, pickle, and sauce receipts.

There have been some rather valiant attempts since the "late unpleasantness," as some Charlestonians still refer to the Civil War, to document Lowcountry cuisine—to get the recipes down on paper before they disappeared forever. They tell a sad tale. *The Centennial Receipt Book* of 1876 has been attributed to Mary Joseph Waring, from one of the colony's oldest families. In it we see meat pies, groundnut cakes and candies, myriad puddings, tea cakes, and pickles. But neither pilau—the "national" dish of Carolina—nor hoppin' john, favorite of master and slave alike, was included in this cookbook, which appeared a mere dozen years after the end of the Civil War.

By the turn of the century some prominent citizens had organized the South Carolina Interstate and West Indian Exposition, hoping to attract worldwide attention to Charleston and to revive its moribund economy, particularly through trade with the Caribbean. Mrs. Samuel G. Stoney compiled the *Carolina Rice Cook Book,* a hundred-page booklet featuring classic Lowcountry rice recipes that was sold as a souvenir for 25 cents. Some dozen rice brokers and grocers advertise in its endpapers, but rice culture as a way of life and the Carolina Rice Kitchen Association, which published the cookbook, would not last another ten years. As Walter J. Fraser, Jr., has written in *Charleston! Charleston!,* "A severe hurricane crashed ashore south of the city on August 28, 1911, causing a 'night of terror' for Charlestonians. Two people were killed and property losses exceeded $1 million. The winds drove salt water into the lowcountry rice fields and, after more than 200 years, ended forever most of the local cultivation of rice."

Still, the homemakers persisted. Anne Sinkler Fishburne, writing anonymously as was the custom for Charleston ladies prior to the Nineteenth Amendment, assembled *Old Receipts from Old St. Johns* around 1919. Her foreword reads:

> *As the swift shuttle of thought brings before me scenes from the past, there are none that I more love to recall than those which have St. Johns Berkeley for a background. United to one another as we were by the ties of blood and tradition, the outstanding feature of our neighborhood was the*

*true spirit of "hospitality sitting with gladness"! The exchange of delicacies
and first fruits of the season was one of the gracious and kindly customs and
much skill went into the concocting of dishes sufficiently delectable to tempt
the most jaded palate, such as strong chicken and beef broth, real calf's foot
jelly and rusk as defies modern short cuts.*

*An Epicure sighingly remarked that one of the serious calamities brought
about by the surrender at Appomattox was the disappearance of Southern
Cookery. Surely this is an exaggeration, but lest it should come true, shall
we not endeavor to preserve the recipes which would otherwise soon be but
a memory?*

A homemade booklet, its covers hand-sewn, of recipes from antebellum
plantations in St. Johns Parish in Berkeley County, just north of Charleston,
it is filled with actual photographs of some of the plantations in the area,
but no chapter on seafood or vegetables!

When the Junior League put together its famous *Charleston Receipts* in
1950, it did not include any of the thirty recipes (or "receipts," as they're
still often called here) for rice bread that had appeared in *The Carolina
Housewife* a hundred years earlier. And marsh hens, or clapper rails, a local
favorite for three hundred years, appear not at all in the new Junior League
cookbook issued in 1986.

Every recipe in this book does not have a written historical antecedent;
this is not a definitive book that offers the entire repertory of Lowcountry
dishes; they are legion. In my version of Lowcountry cooking I use the
philosophies from a bygone era with the traditional foods of the area. I
prefer to think of myself as the Lowcountry's culinary preservationist. And
still, there are limitations: as Anne Mendelson has pointed out, "The most
important factor in giving food a valid local character—faithful use of *good
locally raised ingredients*—can't be translated into recipes." With that in
mind, I hope you will get a strong sense of place as you prepare these dishes.
I know no better food.

2

TOWARD A LOWCOUNTRY KITCHEN

Like all regional foods, the finest elements of Lowcountry cooking—our fresh local seafood, Sieva beans, and green peanuts—do not travel well. But I have cooked collard greens and hoppin' john in New York City and corn bread in Italy, so don't despair. I have suggested reasonable substitutes where I thought they might feasibly imitate original ingredients without sacrificing the integrity of the dish. Befriend your grocer and your fishmonger. Often they are happy to notify customers when seasonal food items are due. Natural foods stores are also good sources of some of the hard-to-find items that I suggest, such as rice flour and fresh yeast. If you frequent restaurants, ask the owners, chefs, or managers if they know specialty food purveyors. Sometimes the item you seek is just enough to help the restaurant meet distributors' minimums, so don't hesitate to ask if they will order something for you.

Before you begin to prepare the recipes in this book, read through these listings of some special ingredients and equipment found in the Lowcountry kitchen. All of the recipes in this book have been cooked at home in my minuscule kitchen; it is not professionally outfitted. But I do have at hand, and take for granted, many utensils and ingredients that most kitchens do not, as a rule, include. Some, such as wood-framed drum sieves (*tamis*) from France, are excesses for the fanatic. Others, such as a kitchen scale, are, I feel, absolutely essential. It's unnecessary to buy the top-of-the-line, state-of-the-art KitchenAid or Robot Coupe, but you will need both a mixer and a food processor. Mine are both inexpensive models; all of the recipes have been checked with these typical home appliances. If you do own the powerful professional-quality mixers and processors, you may be able to cut the mixing times in the recipes. A few notes on useful kitchen equipment are found at the end of this chapter. For every task there is the proper tool. But no tool ever a cook made.

Of all the cooking skills and techniques that typify the Lowcountry kitchen, none is more difficult to describe or teach than the use of one's senses—and not just the sense of taste. Salting and timing the cooking of a simmering pot of hominy or soup can be done through the nose of a seasoned cook; Geechees say, "She has an old hand." A pinch of dried herbs or a handful of fresh ones is tempered by the way it looks; a roast is basted according to its hisses; a steak is done to the touch. Slow down and read recipes carefully so that you have well conceived the results before you begin. Above all, be sensitive to the ingredients and prepare the foods so that all flavors are featured; there is no reason to include an ingredient if you plan to mask it.

Cornmeal is added to batter until it thickens, but freshly ground meal absorbs liquids slowly. Even tightly covered flour often absorbs water from the air in the humid Lowcountry; it should be weighed or, better yet, dried in a low oven and sifted well first. For authentic Lowcountry biscuits and cakes, you must use a southern flour made from soft wheat, low in gluten. But be warned that this flour stales more quickly than others. Store them all in cool, dry, airtight containers for no more than six months. Be careful with cooking times: all ovens and stoves are different. All of these recipes were checked in the Lowcountry, precisely at sea level; water and yeast behave differently at higher altitudes.

The typical Lowcountry meal does not consist of a dizzying array of courses; more often than not it is a plate of seasonal foods. A roast veal chop accompanied by butter beans is found throughout the South; when those beans are served on a bed of rice and garnished with a healthy dollop of artichoke relish, the dish is distinctively Lowcountry. The pantry here is filled with homemade condiments that are taken for granted at most meals. The art of preservation—of canning and pickling and smoking and curing—has a long, uninterrupted history in the real Lowcountry kitchen.

The Lowcountry dinner is served at about two or three o'clock in the afternoon, though that tradition now seems to be reserved for Sundays and holidays as we have become more and more homogenized with the rest of the nation. Breakfast and supper foods are interchangeable, and the popular tea fare of eighteenth- and nineteenth-century Charleston lingers on, with cucumber sandwiches appearing at cocktail parties and sweet rusk now relegated to breakfast. Many of our foods appear as both sweet and savory. Sweet potatoes, benne, and peanuts, for example, all are found in soups, main dishes, and desserts.

For centuries cooks in the Lowcountry have used fine imported ingredients as well as locally produced ones. For authentic and delicious results, do not scrimp: buy the finest olive oil, the most delicious amontillado sherry, and the freshest herbs you can find.

Lowcountry flavors are based on the region's cash crops of today and yesterday. Among those are rice, corn, greens, legumes, root vegetables,

and members of Solanaceae—the nightshade family, which includes tomatoes, potatoes, and the peppers, all native to the Americas. Nothing
matches the flavor of vine-ripened tomatoes; if you cannot find them, I
recommend using canned ones. Unlike their appearance in southwestern
American cuisine, peppers in the Lowcountry are used as condiments rather
than centerpieces, typically spicing a bottle of sherry or vinegar and appearing in relishes and pickles served alongside other dishes. I add a few
fresh hot peppers (poked with a knife in several places to release their fire)
to jars of sherry, olive oil, and vinegar. If you cannot buy fresh peppers
where you live, you may want to buy some commercially spiced oils and
vinegars to approximate those that we make here in the Lowcountry. When
a recipe instructs to "season to taste," I would hope that you would do just
that: most Lowcountry cooks use not only Worcestershire sauce, but soy,
prepared mustard, and pickle juices as well.

Once you have eaten freshly stone-ground whole-grain grits, the bland
degerminated store-bought ones will never do. No perfectly shaped Japanese
persimmon will ever match the flowery aftertaste of a misshapen, ripe,
indigenous one; but I have made persimmon bread with the Japanese variety
in Europe to rave reviews. On one pantry item, however, I can't compro-
mise; when stock—which the French call "the foundation of the cuisine"
(and in French *cuisine* means both the kitchen and the cooking)—is called
for, I demand homemade, not only for flavor but also for the ease of
preparation. Canned and concentrated stocks are simply too salty to be of
use in any reduction. A simmering pot of bones, shells, and aromatic
vegetables changes a house into a home; homemade stocks similarly enrich
soups and sauces. Recipes for basic chicken, fish, duck, vegetable, and
shellfish stocks are included in the section that follows.

Finally, in your efforts to understand the Lowcountry kitchen, consult
other sources as well. A bibliography follows the text. For the scholar
interested in the culinary history of the Lowcountry, I highly recommend
a trip to the rich collections of the South Carolina Historical Society, the
Library Society of Charleston, the Caroliniana collection of the University
of South Carolina, and several other museums housing Caroliniana, such
as the Charleston Museum. For more recipes my workhorses are *The Carolina
Housewife* of 1847 and the Junior League's *Charleston Receipts* of 1950. While
I was working on this book, many people asked me why I was writing a
Lowcountry cookbook when we already have those two marvelous books,
spanning a hundred years of Charleston's history: *real* Lowcountry cuisine
is, after all, right there in those two books, they said. *The Carolina House-*

wife's archaic language is reason enough to rewrite those wonderful receipts so that they are usable today, and although I'm on my third or fourth copy of *Charleston Receipts*, I wanted to eliminate some of the baking powder, cans of soup, and overreliance on commercial products. My Lowcountry recipes present the sumptuous fare of antebellum Charleston for the modern cook.

THE PANTRY

Some recipes in this book call for ingredients that you may not have in your kitchen. Here are notes on special ingredients and sources for those that may be hard to find.

DAIRY PRODUCTS

Milk and cheese are conspicuous in their absence from old Lowcountry cookbooks. Every plantation and many town houses had their "dairy," but animal husbandry was not a major part of Lowcountry farming practices prior to the Civil War. Cows were kept for cream, butter, and buttermilk, but it was just too hot in the Lowcountry for serious cheese making before the age of refrigeration. And according to recent findings, 78 percent of Jews, 70 percent of black Americans, and 83 percent of American Indians are milk intolerant; many of the early Carolinians would have found dairy dishes nauseating.

But refrigeration did come to the Lowcountry, and with it an eager embracing of many foodstuffs such as cheese straws, pimiento cheese, and the holiday classic, eggnog. Ice creams have long enjoyed popularity here. Karen Hess, the culinary historian, has suggested using yogurt to approximate the taste of what would have surely been clabbered milk in the older recipes. In modern recipes calling for buttermilk, try replacing it with yogurt thinned with a little milk or cream.

Butter is unsalted unless otherwise stated; an excellent brand is the rich Plu-Gra, which is available through food distributors to the restaurant trade. Note, however, that most of the commercially available butters in your grocer's dairy case have lots of added water. The Plu-Gra label states that it contains less water and that 25 percent less butter should be used; follow the directions on the package. You might want to check with your local natural foods store for pure butter and fresh cream or whole milk.

Some of the recipes call for clarified butter, which is the pure butterfat separated from the water and the milk solids. It is made by melting butter over very low heat. The clarified butter is the clear yellow liquid. Skim the foam from the surface; discard the milky white substance in the bottom of the pot as well.

Charleston passed an ordinance in 1919 which required the pasteurization of milk (beating Chicago's claim to having been the first to do so by sixteen years); dairy laws in the state have been forever strict since then. The recipes in this book which include cream do not specify heavy, whipping, or light; we seldom see the different grades in South Carolina. Use your own judgment. For an old-time flavor, and in place of whipped cream, try the following substitute for unpasteurized country cream. It will be thick and tart.

HOMEMADE CRÈME FRAÎCHE

This substitute for the real thing is as close as you will get, even better than Paul Bocuse's version. It is from Paola Scaravelli and Jon Cohen's *A Mediterranean Harvest*, a book of delicious meatless recipes.

Mix together 2 parts cream to 1 part sour cream in a bowl. Allow to sit at room temperature for 6 to 8 hours.

Place a coffee filter in a funnel or something equivalent, add the cream mixture, and set aside to drain for 2 to 3 hours, until thick.

Mix in a teaspoon of lemon juice for each cup of *crème fraîche*. It will keep in the refrigerator for about a week.

NUTS

While peanuts, which aren't really nuts, and pecans, which were planted in the Lowcountry only in this century, have become the most popular nuts used in modern Lowcountry cooking, native black walnuts and "English" walnuts from abroad were more popular in earlier times. The nut mixture that I use for my Huguenot Torte provides an intense and rich flavor in piecrusts, as breading, and in ice cream. For the fall holidays, which come quickly on the heels of the nut harvests, sugared and salted nuts appear at the many parties of the season. Perfect pecan halves garnish desserts, salads, and spicy cheese biscuits. Peanuts are boiled, ground for soups and stuffings, and salted for snacks. And walnuts are sugared with freshly squeezed orange juice.

NUT MIX

Mix 2 pounds of shelled pecans, English walnuts, and black walnuts in whatever combination, but with no more than ⅓ pound of the black. My favorite combination is 1 pound pecans, ⅔ pound walnuts, and ⅓ pound black walnuts. Grind the nuts in small batches in a nut grinder or in a food processor fitted with the metal blade, working in quick bursts, until they are evenly ground. Do not blend them too long, or they will become oily. Store what you don't use immediately in airtight containers in the refrigerator. You can freeze nuts, but they lose both flavor and texture when thawed. If you cannot find black walnuts in your grocer's or your local natural foods store, Funsten brand canned black walnuts are available through the Tracy-Luckey Co., Inc., 110–140 North Hicks Street, Harlem, GA 30814.

PORK FAT, OILS, AND SHORTENINGS

My preferred shortening is clean home-rendered lard. For frying it produces the most delicious and authentic flavor, and for baking it produces the flakiest pastry and the most delicately layered biscuits. Rendering lard is incredibly simple. Have your butcher save clean fresh pig fat for you; some butchers do not charge for fat. The butcher also may be willing to run it through the meat grinder for you to save you a step. Put a mere film of water in the bottom of a heavy pan—preferably cast iron—large enough to hold the fat you want to render. (I have a cast-iron roasting pan that is 20 inches long and 4 inches deep; I can render 15 pounds of lard at a time. If you do not own any cast-iron pans, and plan to buy some to outfit your Lowcountry kitchen, this is a perfect way to begin seasoning them.)

Grind the fat and add it to the pan. Put the pan over very low heat or in an oven preheated to 225°. Melt the fat slowly. When the solid matter, or cracklings, turns brown and sinks to the bottom of the pan, strain the lard through cheesecloth or a fine-mesh stainless-steel strainer into sterilized jars. You may fill them to the rims since the lard will contract upon hardening. Cover the jars with cheesecloth to keep out dust and insects, but do not cap them for 2 days. The lard will last for several months in a cool, dark, dry place and even longer in the refrigerator. Weigh lard and butter or measure it by displacement. One-half cup of lard weighs 3 ounces; one-quarter cup or 4 tablespoons is equal to one-and-a-half ounces.

Commercially available lard is often stale; it usually contains questionable additives such as BHA and BHT. John F. Martin & Sons are custom butchers in Stevens, Pennsylvania, who sell pure lard, with no additives. Call Ben Stoltzfus at 1-800-422-8555 for shipping information.

If you don't want to use lard, I suggest that you use rendered goose or duck fat (see page 160) in your pastries and peanut oil for your frying. Both peanut oil and olive oil are called for frequently in the Lowcountry kitchen. Extra-virgin olive oil is specified in a few salads; vegetable oils are occasionally called for. If you are a vegetarian who wants to cook some Lowcountry classics such as okra and tomatoes, sauté in olive oil instead of bacon grease and use the vegetable stock on page 36.

Other pig fat that is used in our cooking is salted "fatback," which is also more correctly called "sidemeat" (hog back is never smoked or salted) and "streak o' lean," from the side belly (called "bacon" when smoked). "Butt's meat" is salted meat from the jowl of the hog. Smoked jowl is called "smoked butt's" or "hog jowl" and is used with greens on New Year's Day. Hocks, when smoked, become "ham hocks." What we call bacon is what everyone else calls bacon, cured similarly to country hams, which are discussed in the meat chapter. Bacon grease (drippings) is always strained; it gives the distinctive crust to our corn bread baked in hot cast-iron skillets.

When you're cooking with these salted and/or smoked meats, note that the foods cooked with them, such as greens and beans, seldom need any salt or pepper; only hot pepper vinegar and various relishes are added when the food is eaten. A nitrite-free bacon is available from Gwaltney's, in Smithfield, Virginia, but it is very salty. Ask for its Williamsburg brand.

STAPLES FOR BAKING

I have cornmeal, grits, and cornflour ground to my specifications in the mountains of Georgia. They are available in 2-pound bags through Hoppin' John's, 30 Pinckney Street, Charleston, SC 29401; (803) 577-6404. Freshly stone-ground and whole-grain, they are delicious. They must be refrigerated or frozen.

Flour. All flour is unbleached all-purpose unless otherwise stated. Flour for biscuits and pastries is made from soft, low-gluten southern wheat. White Lily is a reliable brand. If you cannot find it in your area, write to the company at P.O. Box 871, Knoxville, TN 37901. You will also need bread flour and cake flour, available at most grocery stores. Rice flour is available at natural foods stores. It makes delicious shortbread. Mail orders are taken at Falls Mill and Country Store, Route 1, Box 44, Belvidere, TN 37306.

Be sure to weigh flours when weight measures are given. Two cups of sifted southern flour weigh only 8 ounces; two cups of unsifted all-purpose flour weigh more than 9 ounces.

The weight measures of flour are not always given in the recipes for unleavened crackers or for breads and cakes that are artificially leavened with baking powder. Beaten eggs aren't so forgiving.

Baking powder. You can make your own baking powder with equal parts of baking soda and cream of tartar. Otherwise, use a double-acting, aluminum-free brand such as Rumford.

Yeast. The yeast I use is compressed fresh "cake" yeast. Budweiser makes a good cake yeast. If you cannot find it, go to your baker or local doughnut shop and ask to buy some. It costs pennies and produces incomparable results. Divide the yeast into one- and two-ounce portions. Wrap them well in plastic wrap, then in aluminum foil; they may be stored in the freezer for several weeks to several months.

Eggs. All eggs used in the recipes are large, and they should always be brought to room temperature before being used; but be forewarned that these recipes were tested in the subtropical warmth of the Lowcountry. Warm mixing bowls and eggs by running hot water over them before using them in baking recipes.

Salt. Salt for cooking should be pure, with no additives. Be sure to check the labels. Pickling salt is available in most supermarkets, as are kosher flake salt and sea salt. They are sometimes pure. They are different grinds from different sources; however, most of my recipes are so lightly salted that the slight differences in grain size will not affect measurements enough to alter your results. Recipes usually instruct to salt to taste. Rock salt—ice cream salt—is used in the churn and for baking fish.

VARIOUS INGREDIENTS

Peppercorns. Both white and black are used; the flavors are different. Do not grind the peppercorns until you are ready to use them.

Benne (sesame seeds). Buy hulled raw seeds in bulk from a natural foods store; store them in airtight containers in a cool, dark, and dry place. They will be fresher and less expensive than the tiny jars on the spice rack at your grocer. To roast benne, place them on a baking sheet in a medium (350°) oven or in a frying pan on top of the stove over medium heat. Stir often until all of the seeds are evenly roasted a golden brown, about 15 minutes.

Anchovy and tomato pastes. Buy the imported ones in squeezable tubes.

Prepared mustards. Even the fluorescent American ones are all natural and delicious.

Canned tomatoes. Better for cooking than fresh ones bred only for their shipping qualities and picked before ripe. To be used only when gloriously vine-ripened ones are not available.

Rice. Traditional recipes call for raw long-grain, white rice. Other, more flavorful long-grain white rices such as Basmati and Texmati may be substituted in the recipes, but they are not traditional. Carolina Gold, once revered around the world as the finest, is being grown after a sixty-year hiatus on Turnbridge Plantation in Jasper County, South Carolina. The rice is fragile, delicate, and small-grained and is often broken in the milling process. If you want to try this rare buttery strain, it is available at a premium (proceeds are donated to local charities) from Turnbridge Plantation, P.O. Box 165, Route 1, Hardeeville, SC 29927.

Sorghum and cane syrup. These two types of molasses—made from sorghum cane and sugarcane—are common on the Lowcountry table, though it is becoming increasingly hard to find locally produced syrups. Sorghum is the "Guinea grass" that came to the area with the slaves from West Africa, where it is indigenous. Both sugarcane and sorghum stalks are cut in the fall, ground at mule-driven mills, and boiled and skimmed for the better part of a day until the syrup is pure and the right consistency. Most commercial producers of sorghum molasses are in piedmont regions of the South; sugarcane is grown in Louisiana. Mail orders for sorghum are accepted at Eck & Sons, Route 1, Box 29, Bartlett, KS 67332; for pure cane syrup, contact C. S. Steen Syrup Mill, Inc., P.O. Box 339, Abbeville, LA 70510.

Frozen meats and poultry. At any one time the Lowcountry freezer is apt to hold quail, dove, venison, rabbit, and veal. The finest-quality naturally raised, free-ranging veal, lamb, and poultry are available from Jamie and Rachel Nicoll's Summerfield Farm, SR4, Box 195A, Brightwood, VA 22715; (703) 948-3100. I no longer make beef or veal stock because their *glace de veau*—the pure, concentrated essence of veal stock—is a superior product (just add water!).

Quail is grown in Dalzell, South Carolina, at Manchester Farms. Mail orders are filled by D'Artagnan at (800) 327-8246. To inquire about retailers in your area, call (803) 469-2588. Squab (young pigeon) is related to dove; it has been raised on pure spring water and whole grains at the Palmetto Pigeon Plant in Sumter, South Carolina, since 1923. It is available either fresh or frozen via air freight. Call (803) 775-1204. Palmetto Pigeon also sells *poussin* (young chicken). It is available through D'Artagnan.

Sweet onions. While nearly everyone has by now heard of Georgia's sweet Vidalia onions or Texas 1015s, Wadmalaw Sweets, which are produced on this barrier island just south of Charleston, are perhaps the sweetest ever. The Hanckel family, which owns the farm, also ships various Lowcountry pickles and relishes and tender young asparagus in season (March to May for asparagus, May to June for onions). Write to Planters Three, P.O. Box 92, Wadmalaw Island, SC 29487.

Tea. The only tea grown in America is grown not far from the sweet onions on Wadmalaw Island, some 20 miles from downtown Charleston. The delicate flavor of American Classic Tea comes from its freshness; tea does not improve with age. Write to or call the Charleston Tea Plantation, P.O. Box 12810, Charleston, SC 29412; (803) 559-0383.

Bread crumbs. Store stale dried rolls and leftover baguettes in a paper bag for grating when a recipe calls for bread crumbs. The flavor is infinitely superior to that of commercially packaged crumbs.

Vinegars. The Lowcountry cook keeps several vinegars at hand for use in pickling, preserving, salads, and sauce making. You will need plain white distilled vinegar, apple cider vinegar, rice vinegar, sherry vinegar, and a hot pepper vinegar.

Dried beans. The number of varieties of beans grown in the Lowcountry is mind-boggling. Many of the local varieties are hard to find outside the area. Hayes Food Products in Greenville, South Carolina, packages more than a dozen varieties. Your natural foods store is, again, your best bet.

Arrowhead Mills is a huge supplier of organically raised grains, beans, seeds, and nuts, which are sold both packaged and in bulk; write to or call P.O. Box 2059, Hereford, TX 79045; (806) 364-8522.

Chocolate. Merckens chocolate is available in bulk through retail outlets and cake-decorating supply houses throughout the United States. It continually outranks the readily available European brands in blind tastings. For a supplier in your area, call 1-800-MERCKENS, or write to Roy Merckens, c/o Southern Chocolate Supply Company, 3856 Harts Mill Lane, Atlanta, GA 30319. All of my homemade chocolate recipes call for bittersweet (also called semisweet or vanilla) chocolate. If you aren't up to making your own, Cacao's Handmade Chocolates in Charleston will ship. Call 1-800-441-2402.

Spirits. Most Lowcountry kitchens contain a well-stocked bar. Sherry is called for frequently; the nutty dry amontillado is traditional. Bourbon is a common ingredient; it may be replaced by dark rum.

HERBS AND SPICES

With Charleston's well-documented kitchen gardens, her love of the imported, and her Creole mix in the kitchen, her cooks have long leaned toward highly seasoned fare. The Deas family daybook in the collection of the South Carolina Historical Society was written sometime prior to 1749. It typifies the colony's burgeoning interest in botany, and includes precise instructions for gardening in the subtropical Lowcountry. In February, it notes, "Dung yr ground well, & sow cabbage, savoys, coloworti, salloting of all sorts—carrots, spinago, onions, parsley, beets, scorsonoroot—plant melons & cucumbers, Windsor and half-spur beans, dwarf peas, all sorts of sweet herbs—strawberries, rue, tansie, balm, sage, sorrol, horseradish, plant asparagus, artichokes, set onions and leeks." Thyme, hyssop, marjoram, savory, pennyroyal, mint, and peppers are also mentioned in the fragile manuscript, along with notes on curing scurvy ("take the root of sasafras . . ."), and the reigns of British royalty (ending at George II). "In dry and hot weather," the scribe warns, "cut as few herbs as you can except such as you are to dry for winter."

Today, no self-respecting cook in the "Holy City" is without at least a few mint plants, however minuscule the dooryard; most cooks have an assortment of culinary herbs not unlike those of eighteenth-century Charleston gardeners. Avoid those little bottles of herbs sold at exorbitant prices at the big grocery stores: no telling how long ago they were grown and under what conditions. Many Lowcountry recipes call for a *bouquet garni,* assuming the reader knows to tie sprigs of thyme and parsley to a rib of celery and a bay leaf. Others call for a handful of fresh herbs; the recipes include suggestions.

HERBAL MIX

Though many of my herbs winter well outdoors, as the days get shorter the plants become somewhat scraggly, and I cut them and hang them upside down to dry. Each year my herb garden is different, but the following is a reliable savory herb mixture that can be made with dried organically grown herbs from the natural foods store as well as from homegrown. Each fall I make one big batch of this mixture, which lasts through the winter and spring. I keep a covered pottery jar of it next to the stove, give some to friends, and store any extra in the freezer. The salt helps preserve the fresh flavor. I usually add a few pinches of lavender blossoms, because I like the bitter flavor, but many people do not—and it's not a traditional Lowcountry herb, so I've left it out of the recipe.

MAKES ABOUT 4 CUPS

- 1 cup dried parsley leaves
- 1 cup dried savory leaves
- 1 cup dried marjoram leaves
- 1 cup dried basil leaves
- 1 cup dried thyme leaves
- ½ cup fennel seeds
- ½ cup dried rosemary leaves
- ¼ cup dried bay leaves
- ¼ cup dried tarragon leaves
- ¼ cup salt
- ⅛ cup freshly crushed black peppercorns

Blend all of the above ingredients together well, crushing the larger pieces so that everything is of fairly uniform size. Store in airtight containers in a cool, dark, dry place, freezing what you don't plan to use in a month. Use as you would *herbes de Provence* or Italian seasoning. Remember that the mix contains salt.

QUATRE-ÉPICES

"Four-spices" usually include four of five spices and are commonly used to season forcemeats for sausages and terrines. I include all five. This is one combination of spices, like Seafood Boil (recipe follows), that I try to keep on hand in small quantities. This recipe is a suggestion; quantities and proportions given are typical but not written in stone. Vary the amounts to suit your own palate.

> 2 tablespoons (⅛ cup) white peppercorns
> ¼ teaspoon freshly grated nutmeg
> ½ teaspoon (about 12) whole cloves
> ¼ teaspoon ground cinnamon
> ¼ teaspoon ground ginger

Put all of the ingredients in a spice mill or blender and process until evenly ground. Store in a cool, dark, dry place.

SEAFOOD BOIL FOR SHRIMP, CRAB, & CRAWFISH

Recipes for boiling these shellfish in the Deep South often call for using commercial blends like McCormick's, Old Bay, or Zatarain's and then adding salt. My version of these "boils" combines herbs, spices, and salt (both for flavor and to preserve the mix). Allow ½ tablespoon of the mix for each quart of water, plus half a lemon. For shrimp you will need a quart of water per pound of shrimp.

MAKES ABOUT 1 CUP

> ¼ cup mustard seeds
> 2 tablespoons (⅛ cup) black peppercorns
> 2 tablespoons (⅛ cup) hot red pepper flakes
> 6 bay leaves
> 1 tablespoon celery seeds

1 **tablespoon coriander seeds**
1 **tablespoon ground ginger**
   a few blades of mace, or ¼ teaspoon ground
¼ **cup salt**

Place all of the ingredients except the salt in a blender and blend until evenly ground. Add the salt and blend briefly to incorporate the salt into the seasonings. Store in well-sealed jars in a cool, dark, dry place.

SOUP BASES: ROUX AND STOCKS

Roux

You may notice throughout the book that the soups and sauces are seldom thickened with flour. There is nothing wrong with flour as a thickener if it is cooked properly before it is added. The easiest way to make roux is to put equal parts of flour and fat in a sheet pan and bake at 350° until the desired color is achieved, stirring the mixture every 10 or 15 minutes so that it does not scorch. I use equal parts of rendered duck fat (see page 160) and rendered bacon or pork fat for an intriguing flavor, cooking the roux until it is a rich mahogany color. I remove some from the pan and allow the rest to reach an intense chocolate color. The darker roux goes into seafood gumbos. I freeze it in ½-cup quantities in plastic containers.

Okra is the thickener in my seafood gumbos, and the roux simply provides a rich background to the delicate flavors of the shellfish. Ruth Bronz explains in *Miss Ruby's American Cooking* that roux cooked until it is dark brown loses its thickening ability as the flour is broken down. The roux is added for flavor. According to my mother, the roux also coats the vegetables so that they float and so that you can taste each of them separately.

Stocks

The secret to a good soup is a good stock, said my mother. Flavors are long simmered to mingle in a stock, but each ingredient that you add to that stock to make it a soup should be discernible.

I freeze chicken, duck, shrimp, fish, and vegetable stocks in ice cube trays, then remove the cubes and put them in labeled freezer bags so that I can take a little bit out at a time. Even if I am dining alone, I can pull out a cube or two of stock, reduce it in a frying pan, whisk in some butter, and sauce the meat or fish I am cooking. Homemade stocks take little preparation and cook on their own, virtually unwatched. A vegetable stock is included so that vegetarians interested in cooking Lowcountry may try some of the recipes such as fennel or sorrel soup.

CHICKEN STOCK

This rich Lowcountry stock uses *The Carolina Housewife*'s guidelines of 1 pound of meat to a quart of water. If you want a very clear and light broth, do not brown the chicken or crack the bones and be sure to peel the onion; marrow and onion skins impart dark colors.

MAKES ABOUT 3 CUPS

2 pounds chicken backs, necks, and scraps, with the fat, *or* a chicken
   carcass, with the bones cracked
1 large unpeeled onion, quartered
1 carrot, broken into pieces
1 celery rib, broken into pieces
   a *bouquet garni* of fresh parsley, thyme, and a bay leaf
2 quarts water

Brown the chicken pieces in a heavy-bottomed pot over medium-high heat, taking care not to burn them or let them stick to the pan. Add the vegetables, herbs, and water and simmer, uncovered, for about 1½ hours or until the liquid is reduced by half, skimming any scum from the surface from time to time.

Strain out the solids, cool, and refrigerate the stock.

Remove and discard the chicken fat when it congeals on the surface. Fill an ice cube tray with some of the stock and freeze it to use later. Use the remaining stock in a soup recipe, to cook rice in, or for a sauce.

DUCK STOCK

Duck stock is made exactly the same way as chicken stock (see preceding recipe). Instead of the chicken, use the carcass of a duck, the neck, giblets, and wings, with no fat or skin except the skin of the wings.

SHRIMP STOCK

If you don't live in a place where fresh shrimp can be had, by all means use the shrimp shells, but add some crab and/or lobster shells to the stock to make up for the missing shrimp heads.

MAKES ABOUT 2 QUARTS

- 2 pounds extremely fresh heads-on shrimp
- 1 large *or* 2 small carrots
- 2 celery ribs
  a handful of fresh herbs such as thyme, parsley, basil, oregano, and savory
- 1 medium unpeeled onion, quartered
- 3 quarts water

Remove the heads and shells from the shrimp, dropping the heads and shells into an enameled or stainless-steel stockpot. Cover the shrimp bodies with plastic wrap and store in the refrigerator to use later.

Add the rest of the ingredients and cook the stock, uncovered, at a low boil until the onions are transparent, the carrots are soft, and the stock is pleasantly infused with the shrimp flavor—about 45 minutes. The liquid will be reduced to 2 quarts. Strain out the solids. Cool, then freeze what you don't plan to use immediately.

FISH STOCK

MAKES ABOUT 1 QUART

———

    2 pounds fish heads and bones, with no blood, guts, or gills
    1 celery rib
    1 fresh fennel rib, if available
    1 medium onion, peeled and quartered
    1 leek *or* several scallions, white parts only
2 or 3 fresh thyme sprigs *or* 1 teaspoon dried
    1 quart water
    2 cups dry white wine

Combine all of the ingredients except the wine and bring to a boil. Reduce the heat and simmer, uncovered, for 15 minutes, skimming off any foam that rises to the surface. Add the wine and continue to simmer for 30 minutes. Strain out the solids and discard. Strain again. Freeze some of the stock in ice cube trays, then transfer the cubes to a plastic bag and store in the freezer. Use the rest of the stock within two days or freeze it as well.

VEGETABLE STOCK

MAKES ABOUT 3½ CUPS

———

    1 large leek, well rinsed and chopped
    2 carrots, cut up
    2 celery ribs, cut up
    1 medium onion, peeled and chopped
    1 fennel rib, with feathery leaves attached, if available
      a handful of fresh herbs, 1 teaspoon of Herbal Mix (page 31),
        or 3 or 4 sprigs of fresh thyme and parsley, and 1 bay leaf
    1 garlic clove
3 or 4 black peppercorns
    6 cups water

Bring all of the ingredients to a boil in a heavy saucepan, reduce the heat, and cook, uncovered, at a low boil for 1 hour. Strain the stock well, pressing as much flavor out of the vegetables as possible. Use immediately or freeze for later use.

KITCHEN EQUIPMENT

The Lowcountry kitchen requires a few items that you may not have. These are some of my favorite tools, as well as some that you will need for special tasks such as sausage making.

If you do not have any cast-iron skillets, I advise that you obtain some for authentic results. The typical Lowcountry kitchen has several cast-iron pots and pans, all well seasoned. At the very least, you should have a small (seven- or eight-inch) and a large (ten- or twelve-inch) skillet, well seasoned, for making corn bread with a golden brown crust. Most of my gumbos and pilaus are made in a well-seasoned four-quart cast-iron Dutch oven with its own "self-basting" cast-iron lid. Shop for used cast iron in antique and junk stores; occasionally you can find skillets that already have a good patina. They should have a clean, shiny black interior. If you buy new cast iron, wash it once with soap and water, then render some lard in it according to the instructions on page 25. Wipe out the pan, but never wash it again with soap. After each use, paint the inside of the cast iron with lard or bacon grease, then wipe it out. And if you must wash it, use cold water and a natural-bristle brush. *The Southeastern Wildlife Cookbook*, compiled by the state wildlife department, tells it best:

> *As anyone who's simmered a pot of catfish stew by a riverbank can tell you, a well-seasoned cast iron pot or skillet is impossible to beat for creating exotic flavors in many home-cooked meals. Where other cookware strives to leave no taste in food, the iron pot, when properly seasoned, will instill a distinctive flavor that becomes richer as the seasoning ages over many years of use.*

Other kitchenware should be nonreactive. That means no chipped enamel, unlined copper, or galvanized cookware. Good kitchen pots should be heavy and well made. Heavy aluminum is fine for baking pans but should otherwise be avoided. One of the joys of visiting big cities is browsing in the great cookware stores such as Bridge in New York and Dehillerin in Paris, where you can find heavy, stainless-lined copper pots and wooden whisks to use in them. A particularly useful pan is a heavy, straight-sided sauté pan. A skillet is no substitute.

Invest in a good set of knives and keep them sharp. They will make your life easier in the kitchen and cut working time. An everyday tool kit comes in handy for odd jobs such as opening coconuts. Heavy poultry shears are indispensable.

My refrigerator rarely holds any fresh foods, because I try to shop daily, but it is always packed with half-filled jars of condiments. If you plan to make Lowcountry pickles, relishes, and chutneys, you should process them in a hot water bath to seal them for shelf storage. You then will need an enameled-steel open kettle canner, a canning funnel, and canning tongs, as well as the jars and lids.

For frying I recommend a deep-fry thermometer or a deep fryer with an adjustable thermostat. Buy three or four metal racks for cooling your cakes and cookies and for draining fried foods. A candy thermometer is essential when cooking sugar.

A kitchen scale is probably the most useful—and overlooked—kitchen tool. For baking and preserving it is essential. Krups makes a reliable one with an adjustable dial that reads in both grams and ounces. When you buy a scale, check it to see if it reads correctly by weighing several items from the grocer, such as a two-pound bag of sugar and a pound of butter. Use the same scale throughout a recipe.

If special equipment is needed, the recipe calls for it. Meat grinders, for example, are necessary for making sausages; food processors make mush of most meats. Metal biscuit cutters and U-shaped pastry blenders are carefully designed tools that give much better results than substitutes. I advise you to read recipes all the way through before beginning.

3

SNACKS AND STARTERS

The Lowcountry meal is seldom a series of courses in the French manner, although a sideboard brimming with offerings from soups to nuts is not unusual. The food itself is often the entertainment at social gatherings such as the barbecue, the oyster roast, and the fish fry. Everyone pitches in and joins the cooking, then sits down at the communal table when all the food is prepared.

We take our oysters so much for granted that to serve a few of them as an appetizer before a meal seems an insult to a palate jaded by bushels of them. Most Sandlappers enjoy their oysters straight, opened outdoors around tables made from giant cable spools.

At Christmas in my family, the large meal may begin at any time from midmorning to midafternoon, but outdoors there is a bushel or two of fresh local oysters, iced Champagne, and oyster knives so that we can help ourselves to these "starters" at our own individual speeds. Even the children must fend for themselves. Inside, bowls of roasted pecans and tins of cheese straws shaped like pigs keep hunger at bay.

Except at the most formal dinner parties, the structure of most meals here remains informal. Trays of game pâtés or shrimp paste may be set out with crackers, and celery ribs stuffed with pimiento cheese might be passed, but these starters are mere snacks until we sit down to a dinner of lovingly conceived plates of complementary foods.

Lowcountry soups are more often than not hearty gumbos and stews. Some of our finer vegetable soups, such as sorrel and fennel, make excellent starters (see Chapter 10). Our best soups, such as she-crab, are complicated to make when prepared properly. They make fine beginnings to meals but are often featured luncheon dishes.

Tomato aspic is the one salad eaten with frequency at the beginning of the traditional Lowcountry meal. Harriet Ross Colquitt explained why in *The Savannah Cook Book* in 1933: "No salads are included in this book, because they are not especially Southern, and because we agree with the French that nothing can improve the simple method of marinating with good dressing lettuce, escarole, or endive, and letting it go at that. Adding anything to this is but painting the lily." Salads are treated as vegetables (Chapter 10).

These typical starters are not, then, just "appetizers." Boiled peanuts deserve a category all to themselves. Black bean soup is a common Low-country supper. Corn oysters are fried and served alongside fish in lieu of hushpuppies. These are some of our favorite foods—our preferred snacks.

BENNE CRACKERS

The first recipe, after those for drinks, in *Charleston Receipts* is a benne (sesame seed) "cocktailer" said to have revolutionary powers, at least at cocktail parties. My version shortens the dough with equal parts of butter and lard.

MAKES SEVERAL DOZEN

2⅔ cups unbleached all-purpose flour
1½ teaspoons salt
¼ teaspoon cayenne pepper
¼ pound (1 stick) unsalted butter
½ cup lard, chilled
   about ⅓ cup ice water
1⅓ cups roasted benne (sesame seeds; see page 28)
   additional salt (optional)

Preheat the oven to 300°. Sift the dry ingredients together into a bowl, then cut in the shortening with a pastry blender or 2 knives until it is uniformly distributed. Gradually add the ice water until the dough just begins to hold together (you may not need to use it all). Add the sesame seeds, then form the dough into a ball.

Roll the dough out thin and cut into small crackers. A round wafer is traditional, but I like to use a pig-shaped cookie cutter, lifting the delicate dough with a metal spatula onto a cookie sheet.

Bake for 30 minutes, flipping them over halfway through. If you want a very salty cracker, sprinkle them with a little salt while they are still hot and on the pan. They can cool on the pan. Store in airtight containers.

CHEESE PIGS

These cheese "straws" are one of the best recipes in *Charleston Receipts*. They are unfailingly crisp, easy to make, and perfect with Champagne punches, beer, and cocktails. I nearly always make a batch when I have a party, using a pig-shaped cookie cutter to cut the dough. I have added some red pepper flakes to the recipe.

MAKES ABOUT 100

- ¼ pound (1 stick) unsalted butter at room temperature
- 1 pound sharp cheddar cheese, grated
- ½ teaspoon salt
- ¼ teaspoon cayenne pepper
- ¼ teaspoon hot red pepper flakes
- 1¾ cups unbleached all-purpose flour

Preheat the oven to 350° and get out 2 large cookie sheets. Cream the butter, then blend in the cheese. Work in the seasonings and flour.

Roll the dough out thin and cut into strips or use a cookie cutter. Bake for about 25 minutes or until golden brown. Remove to racks to cool. Store in airtight tins.

SHRIMP PASTE

There are innumerable recipes for shrimp paste, many of them very old and often calling for mace. This unbaked version includes no mace or onion juice, but is otherwise traditional. It is far more delicious than modern versions which call for cream cheese and/or mayonnaise.

MAKES ABOUT 2 CUPS

1½   pounds cooked shrimp (see page 90)
¼   pound (1 stick) unsalted butter
¼ to ½   teaspoon ground dry mustard
2   garlic cloves, finely minced
1   tablespoon amontillado sherry
     salt and freshly ground black pepper to taste

The shrimp should be cool. Peel the shrimp and grind together with the rest of the ingredients in a meat grinder set with the fine disk or in a food processor. Chill and serve on crackers or on white bread with the crusts removed.

PIMIENTO CHEESE

Pimiento cheese is a staple of picnics and lunches throughout the South. It is spread on sandwiches, used as a dip, and stuffed into celery ribs. Set a bowl of it out at a party with crackers and crudités, and it will disappear.

MAKES ABOUT 2 CUPS, ENOUGH FOR 4 SANDWICHES

½   pound sharp cheddar cheese, grated (about 3 cups loosely packed)
½   cup homemade blender mayonnaise (page 310)
¼   cup (1 small jar) sliced pimientos with their juice *or* ¼ cup
     chopped roasted red bell pepper (see page 321)
½   small onion, grated (about 1 tablespoon)
     cayenne pepper to taste

Mix together all the ingredients except the cayenne. Season to taste with cayenne.

HAM PASTE

This recipe demonstrates typical Lowcountry ingenuity in the kitchen. Leftover country ham (which can be frozen) is teamed with chutney to make an intriguing spread for crackers. The recipe, while common, is apparently little known outside the area. It is far superior to "deviled" ham.

> leftover cooked country ham, trimmed of all fat
> Golden Pear Chutney (page 318)
> cream

Put equal parts of ham and chutney through the fine disk of a meat grinder or quickly grind in a food processor. Moisten the mixture with a little cream to make it spreadable. Serve with crackers.

PICKLED SHRIMP

Throughout summer and fall, huge bowls of pickled shrimp grace the food tables at cocktail parties. I like to keep a jar in the refrigerator. The true Lowcountry shrimp salad is composed of pickled shrimp atop a bed of fresh lettuce, with no pasta or mayonnaise in sight. These are delicious!

MAKES ABOUT 4½ CUPS

2 pounds cooked shrimp (page 90)
1 medium onion, thinly sliced (½ to 1 cup)
  bay leaves
1 tablespoon salt
1 cup extra-virgin olive oil
⅓ cup fresh lemon juice
1 teaspoon mustard seeds
1 teaspoon celery seeds
2 garlic cloves, minced

Peel the shrimp, leaving the tails intact, if desired. Combine the remaining ingredients and pour over the shrimp in a quart glass jar (sterilized if you plan to keep them any length of time) with a lid. *Charleston Receipts* suggests making layers of shrimp, bay leaves, and onions. Store in the refrigerator for at least 24 hours before serving. Keeps for up to 2 weeks.

EGGPLANT CAVIAR

Eggplant, or "Guinea squash" as it is called in the Lowcountry, came early to the colony from West Africa, years before Thomas Jefferson supposedly single-handedly introduced it. I suspect that the Sephardic Jews who settled here also brought it with them, for many of our recipes have a Mediterranean feel to them, such as this "poor man's caviar."

I offer this "dip" and bowls of salsa in the summertime, with some chips and crudités, to start off a meal of Frogmore Stew (page 98) or a simple shrimp boil.

MAKES ABOUT 2 CUPS, DEPENDING ON THE SIZE OF THE EGGPLANTS

3 medium to large eggplants
3 heads of garlic
1 medium to large onion, chopped (about 1 cup)
⅓ cup olive oil
1 lemon, halved
1 tablespoon anchovy paste
   salt and freshly ground black pepper to taste (optional)

Preheat the oven to 400°. Prick the eggplants in several places and place them and the whole unskinned heads of garlic in a roasting pan. Bake for about 45 minutes or until the eggplants have softened and collapsed and the garlic gives under firm pressure. The garlic may take about 15 minutes longer to cook than the eggplant.

Score the eggplants deeply in several places so that steam can escape. Place them in a colander or sieve so that the bitter liquid can drain away. Set the garlic aside.

(continued)

When the eggplant is cool enough to handle, begin cooking the onion in the olive oil over medium heat. Peel off the skin of the eggplant and mash the pulp in a bowl. Discard the skins and the liquid that has drained away.

Using a small sharp knife, cut off the bases of the garlic bulbs, exposing the soft roasted flesh. Squeeze all of this flesh into the eggplant and mix thoroughly. When the onions are transparent, add the eggplant and garlic mixture to the onions and olive oil. Add the juice of half the lemon and the anchovy paste and simmer the mixture until it is very thick and dark, about 30 minutes, stirring frequently.

Season the "caviar" to taste with the other lemon half and with salt and pepper if desired. If a smoother consistency is desired, you may run the dip through a food mill before chilling it for an hour or so before serving.

DUCK PÂTÉ

This pâté is made with chicken livers and an entire duck. If the ducks that you buy come with the liver, by all means add it to the forcemeat. If you have access to wild duck, the recipe will be all the tastier (and picking the meat before cooking eliminates the disadvantage of biting into shot); simply adjust the recipe according to the weight of the meat that you have. This is one of the few involved recipes in this book; save it for a special occasion such as a formal holiday dinner for your best friends.

   1 **4- to 5-pound duck**
      about 1 pound chicken livers, cleaned of any sinew or funny
         spots
      grated zest of 1 orange
  ¼ **cup brandy**
   1 **quart water**
   1 *bouquet garni:* **several parsley and thyme sprigs tied in**
         cheesecloth with a bay leaf and a celery rib
   1 **carrot**
   1 **medium onion, quartered**
   2 **garlic cloves, finely minced**
   2 **teaspoons salt**

16 grinds of black pepper
 3 large eggs
 3 tablespoons cream
 ½ teaspoon *Quatre-Épices* (page 32)
 ½ cup chopped black walnuts
   fresh pork fat cut into thin slices
   thin orange slices

Remove the 2 breast pieces from the duck (page 161) and set aside. Remove the wings from the duck and set aside. Remove the skin and fat from the rest of the duck and set aside. Remove all of the meat from the carcass and the legs and cut it, along with the breasts and the skin on the breasts, into small pieces. You should have about a pound of duck meat. Add an equal weight of cleaned chicken livers and grind through the fine disk of a meat grinder. Add the orange zest and brandy and set aside.

Chop the remaining carcass and wings into small pieces and bring to a boil in the water with the bouquet garni, carrot, and onion, skimming any fat or scum that rises to the surface.

Reduce the mixture to ¼ cup, which will take about 45 minutes. Strain out the solids, then add the minced garlic to the reduced broth and reduce by half—until you have about ⅛ cup of glaze.

In the meantime, puree the remaining skin and fat in a food processor and render for about an hour, as explained on page 160 or in a very low oven (170°).

Fold the glaze into the ground meat mixture along with the salt, pepper, the eggs lightly beaten with the cream, and the quatre-épices. Refrigerate, covered, overnight.

The next day, remove the mixture from the refrigerator and fold in the walnuts. Preheat the oven to 300°, line a 1½-quart terrine with the pork fat, and fill with the forcemeat. Garnish with several thin slices of orange, cover tightly with foil, and bake for 2 hours. Remove from the oven, place a heavy object such as a brick or can of food on the pâté, and allow to cool. Refrigerate with the weight overnight, then wait a day or two before serving. This pâté is delicious on toast points.

CURED MEATS WITH FRUITS

Fresh figs, like melon, may be served with cured meats as an appealing first course during the dog days of summer, when they appear on the trees common in Lowcountry dooryards. All over the South, country ham curers sell small packages of thin, odd pieces for biscuits and ¼-inch center slices. I try to keep a package of center slices in my refrigerator; then, when figs are in season, I simply cut the ¼-inch-thick slices into ½-inch strips and serve "raw" with fresh figs.

Thin slices of the duck breast "hams" on page 162 also marry well with figs, melon, or preserved fruit such as Golden Pear Chutney (page 318) or Plum Sauce (page 322).

BOILED PEANUTS

Peanuts, though American in origin, came to South Carolina with the slave trade from West Africa, where they were—and are—frequently used in cooking. No one knows the origins of our singular treat, boiled peanuts, but to those who love them, as I do, there is no better snack. Peanuts are of two types—bunch and vine—and many varieties. I never eat boiled peanuts except when they are in season (July through September), because they are good only when made from freshly dug "green" peanuts—and the small, red-skinned Valencias are the best. Unfortunately, this is a purely regional specialty; green peanuts do *not* travel. And I'm the first to admit that boiled peanuts made from previously parched or dried peanuts are awful. But don't judge all boiled peanuts by them. Soybeans, a major crop in the Lowcountry, are similarly boiled in the shell in Asia; they too are delicious when made with the fresh green soybean still in the pod.

Three pounds may seem like a lot of peanuts; it will feed two boiled-peanut lovers through about two beers.

> 3 pounds freshly dug green peanuts in the shell, preferably the
>   Spanish variety (about 8 cups)
> 3 tablespoons salt
> 3 quarts water

Cook the peanuts, uncovered, over a low boil in the salted water for 1 to 2 hours, until they are cooked to your liking. I like to be able to all but eat the shell.

Let the peanuts sit in the water until the desired degree of saltiness is reached.

CORN OYSTERS

Airy, oblong spoonfuls of freshly shucked corn and egg fried in butter to a golden brown resemble oysters only in shape, but they are equally delicious. Elsewhere these are called corn fritters. They are most commonly served as appetizers, but they can be side dishes, or dusted with powdered sugar and served with fresh fruit as a breakfast dish or dessert (in which case eliminate the pepper). I give here the version unchanged from *The Carolina Housewife* of 1847.

Note to today's cook: It is not necessary to boil fully freshly picked modern varieties of corn; just drop them in boiling water and turn off the heat, then remove the ears when they are cool enough to handle. Clarifying the butter will prevent it from burning, and you may cut the kernels off the cob with a knife, if you prefer, rather than grating.

Grate the corn, while green and tender, with a coarse grater, in a deep dish. To two ears of corn allow one egg; beat the whites and yolks separately, add them to the corn, with one table-spoonful of wheat flour and one of butter; salt and pepper to the taste. Lay them in hot butter with a spoon, and fry them on both sides. It is to be understood that the corn is first parboiled.

The Carolina Housewife, 1847

ROASTED PECANS

When I go to Europe, I always take some roasted pecans with me to give to friends. Roast the nuts with a little salt at a low temperature so that they do not burn. If you are going to add the pecans to another recipe, you may wish to omit the salt, but be sure to include it if you want to make the southern classic, butter pecan ice cream (just fold the nuts into your favorite vanilla ice cream recipe). Both salted and sugared nuts are set out at the myriad parties of the holiday season in Charleston.

MAKES 4 CUPS

---

4 cups pecan halves
4 tablespoons unsalted butter, melted
1 tablespoon salt (optional)
    cayenne pepper or hot red pepper flakes, soy sauce, ground ginger,
        honey, or amontillado sherry (optional)

Preheat the oven to 325°. Spread the pecan halves around on a heavy baking sheet or in the bottom of a roasting pan and bake for 15 minutes. Add the butter, the salt, and any of the other seasonings to the pan, stirring well to coat the nuts. Bake until the nuts are richly browned, 15 to 30 minutes more. Remove them from the oven and stir well again. Cool, then store in airtight containers.

BLACK BEAN SOUP

Columbus found black beans in Cuba in November 1492. Black beans have been a favorite in the Lowcountry since Europeans first settled here. The local version of a soup made from the dried beans is seasoned with a leftover country ham bone and served with fresh lime slices and sherry.

MAKES 10 CUPS OR 6 BOWLS

---

2 cups dried black beans
2 quarts water
1 country ham bone
2 celery ribs, chopped (about 1 cup)
1 medium onion, chopped (about ¾ cup)
1 carrot, chopped
1 or 2 limes, thinly sliced
    amontillado sherry

Cover the beans with water, discarding any that float or look weird. Leave to soak overnight or at least 6 hours, then drain. Put the beans in a stockpot with the remaining ingredients except lime and sherry. Simmer for 2 to 3 hours, until the water just dips below the surface of the beans, skimming foam from the surface as necessary. Remove the bone and puree the soup. This is most easily accomplished with a hand-held blender. Garnish the soup with thin slices of lime and about a teaspoon of sherry per bowl.

SHE-CRAB SOUP

No dish is more quintessentially Lowcountry than our famous she-crab soup, yet judging from the pasty versions served in most restaurants you would think its major ingredient is flour. In *Two Hundred Years of Charleston Cooking*, published in 1930, the recipe is attributed to "Mrs. Rhett's able butler, William Deas, who is one of the greatest cooks in the world." His recipe for a dozen crabs calls for only a teaspoon of flour as thickener in more than 2 cups of liquid. It seems likely that the soup is a variation of a traditional Scottish crab soup—partan bree—thickened with rice. William Deas was the black chef at Everett's Restaurant, where the soup became synonymous with the Lowcountry. His surname would have been given to his ancestors by their owners. The Scottish Deas family has a long and celebrated history in the Lowcountry. The original partan bree calls for anchovies as seasoning. My version is otherwise true to both the original and the Lowcountry. This is a soup for midwinter, when the she-crabs are full of roe.

(continued)

So much misinformation about the taking of female crabs has been published; I hope this will set the record straight. Blue crabs are plentiful from Massachusetts to Texas. It is *not* illegal to take female crabs (called "sooks") in coastal Carolina waters, but it *is* illegal to take crabs less than 5 inches across the back of the shell. Females have reddish tips on their pincers; the aprons on their bellies are broad and triangular (males' are T-shaped). Only female crabs that are "berried," or showing a spongelike protrusion of eggs, must be released. There is no season, no license is required, nor is there a limit on crabs taken on handlines, in dip nets, or drop nets. Further, every head of household in South Carolina is allowed 2 crab pots as well.

MAKES 5 TO 6 CUPS OR SERVINGS

12 to 13 large female crabs
       3 quarts water
    1½ tablespoons seafood boil (page 32)
     ⅔ cup long-grain white rice
       1 quart milk
       1 cup cream
          cayenne pepper, salt, and freshly ground black pepper to
             taste
          amontillado sherry

Boil the crabs, uncovered, in the water seasoned with the seafood boil for 30 minutes. Remove the crabs, reserving 1 cup of the cooking water. Pick the crabs, which should yield about 1 pound of meat and ¼ pound of roe. The roe is bright orange and is unmistakable in the crab shells.

Cook the rice in the milk at a low boil for 30 minutes or until the rice is very soft. Strain the mixture or puree very fine; return it to the pot. Add the reserved crab water and cream and heat the mixture through. Season to taste with a dash of cayenne and salt and pepper. Fill cups with the soup, add a dollop of crabmeat and a sprinkle of crab roe to each, and finish each bowl with a teaspoon of sherry.

SAUSAGE BISCUITS

These are not the sausage sandwiches that you find at fast-food restaurants, but an hors d'oeuvre that is served at cocktail parties. This is really a down-home, trashy sort of food, but everyone loves it. It is a cheese biscuit chock-full of country sausage.

MAKES ABOUT 6 DOZEN

  1 pound country sausage (page 129)
  6 ounces (1½ sticks) unsalted butter
1½ cups grated extra-sharp cheddar cheese
  ¼ cup freshly grated Parmesan cheese
  1 teaspoon salt
1½ cups plus about 2 tablespoons (⅛ cup) unbleached all-purpose
      flour
      perfect pecan halves (optional)

Fry the sausage over medium-high heat until it is cooked through, drain, and allow to cool. Cream the butter and cheeses together. Sift the salt and flour together over the cheese mixture and blend together with a wooden spoon or spatula. Crumble the sausage and mix it in with your hands. Chill the dough for about 30 minutes.

Preheat the oven to 350°. Pinch off small pieces of the dough and roll them into 1-inch balls. Place the balls about an inch apart on baking sheets. If desired, top some or all of the balls with perfect pecan halves, pushing the pecan into the dough and flattening the balls. Bake for 15 to 20 minutes or until they begin to brown. Serve warm or at room temperature. Store in airtight containers for no more than 1 week.

STUFFED GRAPE LEAVES

Dolmades are a traditional Lenten food from Greece—vine leaves stuffed with rice and simmered in a little oil, lemon juice, and water. They have been widely popularized in Charleston, largely through the Greek community's food fairs and festivals, held several times each year. I make the stuffed leaves as an appetizer before a meal of mutton or lamb, using a rice steamer to cook them. Sometimes I simply fill the grape leaves with rice soaked in leftover gumbo or use shrimp or chicken stock to flavor the rice and tuck a freshly peeled small shrimp into each roll as well. (Vegetable stock may be used during Lent.) The following recipe can be made in a pan on the stove or in the oven. See page 305 for directions for preserving your own grape leaves.

MAKES 24 DOLMADES

24 **fresh or canned grape leaves**
½ **cup long-grain white rice**
 1 **cup shrimp stock (page 35) or chicken stock (page 34)**
⅓ **cup olive oil**
½ **cup finely chopped onion**
 1 **tablespoon finely chopped parsley**
    juice of 1 lemon
24 **small shrimp, peeled**

Parboil fresh grape leaves for 4 or 5 minutes, until they turn dark, or soak canned leaves in warm water for about 10 minutes. Combine the rice, ½ cup of the stock, the oil, onion, parsley, and lemon juice in a saucepan. Bring to a boil over high heat, stirring constantly. Lower the heat immediately and simmer, uncovered, for about 10 minutes, until most of the liquid is absorbed.

Place the leaves smooth side down on a work surface. Place a teaspoon of the rice mixture and a shrimp in the center of a grape leaf. Fold in the sides of the leaf, then roll it up, but not too tightly, because the rice will expand. Repeat for each leaf, arranging them in layers in a heavy saucepan. Add the remaining ½ cup of stock, cover the pot, and cook very slowly until most of the liquid is absorbed and the rice is tender, adding water if needed. It will take about 20 minutes (or about 45 minutes in a 325° oven).

4
RICE AND GRITS

Corn fed the Indians of the Lowcountry long before Europeans came; it has been cultivated here since time immemorial. Rice, which shaped the culture in the Lowcountry for more than two hundred years, is so deeply a part of the local kitchen that it appears at the Lowcountry table for very nearly every meal, even though we are now two generations removed from its last cultivation here.

When the rest of the world eats potatoes and pasta, we Sandlappers eat grits and rice. It is true that Lowcountry cooks pride themselves on excellent *pommes frites,* but that is really because we know, as do the Chinese, how to fry. We serve grits, rice, and/or hushpuppies with fried fish. In older manuscripts and cookbooks from the area, recipes calling for potatoes often mean sweet potatoes. The white and the sweet potato are seldom used in our cooking as the basic starch or foundation—only in a few soups and stews do they provide ballast. Even modern potato or pasta salads, ubiquitous at picnics, are just side dishes, typically American but not particularly southern. Barbecue is served with rice. Rice is served at Thanksgiving. Grits are always served on Christmas morning. And, again like the Chinese, children learn early on how to cook rice. It's as natural here as learning to swim.

RICE

The numbers are staggering. By the mid–nineteenth century more than seventy-five thousand acres of land were producing rice in the Lowcountry, yielding 160 million pounds. In 1860 the total national crop of rice was 5 million bushels, 3½ million of them grown here in South Carolina. Nathaniel Heyward, the most productive of the rice planters, owned twenty-three hundred slaves. His friend William Aiken had as many as one thousand on his Jehossee Island Plantation alone. Carolina Gold was considered the best rice in the world, demanded by European royalty and Chinese emperors. It was, as Macky Hill says, the caviar of the early nineteenth century. And he should know: He is a passionate historian and his family owns Middleburg Plantation, where the ruins of the first commercial rice mill still stand on an old rice dike on the banks of the Cooper River and where the lovely old house—the oldest wooden house in South Carolina— stands as the lonely prototype for the distinctive Charleston "single house."

I know people in the Lowcountry who eat rice—or grits—twice a day. And in the days of the rice plantations, either rice or hominy was served in one form or another at every meal. The Lowcountry *was* rice. And while early Carolina cookbooks are filled with recipes for rice—always Carolina Gold—no one had a clue as to how this inimitable variety tasted until Richard and Patricia Schulze started growing it again at their Turnbridge Plantation just inside the state line near Savannah, Georgia, a few years ago.

Avid hunters, the Schulzes had planted rice on their property to attract waterfowl. Fascinated by stories of Carolina Gold, however, they were determined to reintroduce the legendary rice to the Lowcountry. Theirs is a story of research, perseverance, and hard work. After several years they convinced the Rice Institute of the U.S. Department of Agriculture to propagate some seed rice from the few grains of the rare strain that had been stored in its seed bank for sixty years. For three years the Schulzes planted the rice, developing what could be considered a pure strain, first harvested in 1988.

Carolina Gold is fragile. It was often broken in the hulling process, as it is today in the Schulzes' hundred-year-old machine. Its flavor is delicate as well, a buttery, almost creamy rice that stands deliciously on its own. The old cookbooks tell us to wash the rice, boil it in three times the amount of water for ten minutes, then pour off the water and let it steam over a very slow fire for another fifteen minutes. In Charleston today most people have in their kitchens what is called a "Charleston rice steamer" in which the rice cooks in an equal amount of water in a double boiler modified with steam vents. Unfortunately, most of these steamers are made of aluminum, with questionable side effects, and the two biggest manufacturers have discontinued the product. In the steamer, perfect rice cookery is effortless: after twenty minutes over a flame the grains have absorbed all of the water and much of the steam and need only be fluffed lightly with a fork before being served. You can rig a steamer on your own, using a wok, a heatproof mixing bowl, and a Chinese bamboo steamer: Put an inch or two of water in the bottom of the wok. Equal parts of rice and water are added to the mixing bowl and placed on the steamer rack in the wok, then the entire affair is covered with a domed wok lid. But perfect rice cookery is a simple affair in a pot with a tight-fitting lid as well.

Verta Grosvenor, with roots in the Lowcountry, tells in *Vibration Cooking* how she prided herself as a child on her rice cookery: "I was sixteen years old before I knew that everyone didn't eat rice everyday. Us being geechees, we had rice everyday. When you said what you were eating for dinner, you always assumed that rice was there. That was one of my jobs, too. To cook the rice. . . . I could cook it till every grain stood by itself."

When Verta comes to visit, she has a pot of rice on my stove within an hour of her arrival. Her foolproof method has made rice cooks of some friends of mine who otherwise cannot boil water:

> *Use one part rice to 2 parts water. Always use cold water. . . . Soon as it comes to a boil you turn it to a simmer and you cover it with a tight cover. Let it cook for exactly 13 minutes and then cut it off. Let it stand for 12 minutes before serving.*

You might want to salt the water, or you might cook the rice in stock instead. But the timing and proportions in Verta's recipe are classic.

Plain steamed rice invites a host of accompaniments, including okra and tomatoes, Sieva beans, field peas, gravies, and gumbos. In *The Carolina Housewife* there appear more than thirty rice breads and several entries under the heading "Vegetables."

Rice is used in Lowcountry sausages and pâtés as well, but seldom in our sweets. It's the foundation of pilau and the filling for gumbo. When I am drying tomatoes or making catsup in the summer and fall, and have fresh tomato juice, I cook Sieva beans in a large quantity of salted tomato juice, then add rice to the pot for a side dish of beans and red rice, to which I then can add chicken, shrimp, ham, and/or sausage as a pilau for a main dish.

Legumes are cooked with bits of salted or smoked pork and served over rice, with corn bread on the side. A bottle of hot pepper vinegar is passed with the dish, which may alone comprise supper; a richer meal might include sliced tomatoes and a fried pork chop or grilled birds.

Most soups and stews are poured into bowls holding a mound of rice; you will see it throughout the book in snacks, breads, salads, and even in one dessert.

HOPPIN' JOHN

My namesake. Throughout the South this humble dish of "peas" and rice is eaten on New Year's Day for good luck, with a plate of greens cooked with a hog jowl and plenty of corn bread to sop up the pot likker. In Charleston and the surrounding Lowcountry, cowpeas—dried local field peas—are traditional. The classic Charleston recipe for hoppin' john is a very dry version of the dish, but it is served with greens with their juices—or with a side dish of more peas and pot likker.

"One pound of bacon, one pint of red peas, one pint of rice"—thus did Sarah Rutledge begin what may well be the first written receipt for this quintessential Lowcountry dish. As the daughter of Edward Rutledge, a signer of the Declaration of Independence, and niece of Arthur Middleton, another signer, Miss Rutledge was the "Lady of Charleston" who anonymously authored *The Carolina Housewife* in 1847.

Where the name originated is a matter of dispute, and I hesitate to concur with any of the pop etymologies. Still, I believe the dish arrived here with the slaves, who numbered in the tens of thousands in Charleston and on the neighboring rice plantations of the 17th and 18th centuries. Those West Africans were long familiar with rice cultivation and cookery, and the pigeon pea (*Cajanus*), favored throughout Africa, quickly took to the tropical environment of the Caribbean where so many of the hapless Africans were first shipped. *The Carolina Housewife* may have been written by a "Lady of Charleston," but dishes such as hoppin' john were staples in the "big house" that had been brought there by black cooks. Karen Hess, the noted culinary scholar, includes an entire chapter on hoppin' john in her treatise on the Carolina rice kitchen, but one needn't be a historian to understand that the slaves taught the master to love this simple dish.

SERVES 6

1 cup small dried beans such as cowpeas or black-eyes
5 to 6 cups water
1 dried hot pepper (optional)
1 smoked ham hock
1 medium onion, chopped (about ¾ cup)
1 cup long-grain white rice

(continued)

Wash and sort the peas. Place them in a saucepan, add the water, and discard any peas that float. Gently boil the peas with the pepper, ham hock, and onion, uncovered, until tender but not mushy—about 1½ hours—or until 2 cups of liquid remain. Add the rice to the pot, cover, and simmer over low heat for about 20 minutes, never lifting the lid.

Remove from the heat and allow to steam, still covered, for another 10 minutes. Remove the cover, fluff with a fork, and serve immediately.

RED RICE

While you would be hard-pressed to find authentic Lowcountry cooking in any Charleston dining establishment, throughout the South in cafeterias and small, family-owned restaurants there is the lingering legacy of red rice. Most Lowcountry cooks prefer their red rice very plain, the best made with vine-ripened, juicy red tomatoes, rice, and a few fresh herbs from the garden. Other recipes including onion and bell pepper are what most of the country calls "Spanish" rice. Actually red rice is just a tomato pilau. An unattributed recipe in the *Carolina Rice Cook Book* of 1901 calls for stirring the rice, but I prefer recipes in which the rice is never touched with a spoon while it is steaming; fluffed, instead, with a fork when ready to serve, each grain will, per tradition, stand separately.

SERVES 10

½ **pound bacon**
2 **cups long-grain white rice**
2 **cups vine-ripened tomatoes, peeled and chopped,** *or* **1 14½-ounce
    can peeled tomatoes, chopped, with their juice,** *or* **1 14½-ounce
    can crushed tomatoes**
1 **teaspoon salt**
1 **quart chicken stock (page 34)**

Cut the bacon into small pieces and fry until crisp in a large skillet or saucepan that has a tight-fitting lid. Remove the bacon and reserve for garnish. Pour off some of the bacon grease, leaving about ¼ cup of it in the pan. Add the rice and sauté over medium-high heat, stirring constantly.

It will begin to turn white after a few minutes; do not let it scorch or brown. Add the tomatoes and continue to sauté until most of the liquid has evaporated. Add the salt and stock (omit the salt if you're using canned stock). Simmer, covered, for 30 minutes or until the rice is tender. Remove from the heat and allow to sit for a few minutes before serving. Fluff the rice with a fork and garnish with the reserved bacon.

RICE PIE

TO MAKE A CASSOROL OR RATHER A RICE PYE

In the first place you must have a copper Pan well tined. A Tin pan will not do.—Boil 3 pints of rice rather softer than you do rice in Common grease the pan well with Butter and press it (the rice) well into the pan round the sides and bottom and top and put to Bake at the fire turning it round constantly as it will burn. When it is done of a good light brown turn it out on a Dish and cut out in the middle in the middle [sic] sufficient to make room for a rich Fill as a Beef or veal or any thing you please.

Harriott Pinckney Horry, c. 1770

This dish has completely disappeared from the culinary repertoire in the Lowcountry, although the *Carolina Rice Cook Book* of 1901 included 13 recipes. A dish that probably came to the Lowcountry from France, the pie, or rice casserole as it is sometimes called, consists of twice-cooked rice that serves as the shell for a ragout. Rice is boiled until very soft, pressed into a greased pan, cooked again until it forms a golden crust, then turned out and filled with a savory pie filling such as chicken, lamb, or veal.

It is an endearing form of rice cookery, and I hope the simple recipe here for a vegetable pie will help revive the technique both in the Low-country and elsewhere. Serve this pie as the main dish to your vegetarian friends or as both ballast and vegetable with roast chicken or pork. You will need to begin this recipe several hours, or a day, in advance.

SERVES 6 AS AN ENTRÉE OR 8 TO 10 AS A SIDE DISH

FOR THE VEGETABLE STOCK:

1 large leek, dark green part only, well rinsed and chopped (about 2 cups loosely packed)

feathery greens and upper stalks from 3 medium fennel bulbs, cut up (about 2 cups loosely packed)

1 large *or* 2 small carrots, cut up (about 1 cup)

2 celery ribs, cut up (about 1 cup)

½ cup chopped onion

1 teaspoon Herbal Mix (page 31) *or* 1 teaspoon *herbes de Provence* or Italian seasoning plus a few black peppercorns

1 garlic clove, crushed with the flat side of a knife

6 cups water

FOR THE RICE PIE SHELL:

4 cups long-grain white rice

10 cups water

2 teaspoons salt

4 tablespoons unsalted butter

FOR THE FRICASSEE OF VEGETABLES:

¾ pound fresh mushrooms

½ cup dry white wine

4 tablespoons (½ stick) unsalted butter

1 leek, white and light green parts only, well rinsed and finely chopped

2 carrots, peeled and diced (about 1 cup)

3 medium fennel bulbs, trimmed of the bottom cores and stalks and cut into small wedges

1 medium zucchini or yellow summer squash, diced (about 1½ cups)

2 cups cream
1 cup peeled, seeded, and chopped tomatoes *or* 1 small can (14½
      ounces) peeled tomatoes, drained, seeded, and chopped
    salt, freshly ground black pepper, and chopped fresh herbs to taste

To make the stock, bring all of the ingredients to a boil in a heavy saucepan, reduce the heat, and cook, uncovered, at a low boil for 1 hour. Strain the stock well, pressing as much flavor out of the vegetables as possible. You should have about 3½ cups.

To make the rice pie shell, place the rice, water, and salt in a Dutch oven or an ovenproof deep saucepan. Boil the rice in the salted water, uncovered, until it is very tender and soft, about 30 minutes. Place a colander over a bowl and dump the rice out into the colander to drain. (Save the starchy liquid that drains from the rice; it's a perfect soup and sauce thickener.) Fill the saucepan with cold water and let it sit for a few minutes, then rinse it out, scraping up any stray bits of rice. Wipe the pot dry, then put the butter in the pan over low heat to melt. Preheat the oven to 425°. When the butter has begun to melt, remove from the heat. Use a pastry brush to paint the butter over the inside of the pan. When the rice is dry, return it to the greased saucepan and press the rice down evenly into the pot. Place in the oven for about an hour while you prepare the filling.

To make the fricassee, stem the mushrooms and add the stems to the reserved vegetable stock and the wine in a heavy saucepan. Cook the mixture at a low boil, uncovered, for 15 minutes. In the meantime, chop the mushroom caps and heat the butter in a heavy, wide, straight-sided sauté pan over low heat. Add the mushrooms and leeks and sauté until the leeks are almost transparent and almost all of the water has cooked out of the mushrooms, about 10 minutes. Remove the mixture to a platter and set aside. Strain the stock into the pan in which the mushrooms were cooked. Discard the stems.

Reheat the stock to a boil, add the carrots, and cook, uncovered, at a low boil for 10 to 15 minutes, until they just become soft and begin to lose their raw flavor. Remove them from the stock with a slotted spoon and place them on the platter with the mushrooms and leeks. Add the fennel wedges to the boiling stock and simmer for about 3 minutes; then add the squash pieces and simmer for another 3 minutes, stirring often since most of the liquid will have evaporated at this point. Remove the vegetables to the platter. Add the cream to the pan, whisking it in and allowing it to boil until it has reduced to just shy of a thick sauce, about 10 minutes. (The cream will appear to be all bubbles at this point.) Turn the heat to low, then add the tomatoes and the vegetable mixture from the platter. Correct the seasoning with salt, pepper, and the herbs of your choice.

To assemble the pie, remove the rice from the oven. It should have formed a golden crust where it touches the pan. Turn the rice out onto a platter, cut off a lid from the "pie," and scoop out some rice from the center to form a well for the vegetables. Check the fricassee to see if it is thickened to your liking. If not, turn up the heat and reduce one last time. Pour the vegetable filling into the rice pie and serve at once.

RICE TABBOULEH

Tabbouleh has as many spellings as pilau. Alice Marks, one of Charleston's great cooks, used to live in Beirut. Her version of tabbouleh, the classic Middle Eastern cracked wheat salad made with tomatoes, mint, parsley, and cucumbers picked fresh from her garden, has a gradually cooling effect during the dog days of summer when the temperature approaches 100 degrees and the humidity 100 percent in the city. In this version the wheat is replaced by rice for a Lowcountry flavor.

SERVES 8

───

          1 large cucumber
          1 tablespoon salt
          4 cups cooked rice of your choice (see *Note*)
    3 or 4 garlic cloves, to taste
          2 cups loosely packed parsley leaves, preferably Italian flat-leaf
       1½ cups loosely packed fresh mint leaves
          1 large sweet onion, chopped (about 1½ cups)
          3 cups peeled and chopped tomatoes
        ½ cup fresh lemon juice
        ¼ cup olive oil, to taste
             salt and freshly ground black pepper to taste

Peel the cucumber, halve it both along its width and its length, scoop out the seeds with a spoon, and cut each quarter into 4 or 5 strips. Place them in a colander and toss them with the tablespoon of salt. Set aside to drain.

Place the rice in a large mixing bowl and set aside. Put the garlic, parsley, and mint in a food processor and process until finely chopped. Add the garlic mixture to the rice, then add the onion and tomatoes. Toss in the lemon juice, then add olive oil to get the desired consistency. (Don't feel that you must add all of the oil. Many oils are heavy and overpowering. And rices are different, as are rice cooking methods. You don't want the "tabbouleh" to be oily, but you do want to balance out the acidity of the tomatoes and lemon juice.) Refrigerate until about an hour before serving.

If you find that the salad has too much liquid when you remove it from the refrigerator, simply put it in a colander and drain some of it off. Dice the reserved cucumbers, which should be well drained by the time you're ready to serve, and toss into the salad. Season to taste with salt and pepper.

Note: The grains of rice should stand separately. I prefer a very flavorful rice such as a brown Basmati for this recipe.

CAROLINA PILAU

Dishes like this one appear in various cultures as pilaf, jambalaya, and just plain chicken and rice. In Charleston and the surrounding Lowcountry, they started as *pilau,* but they're often spelled *perloo* (though I've seen *purloo, perlo,* and *perlau* as well). The word is pronounced "PER-lo," "per-LO," and "pee-LO," but that *o* is a distinctive Charleston sound—and many people not from here think we are saying "oo." Some people say "oo, la, la"; others say "oh, la, la."

SERVES 8

        1 3½- to 4-pound chicken
        2 quarts water
        ¼ pound (1 stick) unsalted butter
        1 large onion, chopped (about 1½ cups)
        2 cups chopped celery
 2 or 3 large tomatoes (about 1 pound), peeled and chopped
        1 tablespoon fresh thyme leaves *or* 1 teaspoon dried
        ½ teaspoon hot red pepper flakes
           salt and freshly ground black pepper to taste
        2 cups long-grain white rice

Cover the chicken with the water and boil in a large pot, uncovered, for 30 minutes. Remove the chicken from the broth and reserve the broth. Skin the chicken and remove the bones, pulling the meat from the bones. Cut the meat into uniformly sized pieces. Set aside.

Melt the butter in a Dutch oven on top of the stove, then add the onions and the celery and cook over medium heat until the onions start to brown, about 10 minutes. Add the tomatoes and their juice and the seasonings, adding a little more salt than you might think is necessary. Add the chicken meat, the rice, and 1 quart of the reserved broth. Cover, bring to a simmer, and cook slowly, without lifting the lid, for 30 minutes. Serve with a green salad and corn bread (page 219).

SHRIMP PILAU

This dish of rice and shrimp is a classic in the Lowcountry. You will need a rich shrimp stock for an authentic flavor.

SERVES 4 TO 6

- 4 thick slices bacon
- 1 large onion, peeled and chopped (about 1½ cups)
- 4 (about 1½ pounds) ripe red tomatoes, peeled, seeded, and chopped
- ½ teaspoon hot red pepper flakes, to taste
- 3 tablespoons chopped parsley, plus some for garnish
- 1 teaspoon salt
- 2 cups long-grain white rice
- 3 cups shrimp stock (page 35; use the heads and/or shells of the shrimp called for here)
- 1½ pounds shrimp *or* bodies from 2 pounds heads-on shrimp, peeled

In a Dutch oven with a tight-fitting lid, cook the bacon on top of the stove until crisp. Remove the bacon, set aside to drain, and pour off all of the grease except about 3 tablespoons or enough to cover the bottom of the pan. Add the onion and cook over medium-low heat for 5 to 10 minutes, until transparent. Add the tomatoes, red pepper flakes, and parsley and cook for another 5 minutes. Add the salt, rice, and stock, raise the heat for a moment or two, and bring to a simmer. Lower the heat again, cover the pot, and simmer for 20 minutes without lifting the lid. In the meantime, prepare corn bread (page 219), a perfect accompaniment to the pilau.

After 20 minutes, lift the lid and fluff the rice with a big fork while tossing in the shrimp. Cover the pot again and turn off the heat. The pilau will be ready in 5 to 10 minutes, and the shrimp will not overcook.

Crumble the reserved bacon and garnish the pilau with it and some chopped parsley. Serve with a tossed salad and corn bread.

Note: This dish freezes well and is delightful chilled and served as a salad or picnic item. If you are to use it later as a salad, you might stir in a cup of fresh English peas, since their season coincides with shrimp's, as you toss in the shrimp.

GRITS

When I talk about grits or hominy, I am not referring to the bland bleached mush that you buy in grocery stores and see in homogenized restaurants and diners now across the South. Instead I mean the naturally raised whole-grain stone- or water-ground corn grits that have provided major sustenance for the area throughout its history, even here in the Lowcountry where rice was for so long king. Most of the grits that I eat are grown by small farmers in northeastern Georgia and ground to order. They are cooked for a minimum of an hour.

In days gone by, Charlestonians referred to cooked grits as "hominy," because when cooked they resemble the lye-bleached corn that goes by the same name. Grits, nothing more than ground corn, were seldom degerminated or treated with lye. Nearly everyone had a patch of corn, it stores well in the grain, and grist mills were common. Nowadays people pay a premium for whole-grain stone-ground grains with no preservatives. And *grits* is the accepted term throughout the Lowcountry today.

This is not just breakfast fare: grits invite a host of accompaniments from raw egg yolks to cream sauces, gravies, seafood, and hashes. See recipes for shrimp and grits (pages 93–97), fried quail with sausage and oyster cream (page 171), and shad roe in cream (page 85). Along the sides of the plate of grits are fried fish or birds, country ham, and/or eggs. Leftover grits are refrigerated, formed into patties, dipped in egg and then crumbs, fried, and served with various toppings. Chef Philip Bardin at the Old Post Office on Edisto Island has made a name for himself with his updated grits dishes, including an appetizer of fried grits with a topping of light hollandaise and goat cheese.

Allow ½ cup grits for 4 people if the grits are a simple side dish; double the amount for a plate of grits topped with sauce. As the liquid cooks out of the grits, add whatever you have on hand to keep the pot from drying out—water, milk, half-and-half, cream, or stock. I find that a little salt is necessary, but it is easy to oversalt grits in cooking. The solution is to add a little salted butter in the beginning of the cooking. It will not only salt the pot but also keep the grits from sticking.

CREAMY GRITS

SERVES 2 TO 4

2 tablespoons salted butter *or* 2 tablespoons unsalted plus ¼
    teaspoon salt
2 cups water
½ cup stone- or water-ground whole-grain grits
1 to 2 cups milk, cream, half-and-half, water, or stock

Drop the butter into the water in a heavy-bottomed saucepan and bring
to a boil. Stir in the grits, return to a boil, and reduce the heat, allowing
the grits to cook at a low boil for 10 minutes or so, until the grits are very
thick and have absorbed most of the water, stirring occasionally to prevent
the grits from sticking.

Add about ½ cup of the milk or cream to the pot and turn down the
heat, allowing the grits to simmer for another 10 minutes or so. As the
liquid evaporates or is absorbed, add more cream or milk, cooking the grits
until the desired consistency is reached, a total cooking time of at least an
hour. The grits should be piping hot when served, slightly soupy but full-
bodied enough that they do not run on the plate.

AWENDAW

Awendaw, like pilau and rice pie, is a dish specifically Lowcountry, named
for an Indian settlement north of Charleston where both native American
and African traditions survive to this day. Lucille Grant, one of Charleston's
most celebrated cooks, was born and raised the daughter of a fisherman in
Awendaw. They grew okra and caught shrimp, then strung the heads of
the shrimp and the okra pods—for use in soups—in the attic of their house,
where they quickly dried under the tin roof. The technique is West African.
Between Awendaw and Charleston, the Mount Pleasant basket weavers
still make rice fanner baskets from marsh grasses the way they have been
made for centuries.

(continued)

Charleston Receipts warns:

> *Never call it "Hominy Grits"*
> *Or you will give Charlestonians fits!*
> *When it comes from the mill, it's "grist";*
> *After you cook it well, I wist,*
> *You serve "hominy"! Do not skimp;*
> *Serve butter with it and lots of shrimp.*

I offer no improvements to Sarah Rutledge's recipe for "Owendaw Corn Bread," which she published in *The Carolina Housewife* in 1847. This is our classic spoon bread.

SERVES 8

---

2 tablespoons unsalted butter
4 large eggs, very lightly beaten
2 cups hot hominy (cooked grits)
2 cups milk
1 cup cornmeal

Preheat the oven to 375°. In a mixing bowl, add the butter and beaten eggs to the hominy and mix well. Gradually stir in the milk, then the cornmeal. Pour the batter into a 1½-quart soufflé dish or a deep baking pan, allowing room for the Awendaw to rise. Bake for about 45 minutes or until the top begins to brown. Miss Rutledge noted, "The batter should be of the consistency of a rich boiled custard. . . . It has the appearance, when cooked, of a baked batter pudding, and when rich, and well mixed, it has almost the delicacy of a baked custard."

5
FISH

Charlestonians say that their harbor is located where the Ashley and Cooper rivers come together to form the Atlantic Ocean. Their chauvinism notwithstanding, Charleston *is* an important port, which sits above the thirty-second parallel, like other famous ports: Nagasaki, Japan's western-most harbor; Tel Aviv and Tripoli on the Mediterranean; Casablanca on the Atlantic and San Diego on the Pacific; and Shanghai, with whom she has traded for three hundred years. Seafood is quite naturally an important food.

Fish has come to mean a lot more than it did in early Charleston, with the advent of offshore and deep-sea fishing and with flash-freezers aboard the fishing vessels that now bring denizens of the deep to shore after several days out. It also means farming, so that freshwater catfish, trout, and bass, once enjoyed only by fishermen (strict state wildlife laws prohibit the sales of game—even "farm-raised"—and freshwater fish), are now available to both the home cook and restaurants. Though we have seen the numbers of some fishes decimated, particularly the anadromous species such as sturgeon and herring, the modern world has literally brought formerly unknown fish to our shore, iced and fresh enough that we might enjoy it raw, as sashimi, rather than overcooking, which was the norm in the days before refrigeration and internal combustion. According to publications of the South Carolina Wildlife and Marine Resources Department, the commercial value of finfish has exceeded that of blue crabs, clams, and oysters combined since 1981, largely because of the establishment of a resident fleet of offshore snapper-grouper vessels in 1976.

In the Lowcountry there are several inland cypress swamps, with their sinuous black rivers; there are myriad ponds and former rice impoundments; and there are two of the largest man-made lakes in the world, all full of fish.

These are the most contemporary of my recipes, because fish cookery has evolved a more sophisticated, yet simpler style as the varieties available have proliferated. Cobia, for example, is not even mentioned in most fish cookbooks. Taken at offshore buoys, these thirty-pounders have elongated bodies and flattened heads like catfish and shark. I'll never forget my first sight of a cobia off Edisto when I was nine years old, cabin boy to my father and his cigar-smoking, beer-drinking buddies: tossed about and light-headed from the roll of the boat, the engine fumes, and tobacco smoke, I immediately sobered in view of that sharklike cobia. The previous summer I had first tasted marlin in Panama, cubed and simply pan-fried in butter. The white, firm flesh of my first cobia was cooked in imitation of that marlin every night that week, and to this day I remember its nutty, sweet richness. No one ever sells this local "crab eater," a treat to be shared with the finest of friends.

Even though I live on the coast and have fish and shellfish stock on hand, I find it wise to see what is the finest and freshest—the most appealing—at the seafood market before planning my menu. Remember: clear eyes, bright red gills, and a clean, fresh smell are the signs of fresh fish. Have your fishmonger clean the fish for you if you will, but always save the heads and bones for stock. Be sure to ask him to remove the gills as well; some of them don't automatically do it, and it can be difficult for the novice.

If you are a fisherman, gut the fish and ice it immediately upon capture, but do not scale it as the scales will help keep the flesh fresh and firm. I've included two ways to cook fish over three pounds with the scales on. Be sure to save any roe that you find: even strongly flavored roe can be delicious when mixed with sausage. If you have friends who bring you fish, be sure to gut it immediately upon receiving it, keep it well iced, and cook it as soon as possible.

I cook all fish very simply, whether fried, steamed, baked, smoked, grilled, cured, or stewed. The rule is the same to test for doneness, no matter which cooking technique or fish you're using: gently pry the meat with a fork. It is done when it flakes moistly from the bone. With practice, you will learn to tell by touch alone.

The basic cooking methods are followed by notes about some Low-country fish and specific ways to cook them.

GRILLED FISH

Grilling has become the preferred method of cooking fish in the Lowcountry. A light sprinkling of salt, pepper, and olive oil is often the best preparation for grilling most fish—whether whole, steaks, or fillets. Ten minutes of cooking per inch of fish is still a good rule of thumb, but the best guideline is to remove the fish from the grill as soon as the flesh flakes moistly when pried lightly with a fork. Nearly all of our pelagic species of fish grill nicely— marlin, swordfish, king mackerel, dolphin, wahoo, and tuna. The oily flesh of bluefish takes to the coals well, as does shark. Fish over three pounds— say, a sea trout (the southern form of weakfish) or a channel bass (also known as redfish or drum)—grill beautifully when left unscaled. The scales form a seal, and the flesh steams perfectly. The scales come off all at once with the skin to reveal delicate steamed flesh. You can stuff the inside of a fish with sliced fresh ginger or with fresh fennel stalks. You can sprinkle it with lemon juice. Or you can wrap it in banana leaves before you grill it, to impart a tealike flavor. Sometimes I soak shark in buttermilk, and I nearly always marinate king mackerel steaks in lime juice before grilling. Buttery whole pompano are grilled slowly, then served with a piquant green tomato relish (page 325). A few frozen cubes of fish stock (page 36) can be tossed into a frying pan and reduced, then a few dabs of butter whisked in to make a sauce for a nonoily grilled fish. Oily fish are enhanced by a few shrimp simmered briefly in the sweet and sour peach and coconut chutney on page 314.

FRIED FISH

When I think of fried fish, I think mostly of freshwater bream (pronounced "brim") and catfish served with hushpuppies. I might also conjure up fried whiting and hot sauce, a hallmark of black cooks in the Lowcountry, or the very French pan-fried flounder (à la meunière). Two-inch cubes of cobia fried in bubbling clarified butter (page 24) are a favorite as well. And all of these are served with lemon wedges.

The basic recipe for fried freshwater fish is to dip the fillets or cleaned (scaled, gutted, and headless) fish in cornflour seasoned with salt, pepper, and cayenne, then fry in hot grease until done, about 3 minutes on each side. You can buy seasoned cornflour for the purpose or, if you can't find cornflour, make your own by grinding cornmeal in a blender to a finer meal. When the fish is done, put it on racks to drain, not on paper. To make hushpuppies, add the leftover cornflour and some chopped onions to the corn bread recipe on page 219 until the mixture is thick enough to spoon into hot oil. Fry until golden brown.

Saltwater fish such as whiting are dusted in seasoned wheat flour rather than cornflour and are served with a Creole sauce (page 299).

STEAMED FISH

When I lived in the Caribbean, the natives steamed the fishy coral feeders such as oldwife and triggerfish in the same Creole sauce I serve raw with fried fish. Now that we see these reef dwellers in Charleston seafood markets, I not only serve salsa with fried fish but also cover a cleaned whole fish with it and place it in a rice steamer (page 57) for about 10 minutes.

BAKED OR BROILED FISH

If I want broiled fish, I use the gas grill. Sometimes an oven comes in handy, especially if I have a crowd for dinner and I'm out of propane. Baked fish is best when kept simple, and I treat both whole fish and fillets similarly for the oven and the grill.

Preheat the oven to 350°. Sprinkle oily fish with freshly squeezed lemon juice. Salt and pepper the fish and splash with white wine if desired. Place the fish (fillets go skin side down) on a lightly oiled baking sheet or in a baking dish in the center of the oven and bake until the flesh flakes easily with a fork. Thin fillets will take about ten or fifteen minutes; whole fish, about ten minutes per inch of thickness. Test often, so you won't overcook the fish. Serve with lemon wedges or with a lemon butter made by whisking fresh lemon juice and chopped parsley into barely melted butter.

KING MACKEREL ON THE GRILL

As A. J. McClane says in *The Encyclopedia of Fish Cookery*, "To those of us who eat kingfish with any frequency, it's infinitely superior when marinated in lime juice for a few hours, then cooked over charcoal and basted with a garlic butter or suitable sauce." When the kings are running in summer, I save that garlic or chive butter for boiled new potatoes and dress the fish simply with tomatoes.

For each person, have a 1-inch steak weighing ½ to ¾ pound. For each steak you will need one or two limes for the marinade. Marinate the fish for 2 to 4 hours, turning them occasionally, then grill them several inches from the fire for 5 minutes on each side. I put the steaks in a wire grilling basket with halves of small sweet onions such as Wadmalaws or Vidalias painted with olive oil. For the tomato sauce, use 1 peeled, seeded, drained, and roughly chopped tomato for each person—splashed with a little lime juice, oil, and salt and pepper to taste. If you can't get gloriously vine-ripened tomatoes, you may be better off using canned tomatoes.

Serve with green beans and new potatoes.

GRILLED PORGY

Porgy is one of my favorite fishes, and I have been known to eat it three times a week in the dog days of summer that follow the seventeen-day Spoleto Festival USA in Charleston. Porgies have very sweet, coarse-grained flesh that is best when grilled slowly.

Have your fishmonger clean the fish, then cut several deep gashes in the flesh to the bone and fill them with a mixture of fresh herbs, garlic, and olive oil before grilling them over charcoal, on a gas grill, or over grapevine cuttings. A cup of freshly picked mixed herbs from the garden, 2 garlic cloves, and ¼ cup of good olive oil ground together in the food processor should give you enough pestolike mixture to coat two ¾-pound fish. You might sprinkle each fish with fresh lemon juice or with salt and pepper as well if you wish. I usually serve the porgies with sliced vine-ripened tomatoes and sweet corn on the cob.

SEVICHE OF SPANISH MACKEREL

Spanish mackerel that weigh about a pound are perfect for grilling, baking, or broiling, but the oldest Lowcountry recipe we have for them is caveached, or cured in the West Indian manner. In this modern version, the flour and frying of the older receipts have been eliminated; the "cooking" is done by the citrus. The old recipes were formulas for preserving fish in a world without refrigeration. Both the cooking and the breading are unnecessary today.

SERVES 4

2 ¾- to 1-pound Spanish mackerel, filleted, *or* ¾ to 1 pound fillets, with the skin
1 small onion, sliced into thin rings
   salt and freshly ground black pepper to taste
½ cup fresh lime juice
1 large tomato, cut into bite-size pieces
¼ cup olive oil
1 jalapeño pepper, finely chopped

Cut the fillets into 1-inch squares and put them in a nonreactive container such as a glass casserole dish with a lid. Add the onions and salt and pepper. Cover with the lime juice and refrigerate overnight.

The next day, drain off the lime juice, add the remaining ingredients, toss the seviche, correct the seasoning, and allow to come to room temperature. This is delicious as is or served with avocado, called "alligator pears" locally because of their pebbly skins.

SHARK

Walking down Edisto Beach at low tide, you would think that the seas were once brimming with sharks, so numerous are their fossilized teeth, said to be between 7 and 20 million years old. Unchanged through the millennia, sharks have cartilaginous skeletons and an osmotic relationship to sea water that set them far apart from the rest of the fishes. The teeth, which fall out when loosened or damaged, are quickly replaced. Less salty than the water in which they swim, sharks would lose their water by osmosis to the sea if they didn't make urea to provide an osmotic balance. The urea (essentially carbon dioxide and ammonia) is released into the blood of the shark and accounts for the ammonia smell of the flesh. Properly handled shark is a true delicacy. As with most game, however, the field dressing is the primary determining factor concerning its flavor. Shark should be bled immediately upon capture: cut off the tail of the shark and bleed it overboard. If you are hunting shark, the blood will simply attract more. If there is an acrid smell to shark meat, try soaking it in buttermilk or lemon juice (which is acidic and can neutralize the ammonia) before putting it on the grill or into a chowder, or dust the buttermilk-soaked shark in seasoned cornflour and fry in hot grease until golden brown.

CATFISH STEW

Catfish fill the local streams and rivers and are caught by youngsters on the end of cane poles and by good ol' boys with fancy boats and gear. Most of the ones I see have ventured into an upriver crab trap and end up at my fishmonger's. When the South Carolina Wildlife and Marine Resources Department was putting together *The South Carolina Wildlife Cookbook* (now republished by the University of South Carolina Press as *The Southeastern Wildlife Cookbook*) in 1981, it received so many catfish stew recipes from the contributors that 11 were included in the book.

You can make this stew with dressed catfish, but the gelatinous quality you get when you use the head and skin makes the stew a hearty one.

FOR EACH SERVING:
 ½ **pound dressed** *or* ¾ **pound whole catfish**
 1 **potato**
 1 **tomato**
 1 **small onion**
 1 **cup tomato sauce**

FOR THE POT:
 1 **slice butt's meat (salted pork jowl) or other cured fatty pork**
 a pinch of Herbal Mix (page 31)
 fresh or pickled hot peppers or bottled hot pepper sauce to taste

If you're using whole catfish, gut the fish and remove the fins and tail. In a large pot, cover the fish with water and boil until the flesh is tender, about 20 minutes. Remove the pan from the heat, remove the fish from the water, and cool, reserving both the fish and the water. Separate the flesh from the skin and bones and set the meat aside.

Peel and dice the potatoes, tomatoes, and onions. Put the pork in a saucepan large enough to hold all the ingredients and brown the meat over medium high heat until the grease is rendered, 5 to 10 minutes. Add the onions and cook until they begin to become transparent, then add the tomatoes, potatoes, Herbal Mix, tomato sauce, and hot peppers. Add the reserved cooking water and cook uncovered over medium heat until the potatoes are done, about 20 minutes. The catfish breaks apart but holds the stew together with its uniquely gelatinous shreds of flesh. Serve with corn bread (page 219).

FISH CROQUETTES

You can make these fish cakes out of any cooked fish. I spent a lot of my youth on my parents' sailboat. When the weather was bad, my mother would make these out of canned salmon from the ship's store.

SERVES 4

2 cups (½ pound) flaked cooked fish
1 small onion, finely chopped (about ¼ cup)
½ pound (1 average Idaho) potato, cooked and mashed
2 tablespoons (⅛ cup) chopped parsley
1 large egg, beaten
unbleached all-purpose flour
salt and freshly ground black pepper to taste
2 tablespoons (⅛ cup) clarified unsalted butter (page 24)

Combine the fish, onion, potato, and parsley in a bowl. Mix in just enough of the egg to hold the mixture together, then divide the mixture into about 8 patties. Dust the patties in the flour seasoned with the salt and pepper. Then sauté over medium-high heat in clarified butter in a large skillet until golden brown, about 3 minutes per side. Serve with lemon wedges.

HERRING, SHAD, AND STURGEON

The anadromous species of fish—those that live in the open sea but swim up into our rivers to spawn—were important here in the Lowcountry in the old days. Prior to refrigeration, strongly salted and smoked red herring was immensely popular. Henry Laurens, a Charleston planter and merchant who was instrumental in molding the country's Revolutionary politics, was proud of his own and sent them to colleagues abroad.

Smoked herring, locally called "kipper snacks," is commonly found in the butcher's case of a Lowcountry grocer, alongside the cured pork. It is often sold as bait, but it is also eaten as a snack; soaked overnight, sautéed with onions, and added to pilau; or ground and used in croquettes. It is "soul food," a dish of area blacks. The briny cured fish is also cooked like Scottish "tatties an' herrin'," with onions added to the stew of potatoes, herring, and water. These are recipes that come from the Lowcountry's great folk tradition, passed down from mother to daughter, father to son. I have never seen any of them in written form. The one exception is Willie Berry's recipe for Dutch Herring, which follows.

Sturgeon were once so numerous here that there are several 18th- and 19th-century references to the mouths of our rivers so full that one could cross to the opposite bank by walking on the backs of the 10- and 12-foot fish. The roe of the female and the gonads of the male sturgeon, herring, and shad are delicious eating. I can remember my parents sending to Georgetown, on Winyah Bay, an hour north of Charleston, for fresh malossol caviar made from the Atlantic sturgeon to serve at a cocktail party.

Winyah Bay is fed by the Sampit, the Black, the Pee Dee, the Little Pee Dee, and the Waccamaw rivers. Only Cat Island separates the bay from the great North and South Santee. As it is now illegal to take sturgeons along the South Carolina coast, Georgetown caviar is a delicacy of the past. But Howell Boone in Darien, Georgia, processes caviar "the Russian way," from the eggs of Atlantic sturgeon taken in Georgia rivers, so that nearly local caviar is once again available. Write to Walter's Caviar, P.O. Box 263, Darien, GA 31305, or call (912) 437-6560. (Available February to May.)

Harriott Pinckney Horry, whose book of recipes begun in 1770 survives, lived on her Hampton Plantation, now a state park, about 40 miles north of Charleston and 20 miles south of Georgetown. Her travel journals provide glimpses into the homes and inns where she stayed, always with notes on the food. She sampled salmon, trout, and bass in New York, but "tasted none to equal our Santee fish."

Shad begin appearing as soon as the water warms, as early as January in some years. The season lasts about two months as the fish move gradually northward. The roe shad, weighing from 3 to 5 pounds, are caught in our rivers in gill nets. They are both larger and tastier than the bucks, though milt is delectable as well. Recipes abound for the roe of the female, but the flesh of shad is often maligned because of the many bones.

In the Lowcountry shad roe is most often teamed with bacon. For forty years Zelma Hickman has served fresh shad in her unpretentious Edisto Motel restaurant on the banks of the Edisto River in Jacksonboro, South Carolina. She wraps the roe in bacon secured with toothpicks, then places the roe in the "deep freeze" for 10 or 15 minutes to "firm up." The wrapped roe is then deep-fried to a golden brown in clean hot oil.

All roe is easier to handle if it is made firm either by chilling or by simmering it for a few minutes in milk or water. To cook the roe, bacon is rendered in a skillet, then removed and drained. The firm roe is added to the hot bacon grease, flat side down, and cooked slowly until golden brown, then turned once to brown the other side briefly. The roe is then served with the reserved bacon, lemon wedges, and parsley.

The roe of other fish may be treated like shad roe. It is delicious scrambled into eggs or mixed with equal parts of fresh pork sausage and baked like a meat loaf. When shad roe is in season, put several of the larger sets of the roe in the freezer for use in these composed dishes; but cook the fine, delicate sets while they are fresh and in season.

DUTCH HERRING

This recipe comes from *"Don't Forget the Parsley. . . ."*—a book of recipes that for 38 years were prepared by Willie Berry at her Berry's-on-the-Hill restaurant in Orangeburg. The recipe is German ("Dutch"), as were the settlers of Orangeburg. Berry's was a famous stop on U.S. Highway 301, which bore most of the New York–Florida traffic prior to the construction of interstates.

When alewives run up into our rivers to spawn, they are netted for the table. Both the roe and the gonads are delicious. The roe is still canned on the Outer Banks of North Carolina (Harry Wynns Fish Company, Colerain, NC 27924). A few delicatessens stock small kegs (which hold 16 or 17) of the "milkees," which are raw salted male herring with their milt. If you cannot find these "milkers," ask any fresh fish supplier to help you. Serve these on New Year's Eve, as the Germans traditionally do for good luck.

SERVES ABOUT 16

—

   1 keg or 14-pound pail herring (milters)
   2 pounds onions, peeled and thinly sliced
 12 lemons, thinly sliced
   3 cups apple cider vinegar
   3 cups water
1 to 1½ tablespoons ground cinnamon
1 to 1½ tablespoons ground allspice

Separate the milt sacs from the herrings. Put a layer of the fish in a large nonreactive bowl or a 1-gallon glass jar or glazed crock. Alternate with layers of sliced onions and lemons. Squeeze the contents of the milt sacs into a heavy saucepan. Add the vinegar, the water, and spices. Cook, uncovered, over medium-high heat until it thickens, about 10 minutes. Pour over the fish, lemons, and onions, cover, and place in the refrigerator for 1 week before serving. Cut into small pieces to serve as finger food or serve 1 herring with fresh lemon slices to each diner as an appetizer. The herring will keep for an additional week in the refrigerator.

WHOLE SHAD BAKED IN SALT

I learned at an early age to leave large—over 3 pounds—fish unscaled to grill them. The scales form a seal and prevent the outer flesh from burning while the interior steams in its own juices. I learned this similar technique of baking whole unscaled fish in salt in Italy, and I find that it facilitates boning the shad after cooking. You will need a large roasting pan as long and twice as deep as your fish.

SERVES 6 GENEROUSLY

1   unscaled 4-pound fresh roe shad
4 to 5   pounds rock salt

Preheat the oven to 400°. Carefully slit the belly of the shad, remove the entrails and discard, and remove the roe sacs and set aside, keeping the outer membranes intact. Slice the cavity lining along the line of the backbone and remove the dark veins. Remove the gills. Gently rinse the fish inside and out with cold water, taking care not to knock off the scales.

Put a layer of rock salt in the bottom of the roasting pan, carefully lay the fish on top of the salt, then slide the roe back inside the cavity. You may pin or truss the belly of the fish closed if it seems that the roe may fall out. Cover the entire fish well with more rock salt and bake for about an hour or until a thermometer poked into the flesh of the fish reads 125°. Immediately remove from the oven.

The salt may have formed a hard crust. If so, simply crack it open and pour off all the salt. Carefully remove the baked fish to a platter or work surface, using spatulas. Open the cavity, carefully remove the perfectly steamed roe, and set it aside to stay warm while you fillet the fish.

With a thin, sharp blade, slice into the skin of the fish along its dorsal (back) edge from the nape to the tail, cutting along both sides of its dorsal fin, then along the edge of the flesh just in back of the head. Slide the tip of the knife under the dorsal edge of the skin just behind the head and lift the skin up. Grab it with your fingers and pull the entire skin off the side of the fish that is up. You may have to pull it off in several pieces.

There is a center strip of dark flesh running down the lateral line of the shad. If you place the tips of your fingers on this dark meat, you can feel the ends of the extra bones, which seem to float in the muscles. Turn the fish around so that its tail is facing you, then, with a spatula, lift up the dark meat from the fish, beginning near the tail and moving the spatula from the dorsal toward the ventral (belly). It will separate from the white meat; it should also pull out a row or two of bones with it. The remaining bones are easily removed as you carve sections of the delicate white flesh from the fish, always slowly pulling the sections of meat away from the fish at an oblique angle to the backbone—with the dorsal sections removed dorsally and the ventral sections ventrally. The bones attached to the backbone will remain on the backbone. The "floating" bones separate muscle sections and are located about ½ inch below and above the back-bone. After you finish carving the flesh from one side of the fish, turn it over and repeat the process on the other side. As you carve, remove the servings to warmed plates. Serve with Creamy Grits, the roe, fresh spinach cooked with bacon (page 194), and sliced lemons. A lemon butter (recipe follows) is optional. You will find that some people will prefer the fish to the roe.

LEMON BUTTER

MAKES ABOUT ½ CUP

———

¼ **pound (1 stick) unsalted butter**
2 **tablespoons (⅛ cup) minced parsley**
2 **tablespoons (⅛ cup) fresh lemon juice**
1 **teaspoon finely grated lemon zest**

Melt the butter in a saucepan over low heat, then stir in the remaining ingredients.

SHAD ROE IN CREAM

Shad roe poached gently in cream and served over grits makes a delicious rich supper. Round out the dish with asparagus, whose season coincides with that of shad.

  1 cup cream per person
  1 set of shad roe per person
     salt and freshly ground pepper
     Creamy Grits (page 69)

Pour the cream into a heavy sauté pan large enough to hold the sets of roe so that they do not overlap. Gently place the roe flat side down in the pan and bring the cream to a boil, gently shaking the pan so that the roe does not stick. Immediately reduce the heat and simmer the sets, uncovered, shaking the pan occasionally and turning the roe once during the cooking time, until they are cooked through and the cream has reduced to a thick sauce (about 10 to 15 minutes for 2 sets). If you are not sure if the roe is thoroughly poached, slice into it. It should be firm, but still slightly moist. If the roe is not cooked and the sauce is already thick, simply add a little more cream to the sauce and continue the cooking.

Place servings of hot creamy grits on warm plates, then gently remove the sets from the sauté pan to the plates. Correct the seasoning of the sauce with salt and pepper and pour the sauce over the roe and the grits.

SMOKED MULLET AND EEL

One throw of a mullet net—a circular cast net similar to shrimp cast nets but with heavier weights and a larger weave—in a tidal pool on an incoming tide will often yield an entire school of mullet. They are usually cut up for bait, and the heads are used to bait crab traps. But I love freshly caught mullet, panfried for breakfast or cured by smoke, the way I prepare eel. Berkeley County eels are world-renowned, though the industry has suffered

many setbacks in recent years. They are farmed in ponds, but I most
frequently come upon eels that have wandered into my crab pot.

Dealing with a live eel is no easy task. They are strong, and they bite.
Wear a glove and grab the eel from behind the head, then put it down in
a tub of heavily salted water both to kill the eel and to remove the layer
of slime that covers its body. Hang the dead eel by its head, either from a
hook or by driving a nail through its head into a board. Make an incision
into the skin all the way around the head; then, with pliers, pull the skin
off the entire body in one fell swoop. Gut the eel and remove the head.
Leave the tail fin intact. It is then ready to be cured. Proceed as for the
mullet:

SERVES 6 AS AN APPETIZER

¼ cup salt
1 quart water
1 teaspoon dry mustard
1 teaspoon ground turmeric
1 tablespoon sorghum molasses, cane blackstrap molasses, or light or
    dark brown sugar
  juice of 1 lemon
1 small onion, chopped (about ¼ cup)
6 ½-pound freshly caught mullets, scaled and gutted, *or* 1 3-pound
    eel, dressed (see above)

In a nonreactive container such as a glass baking dish or a stainless-
steel bowl, mix the salt into the water and stir until it dissolves. In a small
container such as a coffee cup, add a little of the water to the mustard and
turmeric and mix well to form a paste. Add the paste to the remaining
water along with the molasses, lemon juice, and onion. Stir to combine
all the ingredients. Submerge the fish in the marinade and place a heavy
plate right side up on top of the water to keep the fish under water.
Refrigerate overnight.

Remove the fish from the brine and hang them by the tails in a well-
ventilated, bug-free place while a skin, called the *pellicle*, forms on the
outside of the fish (1 to 2 hours). Soak hickory chips in water and prepare
the smoker. The grates should be clean and brushed with oil; the temperature should stay at about 140°.

Smoke the fish over smoldering chips (see note) until it flakes with a fork. It will take 2 to 4 hours. Serve at once or allow to cool, wrap in plastic wrap, and store in the refrigerator.

Note: If your smoker is an electric model, you may want to wrap the soaked chips tightly in 2 layers of aluminum foil, as my father recommends. Poke holes in the foil before placing it near the heat source. This little distiller will produce a steady supply of smoke for several hours.

STUFFED FLOUNDER

Flounder are gigged, caught on light tackle, and retrieved from crab pots in the brackish waters surrounding the barrier islands that describe the coast of the Lowcountry. They are the one local fish that appears with regularity on local restaurant menus. I prefer the fish simply prepared *à la meunière*—dusted in flour, fried in butter until golden, and topped with lemon and the browned butter from the pan—but stuffed flounder is such a common dish in the Lowcountry that I would be remiss to omit it.

SERVES 4

4 ¾- to 1-pound flounder
1 medium onion, chopped (about ¾ cup)
1 celery rib, chopped (about ⅓ cup)
⅓ cup chopped red or green bell pepper
¼ pound (1 stick) unsalted butter, melted
1 pound crabmeat
2 cups white bread torn into small pieces
2 large eggs, lightly beaten
1 tablespoon chopped parsley
1 ¼-pound center slice boned country ham, about ¼-inch thick,
    finely diced
1 tablespoon amontillado sherry
   salt and freshly ground black pepper to taste
   juice of 1 lemon

Preheat the oven to 350°. Lay the fish bottom side (the white side) up on a cutting board and make an incision in each fish down to the backbone along the center of the fish, stopping just shy of the head and tail. Working at an oblique angle, slip the knife in between the flesh and the backbone and run the knife down the ribs on both sides of the backbone.

Sauté the onion, celery, and bell pepper in a heavy sauté pan in about half of the butter over medium-high heat until the onions begin to become transparent, about 5 minutes. Toss with the crabmeat, bread, eggs, parsley, ham, and sherry, seasoning to taste with the salt and pepper. Remember that the country ham is salty and will impart its flavor to the crabmeat. Stuff the fish with the mixture, brush a glass baking pan with some of the remaining butter, and add the fish to the pan. Mix the rest of the butter with the lemon juice, pour over the fish, and bake for 30 to 45 minutes or until the fish flakes easily with a fork.

6
SHELLFISH

Shrimp are the backbone of Lowcountry cooking. The cries of street vendors calling "Swimpee! Raw swimpee!" fill Charleston's novels and histories. Shrimping is such a popular pastime that long before the sweet little creek shrimp appear in the marshes the K Marts and tackle shops sell out of the five-, six-, and seven-foot cast nets that will haul them in by the thousands of pounds. Every year I hear of more and better baiting techniques. No sooner do I hear complaints of one well-known hole being shrimped out than people start pulling them in from the Battery in downtown Charleston. I have a friend who fills a pair of panty hose with a mixture of pluff mud and fish meal and comes back later to pull out a surrealistic shrimp-covered garment from the banks of the Ashley River where she's left it.

Nothing quite matches the flavor of freshly caught shrimp. They are infinitely better when cooked with their shells on or in precious liquids reduced from their shells, yet few people bother. I was tempted to include just one recipe for shrimp (the only one you really need to know), but will state it simply here as the guideline. It is the classic Edisto Island recipe, always told in Gullah, the dialect of the Sea Islands: *Sree minute, off de hot, out de pot, dey ready.*

It is a perfect recipe, which, translated into plain English, reads:

Bring a pot of seasoned water to a boil. Add unpeeled shrimp. Do not let it come back to a boil. Count three minutes and remove the shrimp. Peel and eat. If the shrimp are to be used in another recipe, such as shrimp paste or pickled shrimp, season the water with salt only. If they are to be eaten plain, add some seafood boil (see page 32). The important thing to remember is never to let the water return to a boil. The three minutes is the time for large (fewer than 25 per pound) shrimp; medium shrimp (35–45 count) need cook for only two minutes; small (more than 50-count), for one. If you are cooking more than two or three pounds, you may have to leave the shrimp in a little longer. They should be pink and firm, but still tender. Immediately pour them into a colander to drain. They will continue to cook after they are removed from the water; taste one. If it is the least bit rubbery, run cold water over the shrimp or plunge them into ice water to stop the cooking, but drain them immediately if you do, and sprinkle some more salt over them.

Old Charleston cookbooks call for a plate of shrimp, which means a pint of peeled shrimp, for dishes such as pilau and soup. When I have not been shrimping myself and am forced to buy shrimp, I always buy from small local vendors—or from the boats—who sell heads-on shrimp caught within the last twenty-four hours and untainted by dubious "preservatives." In cities such as New York you can find fresh heads-on shrimp (I have found them in Chinatown and at Fulton Market in New York City) if you look hard enough, but they too may be coated with chemicals. Shrimp heads rot and fall off very quickly, but when fresh they hold nearly all of the flavor. If you don't live in the Lowcountry or in a coastal area where you can get to the shrimp as soon as they come to shore, you may be better off buying "fresh frozen" shrimp, which are immediately headed and flash-frozen aboard the shrimp trawler so that they may be shipped. If you are simply boiling or sautéing the shrimp, give everyone an extra napkin or a finger bowl and cook them with their shells on. And if the shrimp are to be incorporated into another dish—such as Shrimp Pilau—make a stock out of the shells (page 35).

If shrimp are the backbone, then crab and oysters are the heart and soul of Lowcountry cooking. Crab is my favorite cooked food, but nothing compares to raw Lowcountry oysters. The Lowcountry oyster roast is a unique outdoor celebration. Rustic giant cable spools are common on the lawns of some of our most historic houses: they are the perfect height for opening oysters, which is done while standing. A log fire is built on the ground. Concrete blocks support a piece of sheet metal that sits a foot above the fire. Raw oysters from the surrounding marshes are laid on top of the sheet metal, then covered with soaking wet croaker sacks (so called because they hold the frog-gigging catch, they would be called gunnysacks elsewhere), so that the oysters steam. Packages of saltines and bowls of cocktail sauce (usually "homemade" of tomato catsup and horseradish) and melted butter are placed on the oyster tables, but most Sandlappers prefer the salty local oysters plain. Everyone fends for himself and brings his own oyster knife and glove. We take turns manning the fire; a shovel is the only tool used. Empty shells are returned to the marsh or laid in driveways.

Sandlappers tend to stand at the tables and open raw oysters for an hour before eating steamed ones. They are best when just heated through, so that they open more easily than the raw ones, without having lost their tangy juice. A serious oyster eater can devour a bushel; I get a bushel of oysters for every five people invited. No matter how few guests there are, a keg of beer is always a wise addition. Standard kegs hold 240 eight-ounce cups. At outdoor parties people *will* drink. In the Lowcountry, with its three-hundred-year history of heavy imbibing, you must count on four beers plus one glass of wine per person.

SHRIMP BUTTER

You can easily make this shellfish butter from crawfish, crabs, or lobster, but shrimp are classic in the Lowcountry. Early in the shrimp season, when the sweet, tiny creek shrimp are all you can find in a cast net, you can make this butter without the maddening effort of cleaning the inch-long shrimp. It is true that creek shrimp are the sweetest and must be used for authentic Charleston shrimp and grits, but you can extract their flavor in this way without having to pick them.

MAKES 2 CUPS

1 or 2 tablespoons olive oil
   1 pound shrimp shells and heads *or* 1 pound tiny whole shrimp
   1 large carrot, finely chopped
   1 celery rib, finely chopped
   1 1-inch piece of the white part of a leek, well rinsed and finely
      chopped
   1 shallot, finely chopped
   2 garlic cloves
   2 tablespoons (⅛ cup) tomato paste
   1 pound (4 sticks) unsalted butter, cut into pieces
   1 cup water or shrimp stock (page 35)

Lightly coat the bottom of a large skillet, wok, or Dutch oven with olive oil. Add the shellfish and stir-fry over high heat until thoroughly pink. Add the chopped aromatic vegetables, reduce the heat, and continue to stir-fry until the shallot is transparent, about 10 minutes. Add the tomato paste and stir it into the mixture.

Add the butter, continuing to stir, and the water or stock. Bring to a boil, give it a good stir, turn off the heat, and leave it on the burner for about an hour for the flavors to infuse. Strain the mixture through a fine sieve, pushing as much liquid through as possible.

If you have used whole shrimp, you might want to take the solids and grind them in a food processor, then put them through the sieve again, to extract all the flavor. Refrigerate overnight.

The next morning, lift the congealed butter from the surface of the mixture and heat it over very low heat. Save the remaining liquid for Shrimp and Grits or soup. When the butter is melted, strain it again into an 8-inch square cake pan and refrigerate again. When cold, cut into the desired sizes and wrap well in foil for freezing.

A little of this melted butter over fish is exquisite. A little melted in a pan, with a few peeled shrimp added, makes a perfect topping for pasta, rice, or grits.

SHRIMP AND GRITS

I know of no dish more typically Lowcountry than Shrimp and Grits. Umpteen versions exist for the gravy, from a simple sautéing of the shrimp in butter to complicated sauces made by techniques popular in nouvelle cuisine. Until recently families all over the Lowcountry partook of "breakfast shrimp," as the dish is often called, every morning during shrimp season. Preferred, as always, are the smallest, "creek" shrimp.

I prepare seven or eight versions of this dish; two of them are Charleston classics—the shrimp prepared in melted butter or in bacon grease with onions and peppers. Ruth Fales, who with her husband Scott runs Charleston's Pinckney Café and Espresso, prepares a tomato sauce that points to the renewed interest among young chefs here in fine fresh local ingredients prepared simply. In November, when the shrimp season is at its height and the fall crops of tomatoes are bursting on the vines, she makes a sauce from the heads and shells of freshly caught shrimp and ripe red local tomatoes— a very Franco-Italian and very Lowcountry concoction that she serves over pasta as well as hominy. Other recipes count on the reduction of shrimp stock made from their heads and shells, an amber liquid that perfectly melds the creamy grits and the pink of the shrimp. Directions for cooking gloriously creamy, whole-grain grits, which are a far cry from those packaged "quick" and "instant" grits, can be found on page 69.

CLASSIC CHARLESTON BREAKFAST SHRIMP

This is what most Charlestonians think of as shrimp and grits. The secret to a nonpasty gravy is to cook the flour, which takes about 5 minutes. Even the largest shrimp need only cook for 3 minutes.

SERVES 2

1 cup (½ pound) peeled shrimp
2 tablespoons (⅛ cup) fresh lemon juice
    salt and cayenne pepper to taste
3 tablespoons bacon grease
1 small onion, finely chopped (about ¼ cup)
    about ¼ cup finely chopped green bell pepper
2 tablespoons (⅛ cup) unbleached all-purpose flour
    Creamy Grits (page 69)
¾ to 1 cup hot water or stock (shrimp, chicken, or vegetable)

In a bowl, sprinkle the shrimp with the lemon juice, salt, and cayenne and set aside. Heat the bacon grease in a skillet and sauté the onion and pepper over medium heat until the onion begins to become transparent, about 10 minutes. Sprinkle the flour over the vegetables and stir constantly for about 2 minutes, until the flour begins to brown. Add the shrimp and about ¾ cup water or stock, stirring constantly and turning the shrimp so that they cook evenly. Cook for another 2 to 3 minutes, until the shrimp are cooked through and the gravy is uniformly smooth, thinning with a little extra water or stock if necessary. Serve immediately over the grits.

RUTH FALES'S TOMATO AND SHRIMP SAUCE FOR GRITS, RICE, OR PASTA

MAKES ABOUT 5 CUPS

FOR THE SAUCE:

   5 pounds heads-on shrimp
   ¼ cup olive oil
   2 tablespoons (⅛ cup) chopped garlic
   1 gallon crushed ripe tomatoes (core the tomatoes and run them
       through a food mill or meat grinder)
       salt and freshly ground black pepper to taste

Peel the shrimp and remove the heads, saving the shells and heads and refrigerating the shrimp for later use. In a large nonreactive stockpot, heat the oil until smoking and add the shrimp shells and heads, stirring them constantly and frying them until they all turn pink. Add the garlic and the tomato puree, reduce the heat, and simmer slowly for 2 hours. Puree the mixture well, then strain it until it is perfectly smooth and free of stray bits of shell, about 4 or 5 times. Correct the seasoning with salt and pepper.

FOR SERVING:

       olive oil
   ¼ pound peeled shrimp per serving
   ¼ to ½ cup reserved sauce per serving
       about 1 tablespoon unsalted butter per serving
       freshly ground black pepper to taste
       freshly chopped basil or Italian flat-leaf parsley to taste
       (optional)

Sauté the shrimp over medium heat in a little olive oil, adding some sauce as you turn them from one side to the other. Cook no more than 3 minutes. Finish the sauce off with a little butter and freshly ground black pepper and serve over pasta or rice with a garnish of freshly chopped basil or parsley or without the herbs over grits.

TWO SHRIMP SAUCES FOR GRITS MADE WITH REDUCED STOCK

These two sophisticated sauces are, ironically, the easiest to make: the one, a reduction of shrimp stock bound with butter; the other, stock and cream reduced together.

I

The first of these sauces uses a simple technique popular among the young chefs of France. A shellfish stock is reduced to concentrate its flavor, the shrimp are sprinkled with lemon juice or sherry vinegar, and the sauce is bound with butter, whisked in a little at a time, forming a rich, silken shrimp-colored and shrimp-flavored sauce.

PER SERVING:

    ¼ **pound peeled shrimp**
       fresh lemon juice or sherry vinegar to taste
    ½ **cup shrimp stock (page 35)**
    4 **tablespoons cold unsalted butter, cut into small cubes**
       Creamy Grits (page 69)

Sprinkle the shrimp with lemon juice or sherry vinegar and set aside. In a saucepan over high heat, reduce the shrimp stock by two thirds. Add the shrimp and continue to cook over high heat, turning the shrimp so that they cook evenly, for about 2 minutes. Then add the butter a little at a time, whisking it constantly, until the shrimp are cooked and the sauce is evenly bound and velvety smooth. Serve at once over hot grits.

II

This sauce is so easy to prepare and so delicious, it's a wonder every Lowcountry restaurant doesn't feature it. It takes less than 10 minutes to prepare a single serving.

PER SERVING:

    ¼ **pound peeled shrimp**
       salt and freshly ground black pepper to taste
    ½ **cup shrimp stock (page 35)**
    ½ **cup cream**
       Creamy Grits (page 69)

Season the shrimp with salt and pepper and set aside. Put the stock and cream in a saucepan and bring to a boil over high heat. Add the shrimp and cook until they are just done—about 2 minutes. Remove the shrimp with a slotted spoon and place on top of hot grits. Reduce the liquid at a rapid boil, stirring frequently, until the mixture is the thickness you desire. Correct the seasoning, then pour the sauce over the shrimp and grits and serve immediately.

FROGMORE STEW

St. Helena Island, near Hilton Head, used to have a town center called Frogmore, named after an ancestral English country estate. It consisted of four buildings, including the post office; new residents have changed the official name to St. Helena. In the early twentieth century, Frogmore was the site of booming caviar and diamondback terrapin businesses. The "stew" is named after the old Sea Island settlement.

This Lowcountry seafood boil is usually served on paper plates around newspaper-covered picnic tables outdoors, with plenty of ice-cold beer. Partially cleaned but uncooked crab is sometimes added to the pot at the same time as the corn (to clean crabs live, see page 102). The recipe may be adjusted for more or fewer people by allowing ½ pound of shrimp per person, ¼ pound of sausage per person, 1½ ears of corn per person, and 2 tablespoons of "boil" per gallon of water.

SERVES 8

3 tablespoons commercially prepared shrimp boil such as Old Bay
    Seasoning plus 3 tablespoons salt *or* 3 tablespoons homemade
    boil (page 32)
1½ gallons water
2 pounds hot smoked link sausage, cut into 2-inch pieces (see Note)
12 ears freshly shucked corn, broken into 3- to 4-inch pieces
4 pounds shrimp

In a large stockpot, add the seasonings to the water and bring to a boil. Add the sausage and boil, uncovered, for 5 minutes. Add the corn and count 5 minutes. Add the shrimp and count 3 minutes. (Don't wait for the liquid to return to a boil before timing the corn and shrimp.) Drain immediately and serve.

Note: If you cannot find a spicy hot smoked sausage, use another smoked sausage such as kielbasa and add ½ teaspoon hot red pepper flakes per person. Leftover Frogmore stew helps make a delicious soup. Peel the shrimp, cut the corn from the cob, slice the sausage thinly, then add to simmering duck stock or tomato juice to warm through. Season with fresh hot peppers.

SHRIMP KEDGEREE

Kedgeree was the favored breakfast dish of the Edwardian sideboard in England. The word is borrowed from India, where the dish is made with rice, lentils, spices, and eggs. In England, where smoked fish is added, it might simply be called curried haddie (smoked haddock) and rice. Here too, in the Lowcountry, the dish is a curried rice pie, this one with shrimp; it is served as a supper dish.

SERVES 8

1 large onion, finely chopped
½ cup finely chopped celery
¼ pound (1 stick) butter, melted
1 tablespoon imported Madras curry powder *or* 1 tablespoon
    homemade "curry" mix (page 154)
2 cups cream
4 cups peeled shrimp
2 cups cooked long-grain white rice
½ cup finely chopped apple
    salt, freshly ground black pepper, and cayenne pepper to taste
    freshly grated coconut, chutney, roast nuts, and relish for garnish

Preheat the oven to 350°. In a large cast-iron skillet, sauté the onion and celery in the butter over medium-high heat until the onions are transparent, about 5 minutes. Add the curry, stir well, then add the cream and the shrimp. Remove from the heat and toss the shrimp well in the cream mixture. Toss the rice into the mixture—do not stir it, or it will become sticky—along with the apples. Season to taste. Bake, uncovered, for 45 minutes. Provide grated coconut, chutney, roast peanuts or almonds, and a pickle or artichoke relish as accompaniments.

SHRIMP AND CRAB GUMBO

This is a big, wonderful, messy meal to serve on one of the first cool fall nights, when crab and shrimp are still plentiful but the oysters aren't yet good. Louisiana may claim gumbo, which is a West African word for okra, but in fact okra, a member of the genus *Hibiscus,* entered South Carolina with the slave trade long before Louisiana was settled by Europeans. Lowcountry gumbo eschews the filé powder of the Louisiana version.

12 SERVINGS

FOR THE STOCK:

    12 live crabs

    2 pounds extremely fresh heads-on shrimp *or* 1½ pounds headless shrimp

    1 tablespoon olive oil

    a handful of fresh herbs

    1 gallon water

    2 celery ribs, broken into pieces

    2 carrots, broken into pieces

    2 medium onions, peeled and quartered

FOR THE GUMBO:

    ½ cup dark roux (page 33)

    ½ cup chopped onion

    ½ cup chopped celery

    ¼ cup chopped green bell pepper

    1 pound okra, trimmed and cut into ½-inch pieces

    6 vine-ripened tomatoes (about 2 pounds), peeled and chopped, *or* 1 28-ounce can peeled tomatoes with their juice

    2 fresh jalapeño or other hot peppers

    3 cups long-grain white rice

To make the stock, partially clean the live crabs (see page 102), refrigerating the meat-filled body and claws for addition to the gumbo later. Rinse the backs well in water. Peel the shrimp and remove the heads, refrigerating the bodies for use later. Lightly grease the bottom of a large stockpot with the oil, then add the crab backs and cook over high heat

until they turn red, stirring frequently. Add the shrimp heads and/or shells
and continue cooking over medium-high heat until they turn pink. Add
the remaining stock ingredients and cook at a low boil, skimming as necessary, until the desired intensity of flavor is reached. In about an hour it
will have reduced to about 3 quarts; it should be delicious. Strain out and
discard the solids, reserving the stock.

To make the gumbo, heat the roux in a large stockpot over medium
heat. Add the onions, celery, and bell pepper and cook until the onions
begin to become transparent, stirring constantly, about 10 minutes. Add
the okra and cook, stirring often, until all the ropiness is gone, about 20
minutes. Add the tomatoes and simmer for 10 minutes. Add the hot peppers
and reserved stock and simmer, uncovered, for about an hour.

About 30 minutes before serving, cook the rice in a separate pot (page
57–58). Fifteen minutes before serving, add the reserved crab claws and
bodies to the gumbo and increase the heat. Five minutes before serving,
add the shrimp. Serve in large bowls over fluffy white rice, with hand towels
as napkins.

CRABS

More delicate and versatile than their lofty cousins from Maine, Atlantic
blue crabs are also more common than lobster. Charleston is famous for its
She-Crab Soup, but crabmeat itself is so delicious that I hesitate to team
it with dairy products, especially in warmer weather when crab is plentiful.
When I was a child, crabbing was one of my favorite activities, even when
I knew full well that I could probably catch more by simply putting out the
family trap. In the fifties, when Cap'n Mac Holmes was the patriarch of
Edisto Island, we would visit his children and grandchildren at his old house
on the beach. There we'd sit spellbound by his Gullah tales of hurricanes
and "haints" and fascinated by his cigar box of fossilized shark's teeth,
millions of years old. He was "Granddaddy" to all and headed up the old
"yacht" club down at the wide and shallow mouth of the South Edisto
River, on the southern tip of the island, where we loved to crab. It's no
wonder the Lowcountry saw the disappearance of good homemade chicken
stock, given all the chicken parts we used to pull in crabs on the end of
our weighted cotton twine.

At other times we might go back up inland to Cowpens, a spot midmarsh
off Legare (pronounced "le GREE") Road, where we dangled our strings at

low tide from the dilapidated bridge. Before the onslaught of development in the Lowcountry in the early seventies, I do not remember ever coming home empty-handed from a crabbing jaunt. Crabs were not only plentiful then, but larger as well.

It was on Hilton Head Island, though, that I really learned about crabs; as much as I love Charleston and Edisto, something dramatic happens when you cross Port Royal Sound, a culinary boundary as real as the geographic Fall Line. Perhaps the lack of a bridge to Hilton Head and Daufuskie islands kept their traditions isolated and pure; or perhaps it was the cooking of boating families that was so different, given cramped conditions and limited stores. South of Port Royal, people really know their crabs, and they clean them live.

Many cities claim crabs as their own: Baltimore, New Orleans, Charleston, Savannah, Mobile, Jacksonville, and Wilmington. And we all love a good crab boil. But down around Daufuskie you're likely to be invited to a different kind of crab crack—one that isn't messy at all, because the crabs are cleaned before they are steamed.

If you're the squeamish sort, you can always ice the crabs down for a while before you start—but be sure all of them are alive and kicking before you do. Grab the crab from behind. You may find it easy to grab hold of its last set of legs, which are flattened into paddles for swimming. Or you may want to lay something heavy across the crab or grasp it with big crab tongs if you're afraid (and well you might be: a crab can all but sever a finger). Then, with the crab facing away from you, grab one of its pincers at the joint and twist the entire claw down and off the body. Then do the same with the second claw.

Turn the crab over and pull its apron away from its body. Then, using the apron as its "pop tab," or by inserting a fork into the crab at the edge where the apron is attached, pop the entire carapace off the crab. Discard or save for a stock or to stuff with deviled crab. Pull off the gills and the spongy "dead man," but if the crab is a female with unmistakable bright orange roe, save it. Rip off the mouth and pop the body in half (or use a knife or kitchen shears), then rinse the claws and body halves in cold water.

You now have a crab that is all meat and a little bit of shell, ready to be cooked in half the time and space and to be enjoyed without the sloppiness of boiled whole crabs. You will not need so large a pot, and an inch of seasoned water in the bottom of a pan is really all that is needed to steam crabs. Let it come to a boil and add the claws and the body parts. Cover and steam for about ten minutes. The crabs will cook perfectly in the steam, not absorb water and overcook, and are much safer, cleaner, and better-keeping than traditionally boiled whole crabs. But the best part is in the eating, for picking the meat from a steamed cleaned crab is a simple process. Where each leg is attached to the body, a chamber holds a perfect piece of meat that will come out with little effort and no tools. Clean and cook crabs once this way, and you will never go back to boiling live crabs again—unless you are from Louisiana or Maryland and must have heavily seasoned salts clinging to the shells of your crabs. And for recipes calling for crabmeat (expensive even in Charleston) this method saves a lot of time and fuss (though picking crabs *is* work). (A dozen large, meaty crabs will yield a pound of white lump crabmeat, plus the claws.) But the bottom line is: after you have eaten crabs cooked this way, you will probably find it unappetizing to sit down to crab guts at a traditional boil.

Crabs have inspired a Pulitzer Prize–winning book, an enormous industry, and a world of recipes. In 1988, 6 million pounds of local crabs were harvested commercially in South Carolina. No one knows how many more are taken recreationally. The recipes here were chosen to show off the Lowcountry's particular way with these crustaceans.

Harriott Pinckney Horry's receipt book from Hampton Plantation includes the following, written in about 1770. Today it would be called "Panned Crabmeat" and would be delicious on toast points, which are the "sippets" she suggests.

TO STEW CRABS

Choose three or four crabs, pick the Meat clean out of the body and claws, take care no spungy part be left among it or any of the Shell, put this clean meat into a stew pan, with a little white wine, some pepper and salt, and a little grated Nutmeg, heat all this, well together, and then put in Crums of Bread, the yolks of two Eggs beat up and one Spoonful of Vinegar. Stir all well together, make some toasted Sippets, lay them in a plate and pour in the crabs. Send it up hott.

Harriott Pinckney Horry, c. 1770

CRABS STEAMED IN BEER

Of the varied flavorings and liquids used to steam crabs and other shellfish, beer is perhaps the local favorite. For a dozen crabs, pour a 12-ounce beer into a 3-quart saucepan with a teaspoon or two of seafood boil (page 32). Bring to a boil, add the claws, then the other body parts, cover tightly, and steam for 10 minutes.

A dozen crabs will feed only one or two real crab lovers.

CRAB SOUP

This soup of sweet potatoes, crab, and coconut reflects the strong West Indian influence in the Lowcountry. You can make the soup with prepared shellfish stock—I have used lobster shells from the previous night's dinner—and substitute shrimp or crawfish for the crab. Joann Yaegar of the Primerose House and Tavern in Charleston and I first made this soup for an evening of Lowcountry foods in her restaurant. It is complex in texture and flavor, one of her most requested recipes. I recommend making the soup in the dead of winter, when female crabs are full of roe and coconuts are in their prime. The first time we made this soup, it wasn't as thick as we wanted it, but we didn't want to add another starch or more cream. Joann quickly tossed some raw scallops into the food processor and added them to hot soup bowls—a trick I have used many times since.

If you don't want to cook live crabs, you will need 2 quarts of prepared shellfish stock plus a pound of picked crabmeat. Boil the sweet potatoes with their skins on—or place them in the oven while you are roasting crustacean shells if you make your stock that way. While the recipe calls for a dozen crabs, I use 13—a "baker's dozen." Every fishmonger I know in the Lowcountry gives "broadus," like the Cajun's "lagniappe," and a dozen crabs is always 13.

SERVES 8

FOR THE STOCK:

    3 quarts water

    1 carrot

    2 celery ribs

    1 medium onion, quartered

       a handful of mixed fresh herbs such as parsley, basil, thyme,
         savory, and oregano

  12 large blue crabs

FOR THE SOUP:

    1 small (1¼ pounds) coconut

    2 pounds sweet potatoes, cooked, peeled, and run through a food
       mill or riced

    1 quart cream

       salt and cayenne pepper to taste

   ½ cup brandy, plus additional for serving (optional)

To make the stock, bring the water, vegetables, and herbs to a rolling boil and add the live crabs. Return to a boil and cook, uncovered, for 30 minutes. Take out the crabs and set aside, strain out the solids from the stock, then strain again and return the stock to the stove. You should have about 2 quarts.

To make the soup, punch through 2 or 3 of the eyes of the coconut (see page 245) and let a little of the coconut water run into the palm of your hand to taste for freshness. If sweet and fresh, strain the water into the 2 quarts reserved stock and add the riced sweet potatoes and cream. Begin heating the mixture over medium heat and let it reduce slowly, skimming it as necessary. Remove the shell from the coconut, pare off the dark brown skin, and cut the fresh meat into a tiny dice, adding it to the soup as you go along. You should have 2 cups of the diced coconut. In the meantime, pick the meat from the reserved cooked crabs. You should have about a pound. After about an hour, taste the soup, correct the seasoning with salt and cayenne, and add the brandy. Continue cooking and skimming until the desired consistency is reached. Just before serving, add the crabmeat and a little more brandy if desired to the soup bowls and pour the hot soup over the crabmeat. Serve at once.

DEVILED CRABS

Deviled crabs in the Lowcountry are often called simply "deb'l." Crab recipes in the South invariably call for commercially prepared "crab boils." Although I've included a formula for a homemade crab boil (page 32), in fact I usually improvise, depending on the serendipity of the moment, the projected use of the crabmeat, and the bounty of both my herb garden and my spice rack. Because I steam the crabs rather than boil them, I am partial to a simple addition of salt and hot pepper vinegar to the water, though some Lowcountry cooks add mustard, cloves, bay leaves, and allspice.

The following recipe is from Alice Marks, one of Charleston's great cooks. She packs the devil into crab backs (in Gullah, "barks") or scallop shells, wraps them well in aluminum foil, then freezes them for reheating later. One filled shell makes a rich appetizer or supper dish; serve two as dinner.

MAKES 8 TO 10 SERVINGS

½ cup finely chopped sweet onion
½ cup finely chopped celery
¼ pound (1 stick) unsalted butter
8 saltines, crushed
½ lemon, or to taste
1 pound crabmeat
3 to 6 tablespoons amontillado sherry, to taste
8 to 10 crab backs or scallop shells, sterilized in a dishwasher

Preheat the oven to 350°. Sauté the onion and celery in the butter in a saucepan over medium heat until very limp. Let cool completely, then mix with the saltines. Squeeze the juice of ½ lemon, more or less to taste, over the crabmeat. Lightly fold the crabmeat into the mixture so that you do not break it up. Season to taste with sherry. Pack into shells and bake for about 15 or 20 minutes, until just heated through and lightly browned on top.

BESSIE'S CRAB CAKES

Bessie Hanahan has served as chairman of the Hospitality Committee of the Spoleto Festival USA held in Charleston every spring and has planned dozens of parties for Spoleto. Lucille Grant, one of the Lowcountry's great cooks, frequently cooks in the kitchen of Bessie's historic home on South Battery. I too have helped prepare many meals there. But what many people do not know is that Bessie herself is a fine cook and that her crab cakes know no equal. Bessie is the first to admit that her recipe is likely to change each time she makes it—she might grab a bottle of Worcestershire sauce to season the cakes one time, some fresh herbs from her garden another. Because she dislikes breading in crab cakes, she chills them to hold them together before frying. "They usually fall apart," she says with a laugh, "but you won't taste any better."

I like to serve these on a pool of blue crab sauce. This makes for a very rich, elegant midsummer meal. "And be sure to serve vine-ripened tomatoes as a course by themselves," Bessie adds. I've had that course many times at her house in the sultry days that follow the festival: day-old French bread slices rubbed with garlic and good olive oil and cooked dry in an oven, then topped with more oil, tomato slices, more oil, salt, pepper, and fresh basil.

SERVES 3

FOR THE CRAB CAKES:
    1 **pound fresh crabmeat, well picked over**
    1 **lemon**
    4 **tablespoons unsalted butter**
    2 **tablespoons (⅛ cup) finely chopped sweet onion, such as**
        Vidalia or Wadmalaw
  ½ **cup chopped ripe red bell pepper *or* ¼ cup green**
    1 **tablespoon sherry vinegar**
    1 **large egg, beaten**
      salt, freshly ground black pepper, and other seasonings
        (seasoned salt, Tabasco, Worcestershire, cayenne, fresh
        herbs) to taste

(continued)

TO ASSEMBLE AND COOK:
  2 to 3 tablespoons clarified butter (page 24)
         fine dry bread crumbs

Sprinkle the juice of half the lemon over the crabmeat in a bowl to freshen it. (If the lemon is not juicy, use the juice from the whole lemon.) Melt the butter in a skillet over low heat and add the onion and bell pepper, cooking until the onion begins to become transparent. Add the vinegar, raise the heat, and reduce until the vinegar has evaporated. Pour the mixture over the crabmeat, add the egg, and toss all together, being careful not to break up the big lumps of crabmeat. Season to taste. (I add salt, pepper, cayenne, and about a tablespoon of chopped fresh herbs. Bessie adds seasoned salt, Tabasco, and Worcestershire.) Refrigerate for several hours, or place in the freezer for about 15 minutes.

Put the clarified butter in a skillet over medium heat. Remove the crab cake mixture from the refrigerator or freezer and form it into patties—3 large or 6 small. Roll in bread crumbs and fry for 3 or 4 minutes over medium heat on each side until they are golden brown.

BLUE CRAB SAUCE

This classic sauce is intensely flavored. A little goes a long way. If your crab cakes fall apart while cooking, simply pour the sauce over the top of the cakes for an attractive presentation.

SERVES 3

  6 small *or* 4 large live blue crabs
  3 tablespoons unsalted butter
  ¾ cup good white wine (the wine you serve with the meal)
  1½ cups fish stock (page 36) or crab or shrimp stock (page 35)
      fresh lemon juice or sherry vinegar to taste

Break the claws off the crabs and remove the top shells and gills. Crush the crab bodies with a mallet and begin to sauté in a wide pan with the butter, wine, and stock. Add the claws to the pan as well, but do not crush them as they should be used for garnish. Keep the mixture simmering, but do not let it boil. When it has reduced considerably and has begun to thicken, after 10 minutes, remove the claws and set aside, then strain into another pan. Taste for seasoning and finish off the reduction with a little lemon juice or sherry vinegar to correct the flavor. Serve immediately.

If the sauce is not thick enough or does not want to hold, add a little more cold butter, cut into small pieces, and whisk in vigorously. (An immersion blender works perfectly.)

CRAB HOPPIN' JOHN

This delightful salad of crab, peas, and rice is a perfect summer lunch when served with vine-ripened tomatoes. If you live where you can get live crabs, you can pick the meat from a dozen large, cooked crabs to provide the pound of crabmeat (page 32).

SERVES 8 TO 10

2 cups fresh or frozen black-eyed peas
1 cup water
juice of 2 lemons
1 pound cooked crabmeat
3 cups cooked long-grain white rice
½ cup lightly flavored oil, such as safflower
1 medium onion, finely chopped (about ¾ cup)
2 celery ribs, finely chopped (about ½ cup)
¼ cup chopped parsley or another fresh herb of your choice
salt and freshly ground black pepper to taste

Place the peas and water in a small saucepan and bring to a simmer. Simmer the peas, uncovered, until almost all the water is absorbed, about 30 minutes. They should no longer taste starchy. Set aside to cool. The rest of the water will be absorbed in cooling.

Add the lemon juice to the crabmeat, tossing it lightly, breaking it up, and checking it carefully for stray pieces of shell. Add it to the peas along with the rice in a serving bowl, tossing lightly with the remaining ingredients, blending carefully so as not to mash the peas.

Correct the seasoning and chill. Serve with fresh tomatoes and a bottle of hot pepper sauce.

CRAWFISH

I'm surprised that crawfish (and I have never heard them called "crayfish") cookery never reached the heights in the Lowcountry that it has in Louisiana—the rice fields surely must have been filled with them. Perhaps the slaves whose job it was to keep the fields cleaned of pests threw the crawfish into their pots with the turtles and eels. Or perhaps they were simply destroyed, since Africa is the only continent where these "mudbugs" are not indigenous.

Having been born in Louisiana before moving to the Lowcountry, I have well known how to eat "crawdads" all my life. But only recently, with the advent of Lowcountry crawfish farms, have they entered the local culinary tradition. Locally we now can obtain crawfish even as soft-shells.

Crawfish tails themselves have a very bland, delicate flavor that is enhanced by the use of strong spices. If you plan to use the tails in another recipe, cook them for only about 3 minutes. If, however, you want to have a crawfish boil, add some lemons and an extra tablespoon of spices to the water (see seafood boil, page 32) and boil them, uncovered, for 5 to 10 minutes, depending on their size. The shells of crawfish make the most flavorful of all the shellfish stocks. If you can get live crawfish, buy two or three times the amount you think you'll need (it takes about 15 pounds to feed 4 adults): you can always pick the tail meat out for later use and make a stock of the shells.

Between the head and tail of the crawfish is the bright orange hepatopancreas, which is delicious. It is referred to here as the "fat."

CRAWFISH GUMBO

In this rich, densely flavored gumbo the dark roux provides a complex background to the vegetables, and the rice provides a foil for the intensity of the shellfish stock—with brilliant red crawfish tails garnishing the soup with their buttery sweetness.

MAKES ABOUT 8 SERVINGS

FOR THE CRAWFISH:
- 5 pounds live crawfish
- 3 tablespoons seafood boil (page 32) or commercial seafood boil
- 1 lemon, halved
- 5 quarts water

FOR THE STOCK:
- 1 gallon water
- 1 large *or* 2 small carrots
- 1 large onion, peeled and quartered
- 2 celery ribs
  - a handful of fresh herbs such as parsley, oregano, basil, thyme, and savory plus a bay leaf

FOR THE GUMBO:
- ¼ cup chocolate-colored roux (page 33)
- ¾ cup chopped onion
- ¾ cup chopped celery
- ¾ cup chopped green bell pepper
- 2 pounds okra, trimmed and sliced
- 6 large ripe tomatoes *or* 2 28-ounce cans peeled tomatoes
- 1 teaspoon Herbal Mix (page 31)
  - salt, freshly ground black pepper, and cayenne pepper or hot pepper sauce to taste

TO SERVE:
- 3 cups cooked long-grain white rice
  - reserved crawfish tails and "fat"

(continued)

Put the crawfish in a large pot and cover with salt water. Swirl the pot around (some say the motion will make them seasick). The crawfish will purge themselves. Dump out the water and throw away any crawfish that have not survived the ordeal. Repeat until the water is clear. Add the seafood boil and lemon to the 5 quarts water and bring to a boil. Add the crawfish and boil, uncovered, for 3 minutes. Drain, pick the tail meat and "fat" from the heads, and refrigerate, covered, for use later. You should have about 2½ pounds of shells to use for the stock.

Bring the reserved shells and all of the stock ingredients to a boil in a stockpot, lower the heat, and simmer for about 2 hours, skimming foam off the top as necessary. Strain out the solids and discard. Reserve the stock for later use. You should have about 2½ quarts.

To make the gumbo, put the roux in a large pot and heat over medium-high heat until it is hot. Do not let it cook any more or it will burn. Add the onions, celery, and bell pepper and stir until the vegetables are well coated with the roux. Cook for about 5 minutes, stirring frequently. It is important that the roux not burn. Add the okra and stir until it is coated with the roux as well. Cook for another 5 minutes, stirring.

Add the tomatoes with their juice and stir well. Raise the heat and bring to a boil. Add the herbs, then add the 2½ quarts reserved stock. Lower the heat and simmer the gumbo for 1 hour, skimming if necessary, and breaking up the tomatoes as they cook. Correct the seasoning with salt, pepper, and hot pepper sauce.

To serve, put a big mound of rice in each bowl, cover with a handful of crawfish tails and "fat," and pour hot gumbo over them. Serve with corn bread (page 219) and green salad or in smaller bowls as an appetizer.

CLAMS WITH PASTA

Quahogs are abundant in the salt marshes of the Lowcountry. No clamming license is required for residents, and we are allowed ½ bushel per head of household for no more than two days each week of the nine-month season (September through May). Littlenecks, the smallest grade, are seldom seen locally; they are shipped up north, where they are better appreciated. We are left with the cherrystones, or mediums, and the big "chowders," fit only for what their name implies.

I put the clams in a large bucket of salty water to which I add some cornmeal and black pepper. The clams will purge themselves of sand within an hour. I then steam the clams until they just open in a Charleston rice steamer (page 57). Do not overcook them or they will toughen. A dozen medium-large clams, about 2½ to 3 inches in diameter, will yield 1½ cups clam juice. Figure a dozen clams for each diner. One-quarter pound of uncooked dried flat pasta makes one serving.

FOR EACH SERVING:

- ¼ **pound dried pasta**
- ¼ **cup olive oil**
- 5 **garlic cloves, minced**
- ¾ **cup strained clam juice**
- 1 **tablespoon mixed chopped fresh herbs such as basil, parsley, and oregano** *or* **1 teaspoon dried Italian seasoning or** *herbes de Provence*
- 2 **tablespoons unsalted butter**
- 12 **medium clams, steamed and chopped (about ½ cup)**

Bring a large pot of water to a rolling boil, add a pinch of salt, and return to a boil. Cook the pasta in the water, uncovered, while you prepare the sauce.

Heat the oil with the garlic over medium heat until the oil is permeated with the garlic flavor; do not let the garlic brown. Add the clam juice and herbs and allow about half of the liquid to evaporate. Increase the heat a bit and whisk in the butter. Add the clams, stirring to coat them well, then serve at once over hot cooked pasta. Pass the pepper mill.

OYSTERS

Oysters are prepared simply in the Lowcountry, as often as not eaten raw. I like to dredge them in prepared mustard, dust in seasoned cornflour, and fry. I sometimes make a cocktail sauce for fried shrimp and oysters by reducing the shrimp shells and oyster liquor with a little celery and garlic in chopped fresh tomatoes, spicing it with some horseradish. Oyster pie is a typical dish. It is really scalloped oysters: there is no crust, and the oysters are teamed with crushed saltines and a little butter and seasoning. Oyster soups are also traditional.

OYSTER SAUSAGES

These sausages were once common on Lowcountry tables, when oysters were more plentiful than meat, but few people make them today. They are either made into patties or stuffed into casings and are made with either veal or pork (though Sarah Rutledge made hers with both beef and mutton). I have made them with lamb, using some fresh pork fat, and I have increased the ratio of oysters. The marvelous thing about sausage making is that, as soon as the mixture is ground all together, you can fry a little and taste it to correct not only the seasoning but the ratio of ingredients as well.

If you plan to stuff the sausage, you will need about 4 feet of hog casings. Because this sausage is more delicate than the casing, be sure to poach stuffed oyster sausages rather than fry them. Save the drained oyster liquor in which to poach them, with a little milk added if necessary. Serve with the sweet pepper relish on page 320.

If you plan to make patties, fry them in clarified butter (page 24) until golden brown and serve on a bed of lettuce with lemon wedges.

MAKES 2 POUNDS

1 pint freshly shucked oysters
1 pound fatty boneless pork, cut into 2-inch chunks
2 large egg yolks
½ cup dry bread crumbs
   salt and freshly ground black pepper to taste
   cayenne pepper to taste
   Herbal Mix (page 31) *herbes de Provence,* or Italian seasoning to
      taste
   about 4 feet of cleaned hog casings (optional; see *Note)*

Drain the oysters, reserving the liquor in which to poach the sausages if they are to be stuffed into casings. With your meat grinder set on the coarser setting, run the oysters and the pork alternately through the grinder. Add the yolks and bread crumbs, then season to taste with salt, pepper, cayenne, and the herbs. Mix the ingredients well together, then take a little spoonful and fry it in a pan until golden brown. Taste it and correct the seasoning.

Run the mixture back through the meat grinder set on the finer setting (and with the sausage stuffer attached and the casings tied at one end and placed over the end of the funnel, ready to be filled, if you want stuffed sausages). Tie off stuffed sausages into 4-inch links. Cover the sausages and place immediately in the refrigerator. Use within 24 hours, cooking them as described in the recipe introduction.

Note: Casings, available from your butcher, are sold, sometimes frozen, packed in salt. To clean them, run water from a faucet through them several times until they are free of all salt crystals.

BENNE-OYSTER SOUP

Sarah Rutledge, writing in *The Carolina Housewife* (1847), offered several recipes, including one with peanuts and one with benne (sesame seeds). Here is a modern adaptation of the benne-oyster combination.

SERVES 2

 1 tablespoon benne (sesame seeds)
 1 cup oyster liquor, drained from the oysters
 1 cup cream
12 large oysters, shucked
    cayenne pepper and freshly ground black pepper to taste

On a baking sheet in a preheated 350° oven or in a heavy-bottomed pan over medium heat, cook the benne until evenly browned, about 10 to 15 minutes. Remove to a mortar and grind with a pestle until a paste forms, adding a few drops of oyster liquor or cream if necessary. Heat the cream and oyster liquor together in a saucepan, gradually stir in the benne paste, then add the oysters and continue to heat until the oysters are just curled. It takes only a minute. Season with cayenne and black pepper.

Typically, oyster soups contain oysters, butter, and cream. Some people add celery; others add Worcestershire sauce. I prefer Sarah Rutledge's.

POTAGE AUX HUÎTRES

Bruise in a mortar two dozen fine oysters, very fresh and washed. Put them in some broth, and cook on a slow fire for about half an hour. Pass the soup through a sieve or fine colander, and put in crusts of bread. This soup is more nourishing and more wholesome than any other that is made from meat.

The Carolina Housewife, 1847

7
MEAT

Meat cookery in the Lowcountry comes right out of the country French and English traditions that shaped so much of the rest of our culture. Roasts, *daubes,* and *pot-au-feu* fill all of our old cookbooks and appear on our tables today as they have since Carolina was a colony. For two hundred years our food was typified by this country cooking; it was, for the most part, woman's work.

Butchering, sausage making, and outdoor cooking, however, have become a male province in this modern world. As families have become smaller and as we have become more health-conscious, most of the larger cuts of meat have been relegated to the holidays and special occasions when more than three or four people appear at the table. Today most meat cooking seems to be done on patio grills and smokers—steaks, chops, and tenderloins.

Everyone has so embraced the idea that the South has always eaten pork, pork, and more pork that Dr. Elizabeth Reitz's zooarchaeological evidence to the contrary comes as a surprise even to Sandlappers. Speaking at the opening of the Charleston Museum's exhibition, "The Bountiful Coast: Foodways of the South Carolina Lowcountry," Reitz showed that not only was animal husbandry never a major farming practice in the Lowcountry; but also that duck and veal bones were those most commonly found in her digs in the area.

I usually cook meat like poultry, in a very hot oven or over coals. In no cooking do I make more use of my senses: roasts hiss when they need to be basted; doneness is judged by touch. The stew is ready when it smells and looks "just right." Even so, I recommend that you use an instant-read meat thermometer, available at restaurant supply houses. Check the thermometer to see what it reads in boiling water. If it's not 212°, adjust the temperatures you're expecting accordingly.

Let roasts come to room temperature, then sear them on top of the stove or by beginning the roasting at a very high temperature—450–500°. The structure of the muscle fibers in a piece of meat and its amount of fat, not the weight, determine how—and how long—it should be cooked. Insert the meat thermometer into the meat at its thickest point, without touching the bone, to test for doneness. I like meat rare; you may find that the temperatures that I give are a bit low for your palate. Before you carve a veal, pork, or lamb roast, let it rest for at least ten minutes to relax and become juicy again. With beef, try to relax yourself and let it go longer, even 20 minutes if you can resist the aroma.

I eat rare roast beef when its internal temperature has reached about 130°; 150° is medium. Veal and pork are perfectly pink and delicious at about 140°. I eat lamb and mutton ever so slightly more cooked than beef, at about 135–140°. So that a roast does not stew in its own juices, I use roasting racks and baste the meat as it hisses.

MUTTON AND LAMB

Mutton was far more common than lamb in the Lowcountry of yore, and recipes—most often in a British vein—abound. I frankly prefer the mature flavor of mutton over lamb—especially the lamb that has been bred for the American palate so that it does not, in fact, taste like Old World lamb. I mail-order my lamb and mutton, like my veal and chicken, from Summerfield Farm (page 29), where all the animals are raised naturally. I don't tell friends I'm serving them mutton—a Summerfield leg of mutton is not much larger than a leg of modern American lamb—and they are always thrilled with the flavor and texture. I try to simulate the high temperatures of real spit roasting when I cook mutton, even though I'm actually baking the meat.

ROAST LEG OF MUTTON OR LAMB

SERVES UP TO 20 PEOPLE FOR A 10-POUND LEG

1   leg of mutton or lamb
    several garlic cloves (at least 1 per pound of meat), peeled
½   pound fresh lard or fresh pork fat
1   2-ounce tin salted anchovies in oil
    several large fresh rosemary stems, about 12 inches long, tied
       together to form a brush

Preheat the oven to 500°. Trim the leg of mutton or lamb of all fat. Insert the peeled cloves of garlic throughout the leg, piercing the meat where necessary with a knife but avoiding cutting into the choice cuts. Put the leg in the oven on a large shallow roasting pan. If you have a large roasting rack, put the leg in the rack on the pan. In the meantime, melt the lard on top of the stove in a small saucepan and add the anchovies, stirring them into the melted lard. Let the meat cook for a full 15 minutes to sear the outside well, then turn down the oven to 425°. Dip the rosemary paintbrush in the lard and baste the mutton with the mixture every 10 to 15 minutes. Roast the meat for a total of about 12 minutes per pound, then remove from the oven and allow it to rest for at least 15 minutes before carving. If you can find fava beans, serve as suggested in the recipe on page 183.

LAMB SHANKS IN RED WINE

When fresh local asparagus and green beans first appear as harbingers of spring, I serve them with this hearty dish of lamb shanks and Cream Muffins.

SERVES 4

4 lamb shanks, about ¾ pound each
¼ cup olive oil, more or less
1 teaspoon Herbal Mix (page 31) or *herbes de Provence* or Italian
    seasoning plus salt and freshly ground black pepper
1 cup dry red wine
16 garlic cloves, unpeeled

Remove the excess fat from the outside of the lamb shanks. Cover the bottom of a heavy-bottomed pan or a Dutch oven that has a tight-fitting lid with a film of olive oil and place over medium-high heat. Brown the shanks in the hot oil. Grind the herbs in a spice mill or mortar and pestle and sprinkle over the shanks. Add the wine and garlic, bring to a simmer, then reduce the heat to very low. Cover the pot and braise for 1 to 2 hours or until the lamb is perfectly tender and the meat has begun to fall from the bones.

Remove the shanks to plates. Strain the liquid remaining in the pan, pressing as much of the cooked garlic through the sieve as possible. Return the liquid to the pan, reduce a little over medium-high heat if necessary, and pour over the shanks.

BEEF AND VEAL

Today's veal is a far cry from the young calves that were slaughtered on Lowcountry plantations. I order naturally raised veal that is allowed to walk around and is given only its mother's milk (see page 29 for a source). It is delicious. Decent beef is becoming increasingly difficult to find as more of our small farmers and butchers go out of business each year. Recipes for roasts and stews have changed little through the years, so I have included a few beef and veal recipes that are less likely to be found in other cookbooks.

One of the most amazing flavors I know comes from cooking a steak in Chanterelle Butter. Put a little of the butter in a hot pan, melt it, then add some nice steaks, seasoned with salt and freshly ground black pepper. Sear the steaks on both sides and continue cooking until they are done to your liking. Remove the steaks and set them on a warm platter, then add some bourbon to the pan to deglaze, scraping up any little bits stuck to the bottom of the pan. Stir it all together well, then ignite the bourbon to burn off the alcohol. Pour over the steaks and serve immediately. I jokingly call this fake pecan butter, using what most people would consider a luxury to imitate another ingredient taken for granted in the Lowcountry.

OXTAIL STEW

We are fortunate to have only a few weeks of cold weather in the Lowcountry. Late January and early February, though, can be awfully cold when the rains set in and the temperature hovers at freezing for several weeks. I can remember when few houses were built for the cold, and it slipped in through the windows, under the doors, and through floors and chimneys. It takes only about 3 consecutive cold, gray winter days here before I buy some oxtail joints and make a stew. Oxtail is full of bones, but the meat is indescribably rich and sweet. It is one of my favorite flavors, and it cooks for hours on end, warming the house.

These days oxtails are usually sold already cut up into 2-inch joints, weighing about ½ pound each. Buy at least one joint for each serving. Oxtail dishes are all the more flavorful when begun a day in advance.

SERVES 4 TO 6

½ cup unbleached all-purpose flour
  salt and freshly ground black pepper to taste
4 or 5 (about 2 pounds) oxtail joints, cut into pieces about 2 inches
      long
4 tablespoons unsalted butter
1 *bouquet garni*—1 celery rib, 1 bay leaf, 1 thyme sprig, and 1
      sprig of fresh parsley—*or* 1 teaspoon Herbal Mix (page 31)
1 large *or* 2 small carrots, cut into 1½-inch pieces
4 medium onions, peeled and quartered
2 garlic cloves, peeled
3 cups full-bodied red wine
2 cups beef, veal, chicken, vegetable stock, or water
½ pound small fresh mushrooms, stems removed

Early in the day or the day before, season the flour with salt and pepper
and toss the oxtail pieces in it to coat them lightly, reserving any remaining
flour. In a Dutch oven, melt half the butter and add the bouquet garni,
carrots, onions, and oxtail pieces. Sauté them over medium heat until
everything is richly browned, about 10 minutes. Add the garlic and remaining flour and stir until the mixture is smooth. Add the wine and stock,
mix well again, and bring to a boil, stirring frequently.

Reduce the heat to low, cover the pot tightly, and simmer slowly on
top of the stove or in a slow (300–325°) oven for about 3 hours. Remove
the oxtail pieces from the pot, strain the sauce into a bowl, and discard
the vegetables. If you plan to serve a casual meal with the stew as dinner,
leave the meat on the bones of the oxtail. If you plan to serve it over
noodles, pick the meat from the bones. Refrigerate overnight or continue
the recipe from this point.

Two hours before serving, remove any fat that has risen to the surface
of the sauce, then reduce it in a saucepan until it has the consistency of
cream. Put the remaining 2 tablespoons of butter in a Dutch oven, add the
mushrooms, and sauté over medium-high heat until they begin to lose their
water, about 15 minutes. Add the meat and the sauce to the pot, cover
tightly, and cook over low heat on top of the stove or in a slow oven for
another 1½ to 2 hours. Let your nose be your guide to when the stew is
done; when I smell it, I put the noodles in their pot. Serve hot over egg
noodles, preferably homemade. A historical recipe follows.

TO MAKE NUDELN

Put a quarter of a pound of flour upon the table or in a dish with a little salt, one egg, (or the yolks of three) make of it a hard dough, roll it with a rolling pin as thin as possible, strew flour often under it that it may not stick to the table: the harder the dough is, the thinner you can roll it. Strew on a little more flour, cut it in strips two inches broad, lay one over another. Cut the nudels fine or coarse according to your fancy, and lay them separately so that they may not stick together. (You can make them a few days before you wish to use them; but in this case they must boil much longer, and fresh made are the best.) This quantity put into two quarts of boiling broth, let it boil half an hour, that they may be quite soft. You may also boil them in two quarts of milk, and sprinkle with sugar and cinnamon. *German Receipt.*

The Carolina Housewife, 1847

VEAL OR PORK WITH APPLES AND COUNTRY HAM

Bill Hughes is the best meat cook I know. His *daubes* and stews, roasts and steaks are always simply perfect. He especially does right by veal, the favored meat of early Charleston.

- 1 3-pound shoulder steak of veal *or* 1 3-pound pork loin
   salt and freshly ground black pepper to taste
   unbleached all-purpose flour for dusting
- 2 tablespoons unsalted butter
- ½ cup sliced leek or scallion, white part only
- 3 tart baking apples such as Jonathan or Winesap, sliced
- ½ pound country ham, julienned
- 1 bay leaf
- ½ cup dry white wine
- ½ cup cream

Preheat the oven to 375°. Trim steak of fat, season with salt and pepper, and dust with flour. Melt the butter in a Dutch oven over medium heat and brown the steak or loin on both sides. Remove from the heat and add the leeks, apples, and ham. Add the bay leaf, wine, and cream, then cover the pot and place in the oven for 1¼ hours, adding water if needed during the cooking. Serve with twice-cooked potatoes (page 205).

BRINED BREAST OF VEAL

This is another of Bill Hughes's superb veal dishes. Start this recipe a day ahead.

SERVES 6

1 boned veal breast
4 garlic cloves, peeled and slivered
2 tablespoons (⅛ cup) mustard seeds, crushed
4 bay leaves
1 teaspoon freshly grated nutmeg
1 teaspoon freshly ground allspice
1 teaspoon freshly ground cloves
1 tablespoon freshly cracked black pepper
1 cup chopped onion
1 cup chopped celery
1 cup apple cider vinegar
1 quart water
   unbleached all-purpose flour for dusting
2 tablespoons (⅛ cup) peanut oil
   gingersnaps, crushed (optional)

Trim the breast of fat and sliver skin. Poke holes in the meat and insert slivers of garlic at 2-inch intervals. Place the veal in a nonreactive container and sprinkle with the spices and chopped vegetables. Cover the veal with vinegar and water. Marinate for 24 hours, turning the meat to ensure an even distribution of flavor.

Preheat the oven to 325°. Remove the meat from the marinade, reserving the marinade. Dry the meat, dust it with flour, and brown it in a large heavy pan on all sides in oil over medium heat. Place the meat in a roasting pan and pour in the marinade. Cover tightly with aluminum foil and braise in the oven for 2 hours.

Remove the meat to a serving platter. Check the thickness of the sauce. If it is too thin, thicken it by reducing it in a saucepan on top of the stove. A few crushed gingersnaps whisked into the sauce make a wonderful thickener. Pour the sauce over the meat before serving.

VEAL SWEETBREADS IN
A CREAM SAUCE

In Charleston you often see recipes for sweetbreads teamed with oysters and puff pastry ("patty shells")—too much gilding the lily for my taste. This is a simpler recipe.

SERVES 4

2 pairs of veal sweetbreads
1 teaspoon fresh lemon juice
    salt and freshly ground black pepper to taste
4 tablespoons unsalted butter
4 scallions, chopped (about ¼ cup)
¼ cup amontillado sherry or Madeira
2 large egg yolks
2 tablespoons (⅛ cup) cream

Soak the sweetbreads in cold water in the refrigerator for an hour to clean them. Drain the water from the sweetbreads, then put them in a saucepan, cover with fresh water, and bring to a boil. Reduce the heat and simmer for 3 minutes. Prepare another bowl of cold water, adding a few drops of the lemon juice. Remove the sweetbreads from the simmering water, drain, and plunge into the cold water.

When cooled, remove the fat, the tubes, and the membranes that surround each sweetbread. Slice into ½-inch slices. Season with salt and pepper, then sauté the sweetbreads in the butter over medium-high heat for 3 minutes. Add the scallions and sherry or Madeira and simmer for 15 minutes.

Mix the egg yolks, cream, and remaining lemon juice. Remove the pan from the heat and slowly stir in the egg yolk mixture, scraping the bottom of the pan and swirling the pan around in a circular motion so that everything is coated evenly with the sauce. Serve immediately over toast points, with asparagus.

PORK

Not until post–Civil War poverty swept the Lowcountry did pork become a mainstay here. True, there were always a few hogs around, but many of them were allowed to run free, then hunted as game. When pigs were slaughtered, most of the meat was smoked, and the hams were cured as for country hams, with families using recipes representing their Bayonne, Northumbrian, and German backgrounds. These hams were saved for the "big house" on the plantation, as was the finest bacon; smaller smoked cuts may have been rationed to slaves, but few studies of slaves' diets have been undertaken.

Sausage making was then and is now a typical way of dealing with pork. When we say "sausage" in the Lowcountry, we mean a basic country sausage—usually spicy hot, but a milder version is popular too—that is available from every grocer, both large and small. It comes fresh and smoked, in bulk and in links. Liver pudding, a delicious highly seasoned local forcemeat that puts some hog leftovers to use, is held together with rice and stuffed into the larger casings. It is served warm at breakfast with grits. Souse, a vinegared head cheese, is thinly sliced and served with beer. And blood pudding, a hallmark of the French and Scots who settled along the Cooper River in St. Johns Parish, Berkeley County, was once common fare, though now it is illegal to sell the hog's blood that flavors this creamy sausage.

Sausage making is easy and fun. If you do not have a meat grinder, buy one. Many electric mixers have grinder attachments available; be sure to get a sausage horn as well. Processing meat in a food processor is not the same as grinding it. Food processors make mush of most meats; they work for fine-textured liver pâtés but cannot give you the proper grind for country terrines and sausage.

COUNTRY SAUSAGE

You can fry this sausage in patties, stuff it into casings, or use it as an ingredient in other recipes that call for sausage. I use it in stuffings, in biscuits, smoked in links for gumbos, and as a breakfast meat. Use the recipe as a guide only. The wonderful thing about making your own sausage is that you can season it to taste.

MAKES ABOUT 3 POUNDS

- 3 pounds fatty pork *or* 2 pounds lean pork and 1 pound pork fat
- 1 tablespoon salt
- ½ teaspoon black peppercorns
- 1 teaspoon hot red pepper flakes
- ½ teaspoon rubbed sage *or* 3 or 4 fresh leaves
- 1 teaspoon *Quatre-Épices* (page 32)
- 1 teaspoon Herbal Mix (page 31) *or* 1 teaspoon *herbes de Provence* or Italian seasoning
- 1 teaspoon fresh rosemary leaves *or* ½ teaspoon dried
- ½ teaspoon fresh thyme leaves *or* ¼ teaspoon dried
- 6 to 8 feet of cleaned hog casings (optional; see Note)

If your meat grinder comes with a coarse and a fine grind attachment, grind the meat first through the coarser disk. Put all the remaining ingredients in a spice mill or blender and process until ground evenly. Add the ground seasonings to the meat and mix in well. In a frying pan on top of the stove, fry a little piece of the sausage and taste for seasoning. Correct the seasoning to your own taste. If you think the sausage is too fatty, you may add some more lean meat (and it needn't be pork: veal is fine, and oysters are delicious); you may want more hot peppers.

Put the properly seasoned forcemeat through the fine grinder. If you are stuffing the sausage into casings, follow the directions on page 115.

You can smoke some or all of the sausage—or partially smoke it. And you can freeze the sausage as well.

Note: Casings, available from your butcher, are sold sometimes frozen, packed in salt. To clean them, run water from a faucet through them several times until they are free of all salt crystals.

BLOOD PUDDING

Of all blood, that of the hog is thought the richest, and this is always employed in France in their boudins of this kind, which are excellent.

The Cook and Housewife's Manual (1826)

By the time Meg Dods published her classic of Scottish cooking, black puddings—or blood sausages—were well established in the culinary tradition of Berkeley County, where Scots-Irish and French Huguenots had settled along the banks of the Cooper River. On Barbados, whence came many of the early English settlers and African slaves, blood pudding and souse are still traditional Christmas dishes. Rice has replaced the oatmeal traditional in Scotland and the bread crumbs used in some parts of France (other French thickeners include apples, chestnuts, and spinach) in my version of this surprisingly delicate sausage. This sausage is not heavy like the Cajun and German versions but light and creamy like its French cousins.

It is illegal in most states to sell pig's blood, so the culinary tradition of making blood sausages has all but disappeared. Only in pockets of the Lowcountry where farmers still butcher their hogs will you find someone who knows this old bit of charcuterie. The only current local cookbook in which I have found a recipe is Billie Burn's collection, *Stirrin' the Pots on Daufuskie* (1985), from Daufuskie Island, which is still separated from the mainland by the lack of a bridge. I go to my butcher's on slaughter day with a bucket to catch the fresh blood. He gives it to me to bait sharks, but what I really do is make blood pudding. A tablespoon of salt or vinegar stirred into a quart of fresh blood will prevent coagulation.

I serve these sausages on a cold winter night with spinach and mashed potatoes—half white and half sweet—mixed with a little milk and butter. They also make a fine appetizer, on a bed of caramelized onions.

MAKES 4 1½-POUND LENGTHS OF SAUSAGE

1 cup cooked long-grain white rice
2 cups cream
1 teaspoon *Quatre-Épices* (page 32)
2 tablespoons salt (4 if vinegar instead of salt was used in the blood)
½ teaspoon cayenne pepper
2 quarts fresh pig's blood plus 2 tablespoons (⅛ cup) salt
2 pounds fresh pork fat
2 pounds onions, chopped
6 4-foot lengths of prepared hog casings (see page 115), knotted at
   one end, rinsed well, and placed in a bowl of water

Place the rice in the cream and set aside to soak while you continue with the recipe. Stir the seasonings into the blood. Dice the fat, place ½ pound of it in a heavy Dutch oven, and cook until it melts. Add the onions and cook slowly until the onions are translucent, about 10 to 15 minutes. Remove from the heat. Add the rest of the fat and the rice/cream mixture to the pot. Stir the mixture well and, when it has cooled, add the seasoned blood, stirring well.

Now, put on an apron and cover your work surface with something like a large cookie sheet; you cannot help making a mess with the liquid sausage stuffing. Slip the unknotted end of the prepared casing over the end of a plastic funnel, holding the casing tightly with one hand so that it does not slip off. Ladle the mixture through the funnel into the casing, then tie it off in 4-inch lengths.

Simmer the sausages in water, uncovered, for 15 to 20 minutes or until a pricked sausage oozes brown, not blood. Because the sausages are very fragile, this simmering is accomplished best with a wire basket for deep frying. When cool, wrap well in plastic wrap. They will keep refrigerated for several days or in the freezer for several months.

To cook blood puddings, simply prick them lightly in a couple of places and fry or grill them.

HOG HEAD STEW

Families with deep rural ties might still have a hog killin' or two each winter, with a ritual puddin' pot and hog head stew. The Brunson family of Hampton, South Carolina, has assembled its own cookbook, *Emily's Favorite Recipes*, which contains such country recipes as cane syrup and fried chitterlings. This hog head stew recipe is Emily Brunson's. ("For years I helped Uncle Lloyd Rivers butcher, and this is his recipe.") Liver pudding is similarly made, usually by butchers.

SERVES 20 to 25

2 small hog heads
1 whole liver
1 heart
1 melt (spleen)
2 kidneys
2 ears
　salt and freshly ground black pepper to taste
　cayenne pepper to taste (optional)

Make sure the hog heads are well dressed with the eyeballs and brains out. (Brains may be saved to scramble with eggs for breakfast.) Cut each head into 4 parts and put in a large wash pot full of hot water (over an open fire). When all other parts have been completely cleaned, put them in the pot with the heads. Add salt and pepper. Cook until the meat falls off the bone and the water is cooked down low. Add red pepper if desired. Serve over rice.

LIVER PUDDING

Not every Lowcountry butcher makes liver pudding; even fewer home cooks do. The tradition seems strongest about 70 miles inland, where German and Swiss immigrants settled in the early 18th century. Foots Brodie of Orangeburg and Frank McCormack of Ehrhardt are butchers whose puddings are legend. Closer to the coast, puddin' contains a lot more rice.

Though similar to hog head stew, liver pudding contains no water or kidneys. The meat is highly seasoned with spices and herbs and cooked until tender. The bones are removed, the mixture is run through a meat grinder, and then cooked rice is added as a binder. Sometimes it is stuffed into large casings. It is not the scrapplelike liver pudding from other parts of the South; it is peculiar to the Lowcountry. It is served warm with hot grits.

SOUSE, OR HOG'S HEAD CHEESE

Souse is a traditional Christmas dish both in Charleston and on Barbados, where so many of the city's early settlers and slaves first lived. I put it out on New Year's Day, before the hoppin' john, with beer and crackers, to ward off the ill effects of the night before. *Charleston Receipts* notes, "Have butcher clean head and feet."

SERVES 20 to 30

1 hog's head
4 pig's feet
2 onions, chopped (1½ to 2 cups)
2 bay leaves, crushed
½ teaspoon dried thyme
4 shallots, chopped
2 tablespoons (⅛ cup) white vinegar
1 cup dry red wine
1 teaspoon freshly grated nutmeg
  fresh pig fat cut into ¼-inch-thick slices

Place the head and feet in a big pot, cover with water, and boil until the meat falls off the bones, about 2 to 3 hours, depending on the age of the hog. Remove the head and feet from the liquid and pick out all the bones and fat. Refrigerate the meat and the liquid overnight. The next day, skim the fat from the surface of the liquid. Put the picked meat in a pot, add the remaining ingredients except the pig fat, and add just enough liquid to cover; bring to a boil. Line 3 large bread pans with pig fat and pour the mixture into the molds. Refrigerate until ready to serve. The souse will harden into a jelly that can be sliced.

COUNTRY HAM

Country ham, dry-cured in salt, is the most internationally famous southern food. No wonder: the recipes for curing have not changed in 350 years. Harriott Pinckney Horry wrote down curing receipts from Virginia in her late-18th-century journal. Now, in the late 20th century, curers in Smithfield, Virginia, ship more than 10 million hams each year!

Real ham lovers like me prefer "old hams," aged a year or more. Like so many fine wines and cheeses, they develop character over time. Many ham producers today "cure" hams in 90 days, injecting them with brine rather than rubbing them with salt. Some "country hams" aren't even smoked. When customers other than certified southerners call the toll-free number for one of the big producers I know in Virginia, they are discouraged from buying the old-fashioned cured hams because "they are too salty." John Egerton's essay on country ham in his *Southern Food* (1987) is definitive but melancholy: "the real hams may die out . . . simply because fewer and fewer people will be willing to spend the time it takes to cure, smoke, and age them."

I know two butchers in South Carolina who make old-cure hams, in very limited production. I pay a premium for the old-fashioned hams and cook them in copper boilers made especially for that purpose. When I sell hams in my bookstore, I make sure the buyer knows what he's getting into: cooking a country ham is tough and greasy work. It also comes as a shock to many first-timers to see mold growing on the hams. And no matter how long they are soaked or how much they are glazed, they will always be salty; that is why the slices are invariably served with grits or tucked into yeast biscuits (see recipe, page 223).

Thornton's *Southern Gardener and Receipt Book,* written in Camden, South Carolina, in 1839, included the following curing instructions, which are typical.

TO CURE HAMS

For a score of hams, take about three quarts of salt, one pint of molasses, quarter of a pound of black pepper, and two ounces of saltpetre pulverized; mix well together; lay the hams on a table with the rind downwards; rub the mixture over them with the hand, taking care to apply it to every part where there is no rind; let them lay a week, and rub them over with clear salt, which continue once a week for four or five weeks, according to the size of the hams; they are then ready to smoke; or if you choose, after the mixture is sufficiently struck in, put them into brine for two or three weeks before you smoke them; and when smoked, hang them in a dry place. When a ham is cut for use, hang or lay it where you please, the flies will not touch it. We have practised this method for several years, and have no reason to abandon it.

Southern Gardener and Receipt Book, 1839

To prepare a country ham for the table, you must first soak it at least overnight in cold water. I soak the old hams that I cook for about 2 days, changing the water every 8 to 12 hours. It helps to have a ham boiler, which will fit over 2 burners on a standard kitchen stove. When you're ready to cook, scrub the ham well in warm water, removing all the black pepper and mold. If you do not have a pot big enough to cook the entire ham, you can saw off the hock so that it will fit into a smaller pot; however, you will still need a pot that is deep enough for the ham to be covered in water. Bring the water to a simmer and let the ham cook at barely a simmer, never a boil, for about 15 to 20 minutes per pound or until the meat becomes tender. (Most country hams weigh between 12 and 18 pounds; you will need 4 to 6 hours of cooking time.) Remove the pot from the stove (quite a job in itself; you will probably need two sets of arms) and allow the ham to cool enough to handle, about an hour.

Remove the ham from the water and trim off the skin and all but ½ inch of fat. The ham may be sliced and served at this point. It may also be glazed with brown sugar or molasses or saved until another day and reheated in a 350° oven, with or without a glaze. I never glaze a ham, but I always serve it with a chutney such as the Golden Pear Chutney on page 318.

To carve the ham, place it on a cutting board with the meaty side up. Cut a V out of the ham perpendicular to the bone, near the hock. Use a sharp, thin knife and cut the slices at a 45-degree angle, as thinly as possible.

You may refrigerate cooked country ham for much longer than other, uncured meats. Wrapped in aluminum foil, cooked country ham will last several weeks in the refrigerator. Wrapped in plastic, the ham spoils quickly because moisture is trapped. I freeze cooked ham, but only to use in composed dishes, such as the ham paste on page 44.

A country ham will feed a lot of people. Even as the main meat at a meal, a 15-pound ham should feed 40; the same ham can fill 200 of the biscuits on page 223.

PASTA WITH COUNTRY HAM AND SUN-DRIED TOMATOES

Though I have no historical source for the following recipe, it passes my Lowcountry test: it easily *could* have been cooked in former times, even if I don't have a written antecedent. Cream was abundant, and *The Carolina Housewife* of 1847 contains a recipe for homemade pasta as well as the tomatoes. The recipe, for one person, may be multiplied by the number of people you are serving.

PER SERVING:
- ¼ pound dried pasta of your choice
- 1 ounce sun-dried tomatoes packed in oil *or* 2 sun-dried tomato cakes (page 324)
- 1 cup cream
- 1½ ounces uncooked country ham (about ¼ cup when cut up)
  freshly ground black pepper to taste

While you cook the pasta, crumble the sun-dried tomato patties into the cream, or dice a commercial brand, in a saucepan. Reduce at a low boil, stirring frequently and breaking up the patties as they cook—about 5 to 10 minutes. Cut the ham into little strips and add them at the last minute, just to warm them through. Add a dozen or so grinds of pepper per person to the sauce but no salt. Serve immediately over drained pasta.

LOWCOUNTRY BARBECUE

Barbecue in the Lowcountry means pork, cooked slowly over smoldering wood. It's man's work, and it's an all-night affair. Barbecue restaurants here are open, almost without exception, on Thursday, Friday, and Saturday, from about 11 o'clock in the morning until 9 in the evening—all you can eat. Unsauced meat—three shoulders to one ham—pulled from the bones, then roughly chopped, is eaten on sandwiches or piled high on a plate with white rice covered with "hash," pickle slices, coleslaw, and fried skins. Huge pitchers of iced tea and loaves of white bread share the picnic-style tables with bottles of the traditional reddish sweet mustard-based sauce, as well as a spicy hot thin vinegar sauce. Banana pudding is offered to those who have room for dessert.

When barbecues are given al fresco, the whole hog is cooked over a pit dug in the host's yard. Cinder blocks hold a grill, 4 by 6 feet, about a foot over the coals. The entire pit is covered by a hinged top. An upright 50-gallon drum, with both the top and bottom removed and a grate inserted a foot above the base, holds a roaring fire of green hickory and oak. As embers fall through the grate to the ground, they are removed by shovel to the pit. A split hog is hot-smoked over the coals for several hours, the men taking turns tending the fire and refilling "coozies" (the foam rubber holders for beer cans that keep beers cold and hands warm).

The hash too is cooked outside over a gas burner. Traditional hashes, sometimes called "liver hash," contain a Boston butt (the shoulder), the hog's head, several organ meats, and tomatoes, all cooked for a long time until the meat falls apart and the consistency of the sauce is uniform. Nowadays restaurant hash is likely to contain no hog's head and certainly no organ meats. When invited to a barbecue, I offer to cook the hash. A shoulder, a head, and a liver are simmered in homemade tomato catsup to cover. When the meat begins to fall off the bones, I strain out the solids, then add the shredded, cooked meat of the shoulder to the sauce. It is awfully rich, but people love it over rice.

BARBECUED RIBS WITH ROAST GARLIC

This is the easiest barbecue, and it's absolutely delicious. If you have never eaten roasted garlic, you will be amazed at how sweet and subtle it is. When the pork ribs come off the grill, the soft cooked flesh of the garlic is squeezed out of the bulbs and rubbed all over the meat and onto thick bread slices like butter.

spareribs, at least 1 pound per person
salt and freshly ground black pepper to taste
several whole heads of garlic, about 2 per person

About an hour before cooking, season the ribs with the salt and pepper, then leave them on a platter to come to room temperature. Prepare a wood, charcoal, or gas grill for cooking. A gas grill should be set low and allowed to warm up. Coals should be just ashen, totally gray but glowing orange from within.

Place the unpeeled garlic among the coals and the ribs on the grill, directly over the coals. Cover the grill and cook the ribs for 25 to 30 minutes on each side, turning them once. Remove the ribs and the garlic to a cutting board. Slice the bases off the garlic and squeeze the roasted garlic all over the ribs. Slice the ribs apart with a knife, pile on a platter, and serve.

8
GAME

I don't go hunting very much, but many of my friends do. I know octogenarian ladies who hunt in the Lowcountry; hunting has a long social history here. I *have* killed squirrels trying to rob my bird feeder; they are delicious if they don't live in pine forests. My father and I used to skin and clean the freshly killed squirrels and put them in the freezer until we had enough for burgoo, though I also love them panfried, like chicken or quail.

It is illegal to sell game in South Carolina, but my hunter friends bring me all sorts of meats to cook—mostly venison. I'll take whatever cut I can get; I turn the scraps into burgers. I am fond of raccoon, but it is a real labor of love to prepare. Most of the rabbit that I see is farm-raised; nonetheless I have included a German recipe that is a classic in the Lowcountry. Frog, turtle, and alligator are delicious, but I do not like the texture of those meats after they have been frozen. Recipes included for those meats are typical. Game bird recipes are found in the following chapter.

Squirrel, rabbit, squab, and quail can be interchanged in these recipes.

DEERBURGERS

Deer are once again plentiful in the Lowcountry, thanks to an excellent game management plan. Hunters now take the place of their other predators—wolves and cougars—which we long ago drove away from the region. As numerous as they are, however, the deer are seldom huge animals—and never do they carry any of the fat they might need in colder climes. A deerburger with added fat is the perfect way to serve up the lean odd cuts of venison.

MAKES 4 BURGERS

    1½ pounds boneless venison
    ¼ pound bacon
    1 small onion, finely chopped (about ¼ cup)

2 garlic cloves, minced
  a good handful of fresh herbs such as parsley, marjoram, basil,
     and thyme, plus 1 teaspoon Herbal Mix (page 31)
  salt and freshly ground black pepper to taste

Run all of the ingredients through a meat grinder fitted with the coarse disk, form into patties, and grill on a gas grill, over charcoal, or over a wood fire. Cook, like hamburgers, to your taste. Serve with port-scented tomato catsup (page 326).

PAN-FRIED VENISON TENDERLOIN

There are two thin strips of meat that lie along the inside of the deer's backbone; most people call it deer "tenderloin." It is eaten rare. Start this dish the day before you plan to serve it.

      1 tablespoon mixed dried herbs or 3 tablespoons fresh chopped
           herbs (rosemary, thyme, basil, marjoram, and parsley)
 2 to 3 garlic cloves per tenderloin, peeled
      1 venison tenderloin for every 2 or 3 people
        olive oil
        dry red wine
        bacon grease
        salt and freshly ground black pepper
        unbleached all-purpose flour for dusting

Put some herbs and the garlic on a cutting board and chop together with a chef's knife until the mixture is uniformly minced. Rub the mixture all over the meat.

Lightly coat the inside of a shallow nonreactive container (such as a glass baking dish) with olive oil, then put the meat in the dish. Dribble a thin stream of oil back and forth over the tenderloin, but do not coat it. Pour in about 2 inches of red wine or cover the meat with wine. Cover the dish and refrigerate overnight. If the meat is not covered, turn the meat several times while it marinates.

(continued)

The next day, remove the meat from the marinade and drain well. Lightly paint the inside of a well-seasoned cast-iron skillet with bacon grease and place over high heat. Slice the meat into 1½-inch-thick slices, season with salt and pepper to taste, and dust them lightly in flour, shaking off all excess flour. The pan should be very hot, but the bacon grease should not smoke. Add the steaks to the pan and cook over high heat for about 2 or 3 minutes on each side. Do not overcook. Serve with twice-cooked potatoes (page 205).

ROAST VENISON HAM

Lucille Grant is a renowned Charleston cook whose repertoire of dishes includes most of the Lowcountry classics. Widely sought after for her catering skills, she cooks for hundreds seemingly as effortlessly as she does for her family. She often shares her recipes, many with precise measurements, reciting them without resorting to notes. This is her recipe for a venison haunch, which is the ham or rump roast.

SERVES 6 TO 8

1   4-pound venison ham, bone in
    salt and freshly ground black pepper to taste
1   medium onion
¼   pound bacon
3   bay leaves
5   garlic cloves
1   teaspoon Herbal Mix (page 31) or *herbes de Provence* or Italian
    seasoning

Preheat the oven to 450°. Season the venison ham with salt and pepper. Dice the onion and bacon. Using a chef's knife, chop the bay leaves, garlic, and herbs together until you have a uniform paste. Mix this paste with the chopped onion and bacon. Punch 3-inch-deep holes into the ham at 3-inch intervals using a sharpening steel or similar tool. Fill the holes with the seasoning mix.

Place the ham in a roasting pan, cover well with heavy aluminum foil, and place in the oven. Immediately turn down the oven to 350° and roast for 2½ to 3 hours (or until a meat thermometer registers 140°), basting occasionally. Remove from the oven, remove the foil, and allow to rest for at least 10 minutes before carving. Deer is carved like lamb or mutton.

HASENPFEFFER FOR TWO

I grew up in Orangeburg, 70 miles inland, just inside the Fall Line. Settled in the 1730s by German and Swiss farmers, the town is still largely composed of descendants of those first settlers. Lowcountry cookbooks are filled with *torten*, veal dishes, and other Eastern European favorites such as *hasenpfeffer*. Most recipes call for soaking the rabbits in mild vinegar solutions—a common practice for game. In this version, however, the rabbit (more than likely a frozen farm-raised one) is cooked in the tag end of a bottle of red wine—or in a red wine that was maybe just a little off. So the next winter evening that you open a bottle of Côtes-du-Rhônes and it's not quite what you had in mind, save it for the next night and make this *hasenpfeffer*. I don't recommend cooking with inferior wine; indeed, cook only with wine that you would drink. But if you find, as I have, that each case of wine has one bottle that's not quite as good as the others, save it for this recipe.

SERVES 2

¼ pound bacon, finely chopped
¼ cup unbleached all-purpose flour
1 teaspoon freshly ground black pepper
1 teaspoon Herbal Mix (page 31) *or* ¼ teaspoon salt and a teaspoon
    of mixed dried herbs such as *herbes de Provence, fines herbes,*
    or Italian seasoning
1 2-pound rabbit, fresh or defrosted frozen, cut into quarters, rinsed,
    and patted dry
1 medium onion, chopped (about ¾ cup)
1 cup chicken, veal, duck, or rabbit stock
1 cup dry red wine or wine that is slightly vinegared

In a heavy saucepan that has a tight-fitting lid, cook the bacon over moderate heat, uncovered, until it is crisp. Remove the bacon from the pan and set aside to drain.

Mix well together the flour, pepper, and herbs. Dust the rabbit pieces in the mixture, shaking off any excess. Brown the rabbit in the bacon fat, cooking the pieces until they are evenly browned. Remove the rabbit and set aside on a plate.

Add the onions and cook over medium-low heat until they are transparent, about 5 minutes. Pour in the wine and stock, bring to a boil, and scrape up any bits that may have stuck to the bottom of the pan. Add the rabbit (and any drippings on the plate) and the drained bacon. Simmer the stew over very low heat, covered, until the rabbit is tender but not yet falling from the bones—1 to 1½ hours.

Serve immediately with traditional German fare such as potatoes and cabbage or in the Lowcountry manner with a big plate of rice, using the sauce on the rice. *Hasenpfeffer* means "hare in pepper." It should be very peppery, so don't hesitate to add more to taste.

PEARL EDGE'S ROAST BLACK RIVER COON

I met Pearl Edge at the From Scratch Food Festival in Georgetown, where she served her dish of stewed raccoon. Pearl is a rural mail carrier, director of a 42-member youth choir, and a passionate cook. Her spicy stew of shredded meat bolstered by sweet potatoes is similar to goat and lamb dishes found throughout the African diaspora.

SERVES 8 TO 10

1 medium raccoon, skinned and dressed (dressed weight 7 to 8 pounds)
    white vinegar
⅓ cup unbleached all-purpose flour
¼ cup bacon grease
⅓ teaspoon freshly ground black pepper

⅓ cup chopped celery
½ teaspoon salt
3 cups water
½ medium onion, chopped (about ½ cup)
3 medium bay leaves
6 medium sweet potatoes, baked, peeled, and halved

Preheat the oven to 350°. Wash the coon in vinegar and water before and after cutting it up into about 10 parts. Flour the parts and brown in bacon fat in a large roasting pan over medium-high heat. Add the remaining ingredients except the sweet potatoes, cover, and bake for 2 hours.

Remove the coon from the pot. Remove the meat from the bones, place in a baking dish, and pour the gravy from the roasting pan all around, straining out the solids. Place the potatoes around it all, and bake, uncovered, for another hour.

COOTER SOUP

Cooter, or turtle, soups are of three kinds: a rich turtle stock thickened with roux, a clear broth filled with floating pieces of the white flesh, and a thick chowder enriched with cream, wine, and eggs. All three follow the West Indian model, popular long before Carolina was settled, with hot pepper as seasoning. Cooter is from a West African word, *kuta*, for turtle. Recipes for *turtle* soup mean sea turtles. In the late 18th century Charleston's Henry Laurens sent sea turtles kept alive on purslane to clients in London. Purslane, or portulaca, is a common low-lying succulent that is indigenous to the Lowcountry. It was widely used in salads during the time but is as seldom seen today on the Lowcountry table as these soups.

The terrapin is the turtle of our brackish waters. Sometimes called diamondback, it is the most common turtle found in soups. Farther inland, above the saltwater line, chicken turtles, sliders, and snappers are all prized for their flavor by river folk. No matter which species is used, the female full of eggs is preferred for soups. The following soup is from *Orangeburg's Choice Recipes* of 1948. Though Orangeburg, 70 miles inland, was never rice-growing country, it sits on the edge of one of the largest virgin cypress swamps in the world. A few people still grow small plots of rice for personal consumption in the low-lying corners of fields that abut those swamps. The lack of red pepper is geographical: away from the African influence of the coastal plantations, the Sandlapper palate is never as fiery.

Select a large, live, female terrapin—the rice fields variety being the best. Cut off head and remove shell. Dress by removing skin, intestines, and sand bag. Cut meat into cubes and place together with the eggs from the terrapin into a large pot. Add four quarts of water and bring to a boil. While slowly boiling, add two tablespoons salt, one-fourth pound of cubed salt meat and two tablespoons of whole allspice. Cook slowly for two hours. Just before serving, add one tablespoon black pepper, two tablespoons butter, one cup cream and one-half cup sherry wine. Thicken with two tablespoons browned flour. Strain and serve soup clear. Place one thin slice of lemon and one teaspoon sherry wine in each soup plate.

FRIED FROG LEGS

One of my favorite sports as a child was frog gigging, but I think the real fascination for me was watching the legs move hours after the frog was killed. I used to beg my mother to let me shake salt or lemon juice on them. I've seen the legs of large dead bullfrogs contract so much when sprinkled with lemon juice that they have literally jumped off the counter. Bullfrogs live in all of the contiguous 48 states. Where I grew up, a few blocks from the banks of the Edisto River—the longest blackwater river in the world—they could be almost deafening with their bellows after a rain-storm.

Henry Laurens, a Charleston merchant and planter of French heritage, ate frogs while traveling in Burgundy in the late 18th century; he noted his intent to gather them from his own properties in the Lowcountry. If you too are fond of the frog legs sold in restaurants, you should treat yourself to some fresh ones. Frogs do not do well in captivity; all of the frogs sold in restaurants are taken from the wild, mostly in Southeast Asia. Like other edible amphibians and reptiles, frog meat changes its texture when frozen and thawed, becoming somewhat gelatinous in the process. The difference is as dramatic as the difference between freshly shucked and canned oysters: freshly killed frog is always succulent and delicately flavorful. It is best pan-fried, probably the way Henry Laurens ate it. And frogs are mildly flavored; season them lightly so as not to mask their true character. My mother deglazed the pan with vermouth and sometimes added capers for color and flavor, but neither is necessary.

SERVES 4 TO 6, DEPENDING ON THE SIZE OF THE FROGS

24 (about 4 pounds) individual frog legs
 1 lemon
    unbleached all-purpose flour for dusting
 4 tablespoons unsalted butter
    a little salt and freshly ground black pepper
    dry white wine (optional)
    drained capers (optional)

Put the frog legs in a shallow nonreactive baking dish and squeeze the juice of the lemon all over them. Allow to marinate for about 30 minutes at room temperature. Remove the legs from the pan, pat dry, and dust lightly with flour. Melt the butter in a sauté pan, shake off any excess flour from the legs, and sauté them over fairly high heat in the butter until golden brown, about 4 to 5 minutes on each side. You may deglaze the pan with a little dry white wine, if desired, and you may add some capers, as my father recommends, before pouring the now browned butter over the legs and serving them hot.

SMOKED NUISANCE GATOR TAIL

For 20 years alligators were listed as endangered in South Carolina, but you couldn't prove it by me. The pond where I fished as a child used to get so overrun with alligators that we would call wildlife officials to remove them to distant locations. It was no surprise to find that often the same gators—tagged by the game officers—found their way home from some 100 miles away.

There have been so many developments along the coast of South Carolina in the past 20 years that lands once populated only by gators, bears, and other denizens of the swamp now sport golf courses, tennis courts, and condominiums. Gators appear in people's yards; they steal golf balls, mistaking them for eggs; they are said to have a particular liking for dogs. They are reported to the wildlife department.

Strictly controlled killing of officially designated "nuisance" gators over 5 feet long by a handful of licensed trappers is now allowed. The meat is inspected, carefully labeled, and sold to licensed vendors. It is now a popular appetizer item in area restaurants.

The meat of the alligator does not fare well in the freezer. Fresh or frozen, though, it cooks best slowly, at a low temperature. The flesh is perfectly white, and, like turtle, marries well with spicy hot red pepper. It is most often teamed with a Creole sauce, but I prefer it smoked. If you live near gator farms, try to obtain a skinned tail from a small gator, right at 5 feet. Marinate the meat as you would for smoking fish or poultry and smoke according to the manufacturer's directions on your smoker. This is a general recipe.

MAKES ABOUT 12 SERVINGS

1 cup salt
1 gallon water
1 small (about 5 pounds) skinned gator tail
1 teaspoon cayenne pepper
1 cup vegetable oil

Make a brine of the salt and water in a large stockpot. Coil the gator tail down in the brine and refrigerate overnight. The next day, pour off the brine and lay the tail on a greased rack to dry in a well-ventilated place. (I put a coat hanger through the meat and hang it outdoors.) Allow a thin skin to form on the surface. In the meantime, start your smoker and soak the hardwood chips in water. Thoroughly oil the grates of the grill. Mix the cayenne into the oil and baste the tail with the oil. Place the tail in the smoker and smoke-cook over the chips for about 35 to 40 minutes for each pound of meat. The tail will be cooked when the meat is uniformly white all the way to the bone.

Serve as you would smoked fish—warm as the main course, warm or cold as an appetizer. Store what you don't serve immediately well wrapped in plastic in the refrigerator.

SQUIRREL BURGOO

Southerners in general are a proud lot. Sandlappers in particular are accused of being excessively so. Charlestonians claim so many cultural "firsts" in America that chauvinism here is endemic. Much to the chagrin of Kentuckians, we even claim the first jockey club and racetrack; some swear the julep is ours as well. I've never heard the burgoo claimed in Charleston, but both Brunswick County, Virginia, and Brunswick, Georgia, claim it under their own name. Squirrel is traditional in both the Kentucky and Brunswick versions, yet many recipes omit it.

I love the taste of squirrel, as long as it doesn't live in pines, which give the meat a resinous taste. Farmers with pecan groves often let young hunters practice their marksmanship with .22 rifles among the nut trees; pecan grove squirrels are the most succulent. They are delicious when pan-fried like chicken or quail, but my father puts squirrels in the freezer as he kills them in the fall, then makes a big pot of burgoo with the first vegetables of the summer. Traditional recipes call for 1 or 2 squirrels to feed 6 to 8 people. At my father's house it's a squirrel per person. Once you've got the squirrels, the recipe is utter simplicity.

MAKES 4 LARGE SERVINGS

1 gallon water
4 squirrels, cleaned and quartered, *or* 4 squabs, 2 rabbits, or 8 quail
   unbleached all-purpose flour for dusting
   salt, freshly ground black pepper, and cayenne pepper to taste
2 tablespoons (⅛ cup) bacon grease
1 *bouquet garni:* several parsley and thyme sprigs tied with a bay
   leaf to a celery rib
2 large onions, chopped (about 3 cups)
2 cups fresh or frozen Sieva beans, butter beans, or baby limas
4 large potatoes, peeled and cut into large chunks
4 cups peeled ripe tomatoes with their juice
4 cups fresh corn kernels

Bring the water to a boil in a stockpot. Dust the squirrel pieces in the flour seasoned with the salt, pepper, and cayenne. Brown the pieces in the bacon fat in a large Dutch oven over medium-high heat, then slowly add the boiling water to the pot, stirring constantly. Do not let the water return to a boil. Add the *bouquet garni*, onions, beans, and potatoes, cover the pot, and simmer slowly for about 1½ hours. Add the tomatoes and corn and simmer, covered, for another hour. Serve hot with corn bread (page 219).

9

POULTRY AND
GAME BIRDS

Birds are the preferred meats of the Lowcountry. When John Lawson traveled up the Santee River in the early 1700s, he found the Indians eating crows, blackbirds, buntings, pheasant, woodcocks, snipe, partridge, and pigeons "very fat and as good as I ever ate." He saw sixty-pound turkeys, which the "Indians domesticate and use as decoys." The turkey now at large in the Lowcountry is said to be the closest to the original wild strain.

The snipe, woodcock, and clapper rail are the only shorebirds that continue to be hunted. The snipe hunt is a rite of passage for young men in the Lowcountry. The unsuspecting teenager has heard for years of the legendary "hunt," which he will be allowed to join when "old enough." The youngest member of the hunting party is left alone, unarmed, at night, to cross an expanse of boggy marsh, supposedly to drive the birds toward the "hunters," who await the youngster at a breakfast camp, where they drink beer and revel in their practical joke. Getting through the wetland comes naturally to most; it is considered a test of manhood to endure the humiliation of the joke. It builds character and the all-important sense of humor; it also provides the father the opportunity to offer his son his first beer.

Domesticated birds have always been a part of the Lowcountry barnyard. Early to protect wild species, South Carolina has several successful "game" bird farms. (See page 29 for ordering information.) Roasted, fried, grilled, potted, cured, smoked, and teamed with rice—poultry recipes in the Lowcountry are legion. (See also Carolina Pilau, Chapter 4, page 66.)

CHICKEN

COUNTRY CAPTAIN

Bill Neal, in his book on southern cooking, says that he has heard this dish claimed by an inhabitant of every large southern seaport. Country Captain is a fairly straightforward chicken "curry" from northern India. You find the dish throughout the British Isles as well, but the recipe often calls for "curry powder"—much admired in Britain but unheard of in India. In Charleston fresh exotic spices have always come through our port from afar, so we've always had the luxury of the intense flavor of freshly ground and roasted spices.

If you usually rely on curry powder, you're in for a great treat if you're willing to spend a little extra time. Go to your local natural foods store and buy small quantities of bulk spices, then roast and grind them at home yourself. You will be stunned by the complexities and subtleties on the palate. The East India Company's long history of "country captains" commanding spice ships is preserved today in this legacy of British taste in the Lowcountry. Alfred Huger, a prominent Charleston maritime lawyer, married Margaret Mynderse, whose family had owned the East India Company, in the late nineteenth century. Their son Alfred became a harbor pilot, a modern-day tugboat captain.

Start this dish several hours or the day before.

SERVES 8

TO PREPARE THE CHICKEN AND THE STOCK:
- 1 3½- to 4-pound chicken
  salt, freshly ground black pepper, and cayenne pepper to taste
- 3 quarts water
- 2 to 3 celery ribs, broken into pieces
- 1 large onion, peeled and quartered
- 2 bay leaves
- 2 carrots, broken into pieces
  a few fresh thyme sprigs and other fresh herbs of your choice

Rinse the chicken in cold water and pat dry. Sprinkle it all over with salt, pepper, and cayenne. (I put several peppercorns in a spice mill and grind them, then pinch the freshly ground spice between thumb and index finger, rubbing it all over the bird.) Put the chicken in a large stockpot and cover with the 3 quarts water. Add the neck and other giblets (except the liver) if they are included. (I fry the liver in a little butter as the cook's bonus.) Add the remaining ingredients, bring almost to a boil, reduce the heat, and allow to simmer until the meat is cooked evenly, about 1 hour.

Remove the chicken and allow to cool. As soon as it is cool enough to handle, remove the skin and discard, then pull the chicken meat from the bird, tearing it into small pieces. Put the meat in a covered dish in the refrigerator. You should have a pound of meat, about 4 cups. Crack the bones of the carcass with a meat cleaver and return them to the stockpot. Continue simmering the mixture until it has a distinct chicken flavor (about 30 minutes to 1 hour more), then strain all of the solids out of the stock. Allow to cool, then refrigerate the stock. Remove any congealed fat from the surface of the stock before using.

FOR THE CURRY MIX:
- 1 tablespoon whole coriander seeds
- 2 teaspoons whole cumin seeds *or* 1½ teaspoons ground
- 2 teaspoons hot red pepper flakes *or* 1 large dried pod
- 2 teaspoons ground turmeric
- ½ teaspoon (about 12) whole cloves
- 1 cinnamon stick, broken into pieces
- 1 teaspoon black peppercorns
- ½ teaspoon ground ginger
- 2 bay leaves, crumbled

TO ASSEMBLE THE DISH:
- ½ cup blanched and slivered almonds
- 3 tablespoons peanut oil or clarified butter (see page 24)
- 2 large onions, chopped (about 3 cups)
- 2 large green bell peppers, chopped (2 to 3 cups)
- 2 garlic cloves, minced
- 1 28-ounce can peeled tomatoes with their juice
- 4½ cups reserved chicken stock
- 4 cups reserved chicken meat
- ½ cup dried currants

Roast the whole coriander and cumin seeds in a heavy Dutch oven over medium heat, stirring constantly, until they begin to darken, 2 to 3 minutes. If you are using ground cumin, add it about a minute after the coriander. Remove to a spice mill or blender. Add the rest of the dried spices and bay leaves to the spice mill and grind thoroughly. Dump them out onto a plate; you should have about ¼ cup of the curry mix.

Add the almonds to the pot and roast, stirring constantly, until they are browned evenly. Remove and set aside.

Add the oil to the pot. Add the chopped onion, bell pepper, and garlic to the oil and cook over medium heat, stirring often, until the onions begin to get transparent, about 10 minutes. Put the tomatoes in a blender or a food processor and puree. Add the tomatoes, 2 tablespoons of the spice mixture, and 1½ cups of the reserved stock to the onion and bell pepper mixture and simmer, uncovered, stirring every 5 to 10 minutes so that the vegetables do not stick to the bottom of the pot, for about 30 to 45 minutes or until almost all of the liquid is cooked out.

Add the reserved chicken meat and currants and stir all together thoroughly, then cover the pot and turn off the heat. Store the remaining curry mix in a jar in a cool, dark, and dry place for use in other recipes.

TO FINISH THE DISH:

   1½ cups long-grain white rice, preferably a Basmati type
      remaining 3 cups reserved stock
   ½ teaspoon salt
      chopped parsley for garnish
      reserved roasted almonds for garnish

Thirty minutes before serving, add the rice, remaining stock, and salt to a stockpot that has a tight-fitting lid. Bring to a boil, immediately reduce the heat to a simmer, and cover the pot. Do not stir and do not lift the lid. After 13 minutes, remove from the heat and set aside for 12 more minutes. Meanwhile, reheat the chicken. When the 12 minutes are up, fluff the rice with a fork and spread on a platter, top with the chicken mixture, and sprinkle with chopped parsley and almonds. Serve with Ats Jaar pickles, Dilly Beans, fried eggplant, and traditional curry accompaniments such as roasted peanuts, freshly grated coconut, and a chutney such as golden pear (page 318) or peach (page 314).

ROAST CHICKEN WITH GROUNDNUT DRESSING

I don't know what happened to the West African tradition of pairing peanuts with fowl in the Lowcountry; it just seems to have disappeared. Perhaps this more accessible recipe will revive the pleasant combination of "groundnuts" and chicken. If you don't have any chicken stock on hand, you can make stock quickly the day before by boiling the neck and wing tips of the chicken with aromatic vegetables in 3 cups of water until it is reduced to one cup. Make the corn bread the day before as well so that you have only to assemble the stuffing and roast the bird.

Though I usually roast meats in an extremely hot oven, naturally raised chickens profit from this slower baking, which allows you to cook the dressing separately at the same time. You may want to stuff the bird, which is all right, but if you are using an extremely fatty chicken, I don't advise it as the dressing will become soggy.

SERVES 3 TO 4

FOR THE STUFFING:

    ½ recipe corn bread (page 219)
    ¼ cup chopped onion
    ¼ cup chopped celery
    1 tablespoon peanut oil
       salt and freshly ground black pepper to taste
    ½ teaspoon Herbal Mix (page 31)
    ¼ cup chopped dry-roasted peanuts
    1 large egg, lightly beaten
    1 tablespoon unsalted butter
    1 cup chicken stock (page 34)

FOR THE ROAST CHICKEN:

    1 3½- to 4-pound chicken
       salt and freshly ground black pepper to taste
1 to 2 tablespoons unsalted butter, very soft
    ½ cup dry-roasted peanuts
       cayenne pepper to taste

To make the stuffing, crumble the corn bread into a large mixing bowl. Sauté the onion and celery in the peanut oil over medium-high heat until they begin to become transparent, then pour over the corn bread, mixing it all together well. Add the seasonings, peanuts, and egg and mix. Melt the butter in the chicken stock and pour into the mixture, mixing all together one last time.

Preheat the oven to 425°. Place the stuffing in an 8-inch cake pan or casserole dish. Remove any extra fat from the crop and cavity of the chicken and rub the chicken all over first with salt and pepper and then with the soft butter. In a food processor, grind the nuts very finely, working in quick bursts so as not to render them oily. Pat the outside of the chicken with the finely ground nuts and sprinkle it with cayenne.

Place the chicken on a roasting rack that will suspend the bird above the stuffing. (If you don't have a roasting rack, simply place the chicken on top of the dressing.) Roast for about 15 minutes, then reduce the heat to 350° and cook until the juices run clear, about another 45 minutes. Let the bird rest for about 10 minutes before carving, then serve with a simply prepared green vegetable or salad.

EDISTO FRITTERS

For as long as I can remember, I have stayed at Cassandra McGee's big pink house midway down front beach on Edisto Island. The drive down from Charleston, though less than an hour, is a respite in itself, through marshland and old plantation sites, through tunnels of live oaks with Spanish moss unraveling like gray lace in the amber light of dusk (a friend's son calls it "squirrel hair").

All of my memories of that house involve big meals around the two huge dining tables, and I never know when I go if there will be 2, 10, 20, or no people there. I always take some food but rely on the local vegetable stands to provide me with whatever is in season. I also know where countless blackberries grow, and I know every persimmon tree between Charleston and the Old Post Office on Store Creek. Sometimes I take my cast net and catch shrimp on the way down, just off the road about 10 miles inland. And sometimes I buy fresh fish. But always I cook. Cassandra's roomy, well-equipped kitchen always inspires.

One midsummer Sunday evening I drove down, knowing thunderstorms were brewing (my favorite time to go to the beach). On the way down I pulled several clumps of fresh garlic out of the soil from a long-abandoned homesite where it had once been planted, then stopped at George and Pink's vegetable stand on the island for some fresh vegetables. I telephoned a friend to come down when I found the house empty, and he offered to bring a fryer.

The fryer turned out to be one of those industrial freaks packed with 2 gizzards and 2 livers, so I took advantage of that windfall to experiment for myself. These fritters have become one of my favorite appetizers, and my sister Sue can eat a plateful of what she calls my "gizzard croquettes."

MAKES ABOUT 20 TWO-BITE FRITTERS

 1 package (about 16) chicken gizzards, trimmed of all membrane
      and sinew and chopped (about 6 ounces trimmed)
     about 10 ounces chicken livers, trimmed of all fat and any green
      spots (about 8 ounces trimmed)
 1 medium tomato, peeled, seeded, and chopped
 1 cup dry bread crumbs (about 2 stale or dried rolls, ground)
 ½ teaspoon salt
16 grinds of black pepper
     fresh garlic (see *Note*)
     lard for frying

Finely chop together all of the ingredients except the lard (or mix in a food processor, but not too much), saving some of the bread crumbs to coat the croquettes. Make croquettes about the size of 2 fingers, roll in fine bread crumbs, and fry in hot lard for about 1½ minutes on each side, or until golden brown. Drain and serve immediately on a bed of lettuce with lemon wedges.

Note: Freshly picked garlic is moister and has a more intense garlic flavor than what you can buy, but it is not as harsh. The volunteers we find growing at old homesites often produce just 2 cloves, the entire bulb about the size of a shallot. I would use 1 or 2 cloves in this recipe—of either fresh or store-bought—to taste.

DUCK

Duck has been a favorite in the Lowcountry since colonial days. With the numbers of wild ducks decreasing each year, and bag limits reduced, I rarely see wild ducks at my table. All of these recipes have been cooked with the delicious Pekin varieties of ducks grown in Concord, North Carolina (more widely known as Long Island ducklings). Buy fresh ducks: since they're very fatty, the birds are not drastically affected by freezing, but you will get the added bonus of giblets with a fresh duck. In larger cities, especially those with sizable Asian populations, you may even find fresh whole ducks with the heads still attached. Zooarchaeological digs in the Lowcountry have shown that domesticated ducks played an important role in the local cuisine before the Civil War. I hope these recipes will help bring them back into local favor; duck still seems to be the province of the restaurateur and the hunter.

Most people seem to have a fear of cooking duck, for several unfounded reasons—fattiness and unfamiliarity the most common among them. Paula Wolfert has pointed out that duck fat has only 9 percent cholesterol compared with butter's 22 percent, but of course it's true that duck is rich. I find that I pay about the same for fresh duck that others pay for what I call "grocery store chicken." I remove the fat and render it for use in biscuits and vegetable dishes; I have a meal or two from the breasts; I simmer the legs in port or whiskey and make stock from the carcass—or make the pâté on page 46; so I get several meals from my 4- or 5-pound duck, for just a little more than I'd pay for chicken.

DUCK FAT AND CRACKLINGS

No matter which recipe you use, you will probably want to remove the duck fat and render it for use in another dish. I usually remove the breasts from the duck and leave the skin on them, scraping off any excess fat. The remaining skin of the duck I remove entirely unless I plan to cook the legs separately.

Put all of the skin and excess fat you intend to render in a food processor and puree. Cover the bottom of a saucepan or skillet with water (a couple of tablespoons is enough), then add the pureed duck fat and skin. Heat over low heat until all the water has evaporated and the fat is clear. Strain into a container and keep covered and refrigerated. It will last several months.

Cracklings are crisply cooked skins, which are delicious as snacks and as garnishes for salads and vegetable dishes. The easiest way to make cracklings is to place pieces of skin that have been scraped of excess fat on a cookie sheet, spread them out flat, sprinkle them with cayenne pepper and salt, and bake in a 400° oven until they are crisp, about 20 minutes. A small roasting pan with a raised perforated insert will allow juices to drain off, so that the meats being roasted do not sit in their own fat. As with most foods cooked in fat, it is best to drain the cracklings on a rack (or in the roasting pan with the raised bottom) rather than to put them on paper towels, where they would reabsorb the fat.

DUCK BREASTS

I prefer duck breasts cooked quickly and separately from the rest of the body or cured in salt and served as you would serve prosciutto. To obtain 2 boneless breasts from a duck, place a whole unskinned duck on its back, with its neck end toward you, on a cutting board. Slice down the very center the full length of the bird, through the skin and flesh to the breastbone, then down along the breastbone on each side. Attached to the breastbone is a narrow strip of meat that has a tendon running through it. The breast halves will easily separate from this "tenderloin." Bring the tip of the knife down to the wishbone, which forms an arch around the neck cavity, and cut the breast meat free from it on each side. Then, holding a breast half in one hand and the knife in the other, pull each breast half away from the rib cage, running the knife over the "tenderloin" and along the rib cage. Pull the halves out away from the body and slice them free from the wing joints. At this point you may use kitchen shears, if you prefer, to cut around the breasts to free them completely from the body. This method may be unorthodox in butchering circles, but it is easy for even the novice and eliminates the possibility of cutting into the flesh of the breast. If you're using the rest of the duck within the day, sprinkle it with salt and return it to the refrigerator. Or wrap it well and freeze it— or store in the refrigerator for use within two days.

DUCK BREAST HAMS

Serve thin slices of this "ham" with melon or with preserved fruit such as Golden Pear Chutney or Plum Sauce.

> 2 duck breasts, with skin
> 1 tablespoon salt
> 1 teaspoon Herbal Mix (page 31)

Rub the duck breasts with a mixture of the salt and herbal mix. Place the breasts on a nonporous plate in the refrigerator overnight. The next day, drain off any liquid that may have accumulated, wipe the breasts dry, and wrap each one in several layers of cheesecloth. If you live in a cool, dry climate, you can hang them in an airy place to cure. In the Lowcountry we must refrigerate them, suspended, so that they don't touch each other or other objects. They will be cured in about a week. Remove them from the cheesecloth and slice as thinly as possible.

DUCK BREASTS ON THE GRILL

Sunny Davis is from Walterboro, South Carolina, near the black and sinuous Ashepoo River, about an hour from Charleston. She comes from the Lowcountry Barnes family, one of those few who have not lost their rural traditions. The Barnes sisters—Erlene, Rena, Lessie Rae, and RuRu—are all great cooks, and their brother Russell is a stalwart for tradition. Whenever I have a question about *real* Lowcountry food or farming, I call a Barnes. Russell still renders his own lard in an outdoor kettle, stirring it all day with what looks like an oar but is in fact a "lard paddle." He also grows his own cane and grinds and boils his own syrup from it.

Not surprisingly, Erlene's daughter Sunny is also a great cook. Her boiled peanuts, her okra and tomatoes, her hoecakes, and her pickles are the best. But when it's her birthday, I grill for her. One year I cooked two dozen duck breasts on the grill, then another dozen when a late-night crowd arrived. This is a wonderful dish, wonderfully simple to prepare. These grilled breasts are prepared similarly to the porgies on page 76, but the ducks improve by being seasoned in advance. Begin the recipe several hours before serving.

SERVES 1 OR 2

1 **set of duck breasts, with skin**
1 **cup mixed fresh herbs such as basil, parsley, oregano, and thyme**
2 **garlic cloves, peeled**
¼ **cup olive oil**

Slice the skin of each duck breast down to, but not into, the flesh, in 3 or 4 evenly spaced places and place on a nonreactive plate. Grind the herbs, garlic, and oil in a food processor until ground evenly. Coat the duck breasts with the mixture, cover, and refrigerate until ready to grill.

Build a charcoal fire off to one side in a covered grill and let it burn until the coals are all evenly gray.

Place the duck breasts, skin side down, on the grill several inches over the fire and cook them until the skin is seared and cooked crispy brown, about 4 or 5 minutes. Fat from the duck may drip into the coals and ignite. If so, move the breasts to the side of the grill away from the fire and cover the grill. Close all of the grill vents if necessary to kill the flames. After the skin side is cooked, turn the duck breasts over and place them on the fireless side of the grill. Continue cooking for no more than 3 minutes. The breast should be rare, springing back when poked with a finger. Slice diagonally into several pieces, through the slashes already made in the skin. Serve immediately.

DUCK BREASTS WITH LEEKS AND PEARS

You will need a Chinese bamboo steamer or its equivalent for this recipe. As the pears need not be ripe, you may make this at any time of the year, but in the Lowcountry I make it in late summer when our hard local pears are in season.

SERVES 2

2 leeks
1 cup duck stock or chicken stock (pages 34–35)
1 set of duck breasts with skin
  salt and freshly ground black pepper to taste
3 partially ripe pears

Cut off most of the green from the leeks and slice them vertically in half down to the base. Rinse them thoroughly under cold running water until they are free of grit, then cut off the base and slice them into thin vertical strips. Put them in a skillet or wok over which a bamboo or stainless-steel steamer will fit, cover with the stock, and bring to a boil. Reduce to a simmer.

Slice the skin of the duck breasts in several places down to, but not into, the flesh. Sprinkle the breasts with salt and pepper. In a hot frying pan, sear the duck breasts by cooking them skin side down until the skin is crispy and brown. Remove the pan from the heat and turn the breasts over to sear quickly on the other side, then remove the breasts to the steamer, skin side up.

Peel, halve, and core the pears. Slice them into thin vertical slices. Add the slices to the leeks, put the steamer with the breasts on top of the pan, cover the steamer, and steam the breasts in the leek and pear vapors for about 7 minutes. The breasts should be medium-rare; clear juices should flow when sliced. Slice the breasts diagonally and serve with the pear and leek mixture. I serve this dish with green beans that have been parboiled, then stir-fried quickly with some ginger and garlic in the fat rendered from the searing of the duck breasts.

CRÊPES WITH WHISKEY DUCK

After I've grilled a duck's breast and made stock from the rest of the carcass, I am likely to make a pâté from the legs (page 46) or simmer them in spirits. Airy crêpes seem the logical foil for this late-night supper of duck legs simmered ahead of time in whiskey—bourbon or sour mash.

SERVES 2

FOR THE DUCK:
- 1 set of duck legs, with skin
- 1 small to medium onion, chopped (about ½ cup)
- 1 cup bourbon or sour mash whiskey
     unsalted butter or cream (optional)

FOR THE CRÊPES:
- ½ cup unbleached all-purpose flour
    pinch of salt
- 1 large egg
- ½ cup milk
- ¼ cup shelled pecans
- 1 tablespoon unsalted butter, melted
    vegetable oil

The day before you want to serve the crêpes, sear the duck legs in a hot heavy-bottomed saucepan, browning them as evenly as possible all over. Remove and set aside.

Lower the heat to medium and add the onions, cooking them until they are transparent, about 5 minutes.

Add the duck legs and whiskey, cover, and simmer for 1 hour. Remove from the heat, cool, and refrigerate overnight.

When you're ready to serve, remove the fat from the top of the duck mixture along with the duck skins and discard both. Remove the meat from the bones, discard the bones, and return the meat to the pan with the onion and whiskey mixture. Slowly reheat the duck while you make the crêpes.

To make the crêpes, stir the flour and salt together in a bowl, then make a well in the center. Add the egg and a little of the milk and stir together with a wooden spoon, gradually adding a little more of the milk until it is all incorporated into the batter. Finely chop the pecans. Add half the nuts and the melted butter to the batter and stir until perfectly smooth.

Heat a small amount of a flavorless oil in an omelet or crêpe pan until it is very hot but not smoking. Swirl the oil around in the pan to completely coat the bottom and part of the sides, then pour off any excess oil. With a ladle, quickly pour about 2 tablespoons of batter into the hot pan and swirl the batter around to coat the bottom of the pan. Cook until the edges begin to pull away from the pan; then, using your fingers or a spatula, flip the crêpe to cook on the other side. It may take several minutes to cook on the first side, a matter of seconds on the other; every stove and pan is different. As the crêpes are finished, place them on a plate over the pan of warming duck—or in a low oven—to keep them warm. The recipe will make 6 to 8 crêpes. Add some butter or cream to the duck filling to extend or flavor it if desired.

When the crêpes are done, taste the duck for seasoning, correct with salt and black pepper, and fill the crêpes, gently rolling them up. Sprinkle each with a few finely chopped pecans.

DUCK AND SAUSAGE GUMBO

Duck and sausage gumbo is one of the most widely copied recipes in the South, as it does not depend on the fresh shellfish that so many other gumbo recipes demand. It is an ideal way to feed several hungry mouths with inexpensive duck and sausage, and it is absolutely delicious. In slight imitation of a Vietnamese idea, I hold the duck breasts out of the soup until the last minute, then sear them and the sausages just before adding them to the gumbo. You will need to begin this recipe several hours ahead or the day before you plan to serve it.

SERVES 8

FOR THE DUCK AND STOCK:

- 1 4- to 5-pound duck
  salt, freshly ground black pepper, and cayenne pepper to taste
- 3 quarts water
- 1 large onion, quartered
- 1 large *or* 2 small carrots, broken into pieces
- 2 celery ribs, broken into pieces
  a handful of fresh herbs such as parsley, thyme, savory, and oregano
  unbleached all-purpose flour

FOR THE GUMBO:

- ¾ cup duck fat roux
- 2 garlic cloves, minced
- 1 cup chopped onion
- 1 cup chopped celery
- 1 cup chopped green bell pepper
- 1 pound okra, trimmed and cut into 1-inch pieces
  about 2 quarts reserved duck stock
  salt and freshly ground black pepper to taste
  chopped fresh hot pepper or hot pepper sauce to taste
  reserved duck breasts and picked duck meat
- 1 pound spicy smoked sausage, cut into 1-inch pieces
- 3 cups cooked long-grain white rice

Several hours or the day before serving, remove the duck breasts, with skin attached, from the duck (see page 161). Sprinkle with salt, pepper, and cayenne and place on a nonreactive plate, covered, in the refrigerator. Remove the skin from the rest of the duck and set aside.

Put the carcass and the remaining ingredients except the flour into a stockpot on top of the stove, bring to a boil, reduce the heat, and cook at a low boil until the duck is tender, about 1 hour, skimming fat and scum from the surface as necessary. Strain the stock and pick all the meat from the carcass. Set the stock aside to cool and refrigerate the meat.

While the stock is cooking, render the duck fat as described on page 160, then combine it with an equal amount of flour to make a dark roux (page 33). Refrigerate the roux and stock until the next day or continue with the recipe.

About 2 hours before serving, heat the roux in a large Dutch oven, then add the garlic, onions, celery, and green pepper. Cook over medium heat until the onions begin to become transparent, stirring constantly, about 10 minutes. Add the okra and cook until all ropiness is gone, about 20 minutes, stirring often. Gradually add the stock, stirring it into the mixture, and simmer, uncovered, for about an hour. Taste the soup for seasoning and adjust to taste, remembering that the soup will have the seasoned duck breasts and sausage added later. About 30 minutes before serving, add the picked duck meat to the gumbo pot.

Score the skin of the duck breasts down to, but not into, the flesh in several places. Put them skin side down in a medium-hot frying pan and cook them for several minutes, until the skin is crispy and brown. Turn them over and cook them briefly on the other side. Set aside on a plate. Place the sausage in the skillet where the duck breasts were cooked and cook the pieces in the duck fat until they are nicely browned all over, about 10 minutes. Slice the duck breast into thin strips and add it and the sausage to the gumbo. Serve in bowls over fluffy white rice.

GAME BIRDS

QUAIL WRAPPED IN VINE LEAVES AND GRILLED OVER VINES, WITH SPICED GRAPES

This simple recipe uses the leaves, vines, and fruit of native grapes. Serve one bird per person as an appetizer or 2 as a main dish, accompanied by rice cooked in a broth flavored with the quail trimmings. Begin the recipe several hours before serving, defrosting the birds if they are frozen.

SERVES 4 AS AN APPETIZER OR 2 AS AN ENTRÉE

4 quail
1 quart water
  herbs to include several sprigs of fresh parsley and thyme,
    plus a bay leaf
1 small onion
1 small carrot
1 small celery rib
  salt and freshly ground black pepper to taste
  Herbal Mix (page 31) or *herbes de Provence* to taste
  olive oil
4 to 8 preserved grape leaves (page 305)
  dried grapevine cuttings

Trim the neck and wing tips from the quail. Add the trimmings and any giblets to the water in a small stockpot. Add the herbs and the aromatic vegetables and bring to a boil over high heat. Reduce the heat and cook, uncovered, at a low boil until the liquid is reduced by half. Strain out the solids and reserve the broth.

(continued)

While the broth is cooking, salt and pepper the birds inside and out, then place in a nonreactive pan. Sprinkle herbs to taste over the quail, then coat with olive oil, rubbing the oil evenly over the flesh. Place in the refrigerator to marinate for several hours.

Start a charcoal fire. Remove the birds from the marinade and set aside. Rinse the preserved grape leaves in warm water, pat dry, then place the leaves in the marinade. Wrap the birds well in oiled leaves, securing with toothpicks if necessary. I simply place the birds in a wire basket designed for grilling fish.

When the coals are hot, add dried grapevine cuttings to the fire if you have them. Wait for them to ignite—they burn hot and quickly. Place the birds on the grill several inches from the fire and grill them for about 10 to 12 minutes, turning them frequently so that they do not burn. Serve them hot right off the grill.

Paula Wolfert in *The Cooking of South-West France* suggests serving grilled quail with lemon wedges. A small amount of sweet and tart spiced grapes (page 306) complements the slightly bitter and tealike flavor of the vine leaves and smoke. This dish should be eaten with the hands; be sure to place a finger bowl of water and lemon on the table.

FRIED QUAIL WITH SAUSAGE AND OYSTER CREAM

Throughout the South, former cotton plantations remain as large tracts of land maintained as hunting preserves. The quail is a small game bird that spends most of its time on the ground. Often called "partridge," it is favored for its delicious white flesh. Serve one of these birds to each person as an appetizer for a big celebratory meal such as Christmas or a rehearsal dinner, or two as the main course.

SERVES 4 AS AN APPETIZER, 2 AS A MAIN COURSE

    4 quail, dressed for cooking
      unbleached all-purpose flour for dusting
      lard or oil for pan-frying
    1 cup shucked oysters and their liquor
    ¼ pound country sausage (page 129)
    1 cup cream

Preheat the oven to its lowest setting and place a cooking rack over a sheet pan in the oven. Rinse the quail, pat dry, then dust in the flour. Do not season the flour; the sausage is very salty and spicy.

Fry the quail in a small amount of oil or lard in a skillet over high heat until they are golden brown, turning once, about 10 minutes. Remove to the rack in the oven to keep them warm while you prepare the cream sauce.

Drain the oysters and set aside, reserving the liquor. Put the sausage in a saucepan and cook over medium-high heat until all of the grease is rendered out and the sausage is evenly browned. Remove the sausage from the pan and allow it to drain. Pour off the grease and discard.

Add the cream and the oyster liquor to the pan and reduce over high heat until the sauce is just shy of the desired consistency, stirring often and scraping up any brown bits stuck to the bottom of the pan. Lower the heat and crumble the cooked sausage into the cream. Add the oysters, heating the sauce through until the oysters just begin to curl, just a minute or two. Remove the birds from the oven to plates. Pour the sauce over the birds, dividing the oysters and bits of sausage equally among the plates.

FRIED WILD TURKEY

Fried chicken is usually considered *the* southern dish. Sarah Rutledge included three recipes in her 1847 Charleston cookbook. The Junior League's recipe (1950) calls for panfrying the chicken, covered. The chicken steams as it fries; it is very moist. I prefer deep frying, which, strange as it may seem, is a *dry* cooking technique. A whole wild turkey is deep-fried in this recipe, which I've never seen outside the South. You may find it more manageable to fry a domestic turkey breast (see *Note*).

Wild turkey is so delicious; it has a fuller, nuttier flavor than the domesticated birds. If you have an outdoorsman in your family who occasionally brings home a wild turkey, then you probably also have an outdoor gas burner and huge 10-gallon pots. This is one of the easiest and most unusual recipes in the Lowcountry, and it's particularly delicious. I prefer fried turkey to smoked.

Wild turkeys usually weigh between 15 and 20 pounds. Cleaned, they are smaller than the modern hybrids, and their breasts are not nearly so large in comparison to the rest of their bodies. Begin the recipe a day in advance. *Do not attempt these recipes indoors.*

    1 wild turkey, dressed for cooking
    6 lemons
       salt, freshly ground black pepper, and cayenne pepper to taste
    2 teaspoons Herbal Mix (page 31) or Italian seasoning
 1½   cups vegetable oil
   20 pounds potatoes
    5 gallons vegetable oil or lard for frying

Rinse the turkey well in water, pat dry, then place in a large roasting pan. Halve the lemons, then rub them all over the turkey, both inside and out. Squeeze all of the juice out of the lemons over the bird. Season the bird well, inside and out, with salt, pepper, and cayenne. Mix the herbs with the 1½ cups oil and pour all over the turkey, using your hands to rub the bird well with the oil and mixing the oil and lemon juice together. Cover the bird with aluminum foil and marinate overnight in the refrigerator, shaking the pan occasionally and basting with any of the oil mixture that sits in the bottom of the pan.

One-and-a-half hours before serving, remove the pan from the refrigerator and place the turkey on a rack to drain and to come to room temperature, about 30 minutes. Peel and roughly chop the potatoes and place them in the marinade. Over an outdoor gas burner, heat the oil or lard in a 10-gallon pot, preferably one with a removable fry basket. The grease should be very hot, about 365°.

Make sure the turkey is well drained, then slowly and carefully lower the entire bird into the oil. Cook for about 3 minutes per pound or until it floats on the surface and the entire surface is crispy and browned. A meat thermometer inserted into the thickest part of the bird, not touching a bone, should register 180°. Carefully remove the turkey from the grease, then slowly and carefully add the potatoes to the hot grease, cooking them while the turkey rests until they are browned all over and semisoft in the center.

Note: You may also fry a 5-pound turkey breast in 2 gallons of oil in a 5-gallon stockpot, but don't try cooking it indoors; it's too easy to start a fire. The breast will need to cook for 4 to 6 minutes per pound.

ABOUT FRYING

Deep frying is an art in the Lowcountry. Foods that are deep-fried in clean hot oil or lard are crisper and less greasy than those that are sautéed or panfried. The oil must be fresh; there must be enough of it so that the foods are not crowded. Never fill a pot more than half full, or you risk a fire. If some spilled oil should ignite, use salt or baking soda to extinguish it, never water. You can clarify oil for reuse by slowly reheating it, then straining it well. Store it in the refrigerator and be sure to check it for rancidity (by smelling it) before using it only once more.

Proper temperature is essential for perfect frying. Use a deep fryer with a thermostat or a heavy, deep pot and a frying thermometer. Foods that have been cooked previously, such as fish cakes and croquettes, cook at 390° for about 2 minutes. Other foods, such as hushpuppies and fish, fry at 365–370° for 2 to 5 minutes. Perfect French fries are the pride of many Lowcountry cooks. They are fried once at the lower temperature, well drained, then fried crisp and brown at 390°.

SMOTHERED MARSH HENS

In her foreword to the University of South Carolina's 1976 facsimile edition of *Two Hundred Years of Charleston Cooking*, Elizabeth Hamilton nonchalantly noted: "This fishy bird presents a problem, but cooked properly and served on points of toast with broiled mushrooms and cheney briar it is enough to set the most fastidious of gourmets talking for years. If you can't find cheney briar, fresh asparagus will do."

If you are not a Sandlapper, you've probably never heard of marsh hens or cheney briar. The bird is the clapper rail, *Rallus longirostris,* of our salt marshes. Its loud clatter and low, slow flight makes it an easy target for gunners, but laws forbid the use of motors on boats when hunting the marsh hen. Marsh hunting is quintessentially Lowcountry: one must have a keen eye to discern the skinny, well-camouflaged bird among the marsh grasses; be acutely familiar with the tides, shoals, and currents of those backwaters; and be willing to persevere for hours in biting autumn winds. Although marsh hens are chicken-size, they only weigh about ½ pound when dressed, and the breasts are small. Mrs. Hamilton warns, "You don't pluck a marsh hen, you peel it." The birds are then soaked in a vinegar solution or parboiled to remove the fishy taste.

Cheney briar, or greenbrier, is the young shoots of various species of smilax, a member of the lily family of plants. Generally considered pests, the plants scramble over thickets and trees, entangling and strangling everything in their path. William Bartram, traveling in Carolina in the 1770s, found Indians crushing the roots to make a gelatinlike thickener for their stews. More intriguing are the asparaguslike tender young shoots, which are sometimes offered for sale at the Charleston Farmers Market.

SERVES 4

4 marsh hens, skinned
1 cup unbleached all-purpose flour
   salt and freshly ground black pepper to taste
4 tablespoons unsalted butter
2 medium Vidalia, red, or other sweet onions, sliced
1 *bouquet garni:* several parsley and thyme sprigs tied in cheesecloth
    with a bay leaf and a celery rib
2 cups chicken stock (page 34) or water

Place the birds in a large pot, cover with salted water, bring to a boil, reduce the heat, and cook just long enough for the blood to cook out and for a fork to be inserted into the flesh easily, about 10 minutes. Remove the birds from the water and drain well.

Season the flour with salt and pepper, then toss the birds in the flour, coating them well. Melt the butter in a Dutch oven over medium heat, add the birds, and brown well on all sides. Remove the birds and set aside, reduce the heat to very low, and add the onions. Cover the pot and let the onions cook very slowly for about an hour, until they are almost totally melted.

Add the *bouquet garni*, the birds, and the stock and stir everything together well, covering the birds with onions. Cover and cook for another hour over very low heat. Remove the cover. If the sauce is too thin, brown some of the leftover flour in a frying pan, then add a little of the sauce to the pan, whisking well. Return the roux to the pot and mix in well. If the sauce is too thick, thin with a little milk or cream. You can run the smothered birds under the broiler, if desired, before serving them hot over steaming hot white rice, with a side dish of steamed and buttered cheney briar or asparagus.

ROAST SQUAB WITH RICE PILAU

Remember that squab (young pigeons), rabbit, pheasant, quail, and squirrel may be interchanged in recipes. Blanche Rhett's recipe, below, begins the 20 pages of pilau recipes in *Two Hundred Years of Charleston Cooking*. She assumes your Lowcountry kitchen will contain some mustard pickles. A standard mustard pickle formula is included in the Ats Jaar recipe.

SERVES 6 TO 8

6 slices bacon
1 onion, chopped (about 1 cup)
¾ cup chopped celery
2 cups long-grain white rice
1 quart chicken stock (page 34)
4 large eggs
  salt and freshly ground black pepper to taste
4 squab, dressed
  mustard pickle juice (page 325)

For the stuffing, use a rice pilau made as follows: Dice the bacon and cook in a skillet until crisp. Remove the bacon, add the chopped onion and celery to the bacon drippings, and let them brown over medium heat. Cook the rice in the chicken stock until tender. Add the bacon and the onion and celery mixture. Beat the eggs and add to the rice, stirring well so that the heat of the rice cooks the eggs. Season with salt and pepper.

Preheat the oven to 425°. Stuff the squab with the mixture and make mounds of the remainder in a roasting pan. Lay the squabs on top of the mounds of stuffing. Bake for about 25 minutes, basting the squab frequently with mustard pickle juice. The mustard pickle adds a piquancy to the squab and combines well with the pilau stuffing.

10
VEGETABLES

The misconception that southern cooks have always overcooked their vegetables continues, despite a large amount of evidence to the contrary. The overcooking and oversalting that are often associated with the South in fact arrived along with poverty after the Civil War, when the Lowcountry lost many of its farms and its people began to depend on bland dried and canned goods. But antebellum cookbooks, diaries, and farm journals note in no uncertain terms precise gardening techniques and short cooking times for nearly all the green vegetables. I dare say there's not a vegetable grown today that early Sandlappers did not themselves cultivate, and with relish.

The Deas family daybook, in the collection of the Historical Society of South Carolina, was written in the Lowcountry sometime prior to 1749. Its precious yellowed pages mention several varieties of cabbages and beans, spinach, salsify, black salsify, onions, beets, melons, cucumbers, peas, strawberries, artichokes, leeks, radishes, cresses, various greens, peppers, turnips, carrots, and virtually every herb.

In no season is the Lowcountry table without fresh local vegetables. Green beans grow a full ten months some years. Collards are available in all but the hottest months. Our subtropical climate produces two seasons of summer vegetables such as beans, corn, and tomatoes. Yet in many of the older cookbooks, and particularly in unpublished private manuscripts and journals, vegetables—like seafood—are conspicuously absent. It was assumed that you already knew how to prepare this daily fare.

Salads are absent as well, but both household inventories and shipping records in Charleston indicate a long love affair with olive oil. In spite of British embargoes that prohibited the colony's trade with other nations, earthen jars from the Mediterranean have been discovered in several archaeological digs here, belying their success. When John Bartram, the great naturalist, visited the home of Henry Laurens in 1765, he found a "fine growing young olive tree, very luxuriant, 15 foot high; the diameter of the bows 15½ foot; circumference of the bole 13½ inches," but the soil would prove too rich for the trees to produce.

Lemon juice or sherry vinegar traditionally complements the olive oil as the dressing for salad greens. I finely slice freshly dug sweet radishes, then leave them to marinate in olive oil, lemon juice or vinegar, and salt and pepper, adding them to a bed of clean, crisp lettuce leaves just as they are served. Salad greens must be washed and perfectly dried before dressing, or the oil will not cling to them. The modern-day salad spinner is one of the kitchen's best tools. Buy the centrifuge kind that has a string pull; it washes and dries the greens at the same time: a hole in the top lets running water in; holes in the bottom allow the water to run out.

ASPARAGUS

Asparagus, both wild and cultivated, graced the tables of rich and poor alike before 20th-century agriculture came along. Though native to Europe, it has escaped cultivation and has naturalized all over the world. Once asparagus gets started, it produces for many, many years to come. For the best flavor, buy tender young asparagus.

Bend each stalk of asparagus near the base. The end will snap off just at the point above the woody part. Tie a bundle of the vegetables together with twine and place, tips up, in a tall pot with 3 or 4 inches of boiling water, covered. Take them off the fire the instant that the tips become tender, 5 to 10 minutes, depending on the size of the stalks. The tips will have steamed and the thick bases boiled perfectly. Remove the asparagus immediately, untie the bundle, and serve hot with melted butter; or spread the stalks out on a kitchen towel to cool and serve as a salad with peanut dressing (page 315).

BEANS

Some beans will grow 10 months out of the Lowcountry year. They are important crops on the Sea Island truck farms south of Charleston. All kinds are grown in the Lowcountry, from the tiniest "lady peas" to big Old World favas. Beans that are eaten whole, cooked in the pod, are usually called "green beans," "string beans," or "pole beans"; two recipes follow. Tender young green beans are also "jarred," as Geechees call canning (see Dilly Beans).

Shelled beans, often called "peas," might be any of more than 300 varieties grown here. These are not English peas—though we do grow them as well—but crowder peas, black-eyes, butter beans, Sieva (also called Sewee and pronounced "sivvy") beans, field peas, and whippoorwills—all members of the *Phaseolus* genus, the beans. Sieva beans are the smallest of the lima beans, a delicious butter bean that has no equal. They are said to have been grown here by the Sewee Indians when Europeans arrived, though all lima beans supposedly originated in South America. Real Sandlappers know that the best beans of all are the volunteer field peas that come up in the soybean fields in the fall. Field peas (called "cowpeas" when dried), black-eyed peas, and crowder peas—beans as well—are cooked, like butter beans, with a piece of cured pork and served over rice. Made with dried peas in wintertime, the dish becomes hoppin' john.

Peas and rice appear in equatorial cuisines around the world, and the complete protein this combination provides is legend. The West African slaves would have been familiar with pigeon peas and rice, an African dish that remains unchanged in the Caribbean, where the *Cajanus* genus, of which they are specific, will grow; it has been suggested that hoppin' john (page 59) is a bastardization of the French *pois à pigeon*. In the Bahamas, "Hop and John" includes Guinea corn, or sorghum, as the grain and black-eyed peas as the legume. The one remaining local vendor of produce in the city Market now sells dried "13-Bean Soup Mix," as a sort of homage to our culinary heritage, but even the vegetables she sells are from Florida. Fortunately, in the summer of 1989 a Charleston Farmers Market was begun again at Marion Square, in the center of the city. The first crop of butter beans and crowder peas comes in June or July (there is another crop in the fall); I gladly pay a premium for hand-picked, shelled peas. I blanch some of them for a few minutes and freeze in plastic bags for winter use. All the others I cook in similar fashion:

SERVES 8 TO 10

2 quarts water
about 1 pound cured meat (see *Note*)
2 pounds shelled butter beans or crowder peas

Put the water and cured meat in a pan and bring it to a boil. Cook, uncovered, at a low boil for about 30 minutes or until the water is flavored by the meat. Then add the peas, return to a boil, reduce the heat, and simmer, uncovered, for about another 30 minutes, until the peas are just tender.

Seldom do I eat the peas on the same day they are cooked. The most typical Lowcountry meal of summer might include peas and rice, sliced tomatoes and cucumbers, corn bread (page 219), and fried okra. Serve the peas over rice, with plenty of pot likker (the corn bread will sop up what the rice doesn't).

Relishes are always served with peas and rice. Corn relish (page 298) goes well with Sieva beans and rice; fresh peach and coconut chutney (page 314) complements field peas and rice. With the fall crop of butter beans, artichoke relish (page 294) is more appropriate.

Note: In summertime I use smoked neck bones, but in the winter I might use a hock or "butt's meat" (salt pork from the jowl). If you use salt pork or streak o' lean or butt's meat, you'll need to cut it up, "fry it out," then pour off some of the fat before adding the water.

GREEN BEANS AND BENNE SALAD

I serve this salad all year long, to rave reviews; there is never any left. It is an absolutely delicious combination of flavors that complements all sorts of meals.

SERVES 8

 2 pounds young green beans, stemmed but with the tender young
      green tip intact
 ¼ cup benne (sesame seeds), roasted (see page 28)
 1 teaspoon hot red pepper flakes, to taste
 ¼ cup extra-virgin olive oil
 2 tablespoons (⅛ cup) fresh lemon juice
 2 garlic cloves, finely minced
      salt and freshly ground black pepper to taste

Plunge the beans into a large pot of rapidly boiling water and cook them, uncovered, until they just become tender, about 3 to 5 minutes. Taste them frequently and do not overcook them. When they just lose the raw flavor, immediately pour them into a colander and rinse them thoroughly in cold water to stop the cooking and to retain the bright green color. You may wish to have some ice water handy if your kitchen is warm and your tap water, like mine, is not cold. Set aside to drain.

When all of the water has thoroughly drained from the beans, toss them with the remaining ingredients and serve at room temperature.

FAVA BEANS

Fava beans—also known as Windsor or broad beans—were *the* beans of the Old World before the European discovery of America. Our earliest records of gardening in the Lowcountry include favas—and they stayed popular for a long, long time. They are easy to grow, and they are absolutely delicious—at once buttery and fresh on the palate—but they are a pain to prepare. A half bushel of large, mature pods yields but a few cups of beans—and then they too must be shelled of their bitter outer layer. When I lived in Italy, we ate fresh young unpeeled favas raw with delicate salami from Sant'Olcese, but you are not likely to find early favas in this country. In Mediterranean countries a puree of favas is a traditional accompaniment with roast meats—and you can do that with dried or canned beans available in certain markets. But if you can get fresh favas in the height of summer, try this old Lowcountry dish of the beans warmed with onions and tomatoes.

SERVES 6

5 pounds fresh fava beans
1 tablespoon olive oil
1 medium chopped onion, about ¾ cup
4 vine-ripened tomatoes, peeled and quartered (about 1½ pounds)
   fresh marjoram and/or oregano
   salt and freshly ground black pepper to taste
   vinegar or fresh lemon juice to taste

Shell the beans and bring a pot of water large enough to hold them to a boil. Add the beans, return to the boil, and turn off the heat. When the water has cooled, you should be able to slit the bitter outer skin with a fingernail and remove the delicious inner bean.

When all of the beans are extracted, heat the olive oil in a large skillet and add the chopped onion, cooking until it becomes transparent, about 5 minutes. Then add the beans, tomatoes, herbs, and salt and pepper. Cook very slowly, uncovered, just to heat the vegetables through. You do not want them to be cooked but merely warmed. Adjust the seasoning with a little vinegar or lemon juice before serving.

FRIED BEAN CAKES

Refried beans appear in most tropical and semitropical countries where legumes are common cash and food crops. I am amused by a California chef's claim that he invented the bean cake, when old recipes are legion in the South.

The following recipe is from Richard Perry, who manufactures pasta in Charleston.

MAKES 8 BURGER-SIZE PATTIES OR 2 DOZEN SMALL ONES

3 cups cooked and drained (leftover) beans or black-eyed peas
1 large egg *or* 2 large egg yolks
1 teaspoon dried thyme
1 tablespoon chopped fresh basil
1 tablespoon chopped fresh oregano
1 small red onion, diced (about ½ cup)
2 large garlic cloves, very finely minced
1 scallion, chopped
½ roasted, peeled, and seeded jalapeño pepper, finely minced
   unbleached all-purpose flour
   vegetable oil or clarified butter for panfrying (page 24)

Mix together all of the ingredients except the flour and oil, mashing the beans with a fork or by hand. Form into patties, coat with flour, and fry over medium-high heat in a small amount of oil or clarified butter until browned, about 1½ to 2 minutes on each side.

I prefer to serve these cakes with roasted red pepper puree (page 321) or a sun-dried tomato mayonnaise (page 310). Richard notes that you may add shrimp, country sausage (cooked, drained, and crumbled; page 129), bacon, diced meat, or vegetables to the mixture to add flavor and texture.

POLE BEANS AND NEW POTATOES

In the Lowcountry pole beans are any of a number of varieties of snap beans that are larger than everyday green beans. Kentucky Wonders are a favorite variety. Try to find tender beans that do not have a heavy "string"; they will cook in the same amount of time as the potatoes. There was a time when pole beans were boiled all day; it is not necessary with the delectable modern hybrids.

This simple recipe produces delicious results; it always surprises the first-time cook. Note the small amount of water; the beans sit in the water, but the potatoes steam.

SERVES 4 TO 6

2 pounds pole beans
2 pounds of small new potatoes
1 smoked ham hock, about ½ pound
⅓ cup water

String the beans. Peel the potatoes or cut them in half. Put the beans in the bottom of a heavy saucepan. Add the potatoes, hock, and water. Simmer, covered, until the potatoes are done, 30 to 45 minutes.

BEETS

Nothing else in the spectrum of the vegetable kingdom can touch the deep magenta of beets. From midsummer through the fall in the Lowcountry, freshly dug beets are a colorful addition to a plate of summer greens and yellows. Choose beets that are small and firm. Trim the stems about 2 inches above the bulbous root and leave the pointed root intact. Boil or bake them whole and unpeeled so that they retain their color. When tender, cool them under running water and drain. Top the roots and pare them. If small, serve whole; if large, slice the beets before dressing them. The following sauce is a pickle that enhances the beets' intense flavor, whether served hot or cold.

SERVES 4

½ cup white vinegar
½ cup water
¼ cup sugar
1 teaspoon salt
  freshly ground black pepper to taste
2 cups cooked and peeled beets (sliced if large)
2 tablespoons unsalted butter (if served hot)

Boil all of the ingredients except the beets and the butter for 5 minutes. If you're serving the beets cold, pour the pickle over them and let them sit, covered, in the refrigerator overnight. If you're serving them hot, continue to reduce the vinegar mixture, then whisk in the butter to make a sauce of the desired consistency. Pour over the beets and serve at once.

CARROT AND ORANGE SALAD

This salad has a North African feel to it. The recipe may have entered the culinary vernacular with the Sephardic Jews in Charleston. In Morocco the salad would include cinnamon. Blanched thinly sliced onions are a welcome addition as well.

SERVES 4 TO 6

¾ pound large juice oranges, such as Valencias
1 pound carrots, peeled and grated
2 tablespoons (⅛ cup) olive oil
20 grinds of black pepper
   salt to taste
   fresh lemon juice or sherry vinegar to taste
1 medium onion, thinly sliced and blanched (see *Note*)

On a cutting board, slice the top and bottom off each orange with a thin, sharp knife. Slice the peel and white pith of the orange away from the orange, cutting into the flesh as little as possible. Over a mixing bowl, with the orange held in one hand, cut each orange section free from all membranes. Begin by making a slice as close as possible to one of the membranes, down to, but not into, the center of the orange. Make a slice down the other side of the same orange section, just inside the membrane. The section should be released.

Rotate the orange a little and move to the next section. Cut the far side of that section with a slice just like the last one. When the knife reaches the center of the orange, pull the section out and away from the other membrane with the knife blade. Continue with the remaining orange sections, allowing them to fall into the bowl.

Add the carrots, olive oil, and pepper. Taste and season with salt, then splash with a little lemon juice or sherry vinegar. Toss in the onion if desired. Serve immediately at room temperature.

Note: To blanch onion slices, pour boiling water over them in an empty pot. Drain immediately.

CORN

Summer is my favorite time of year. I love the heat, I love the humidity, and I especially love the fresh fruits and vegetables of the season. The first tomato crop peaks, the first of the peaches appear, and those wonderfully sweet ears of corn ripen as the solstice arrives.

The hackneyed saying that the best way to cook corn is to have a pot of hot water in the cornfield is not just an old wives' tale: the sugar really does start breaking down as soon as corn is picked. If you don't live near a cornfield, you will be better off buying corn from chilled bins in your supermarket. I usually buy a bushel or 2 of corn, quickly blanch the ears, cut the kernels off, and freeze them in plastic bags—one of the few foods I put away in a fairly natural state for use later. I am especially fond of the sweet corn varieties such as Silver Queen and How Sweet It Is, which, when truly fresh, need only be warmed through. I might put up some corn relish (page 298) as well, but most of the corn that I eat is in season and on the cob.

To cook corn on the cob, bring a large pot of water to a rolling boil, drop in the corn, cover the pot, and turn off the heat until ready to serve. It will be ready to eat in a few minutes and will not overcook.

SLICED CUCUMBERS

This simple dish is amazingly cool and refreshing. Choose fresh, firm, but not too large cukes and serve the salad with fish dinners in the summer. Do not use waxed cucumbers and do not peel them.

SERVES 8

4 unwaxed cucumbers, unpeeled
  ice cubes
1 cup rice vinegar (available from Oriental grocers)
  salt and freshly ground black pepper to taste

About 30 minutes before dinnertime, slice cucumbers thinly into a bowl—you should have about 4 cups. Cover with ice cubes and place in the refrigerator. About 5 minutes before serving, remove the ice from the cukes, drain well, and splash them with the vinegar in a serving bowl. Season with salt and pepper and toss again.

FENNEL

A common plant in 18th-century Charleston kitchen gardens, fennel— or finocchio—had all but disappeared from local tables until recently. It was once so commonly planted in the Southeast that it has naturalized in some areas. Old homesites along riverbanks are often dotted with the feathery, dill-like stalks of "wild" or "dog" fennel. Native to the Mediterranean and southern Asia, finocchio probably came to the Lowcountry with early Greek settlers, though by 1957, when Charleston's Ladies of the Philoptochos Society compiled the excellent *Popular Greek Recipes*, it was no longer mentioned.

Fennel's flavor is often compared to that of licorice (which belongs to a completely different plant family) or to anise (only vaguely related), and many grocers have the annoying habit of marketing it as anise, adding to the confusion. Some might find fennel's sweet, celerylike crispness more to their liking than the bittersweetness of aniseed. When I lived in Italy, we would dip chilled fresh ribs of raw fennel into salted olive oil as an appetizer, in the same way we Sandlappers might dunk celery into pimiento cheese. Perhaps *the* classic preparation is *à la Grecque*, poached in a seasoned court bouillon and served chilled. In southern France fish is grilled over a fire of the dried stalks. You can stuff fresh stalks into the cavity of whole oily fish such as blues or Spanish mackerels for a similar effect.

COLD FENNEL SOUP

Buy fennel bulbs with the feathery stalks attached. I buy an extra fennel plant and make stock the night before with the fennel as the predominant aromatic in the stockpot.

SERVES 4

4 cups chopped fennel bulb
1 leek, white part only, thinly sliced
3 tablespoons unsalted butter
4 cups chicken, vegetable, or duck stock (pages 33–37)
1 pound potatoes, peeled and diced
  salt to taste
½ cup loosely packed fennel leaves
  cream (optional)
  fennel leaves, fresh dill, or chives for garnish

In a saucepan, sauté the fennel and leek in the butter over medium heat until the leek is transparent, about 10 minutes. Add the stock, potatoes, and salt. Simmer, uncovered, until all the vegetables are tender, about 45 minutes.

Put the fennel leaves in a food processor and finely chop, then add the soup in batches and puree it. Correct the seasoning and add some cream if desired. Chill, then serve in chilled bowls with a garnish of more fennel leaves, fresh dill, or chives.

GREENS, OR LEAFY GREEN VEGETABLES

I can think of no vegetables more southern than greens, no food dearer to the soul of the Lowcountry. Collards, spinach, mustard and turnip greens, beet tops, kale, dandelion, dock, sorrel, chard, and cabbage—and innumerable potherbs—appear throughout the year on the tables of rich and poor alike. Meggett, South Carolina, about 20 miles south of Charleston, was once known as the Cabbage Capital of the World, and Toogoodoo Farms, nearby, continues to produce not only cabbage but also kale, mustard, collards, turnips, and spinach.

It is said that greens are best after a frost, which means after Thanksgiving in the Lowcountry—after Christmas in Charleston. But even in the slick gourmet markets you see big bunches of locally grown greens throughout the year. Pickup trucks piled high with greens for sale are a common sight in Charleston, especially in black neighborhoods.

Wild dock is cooked similarly to the spinach recipe on page 194. Folk wisdom says that it will purify the blood, tighten loose teeth, and improve eyesight. Lowcountry "root doctors" still exist. Their prescriptions often include greens. Dr. Julia Morton has written a book entitled *Folk Remedies of the Low Country,* which tells of soups made with the young leaves of "wild okra," sassafras, and "dog's tongue."

Eating hoppin' john on New Year's Day will bring good luck, but it is the greens that accompany the meal that ensure financial reward. And on that day those greens must be cooked with a smoked hog jowl and served with corn bread and twice-baked sweet potatoes. If you ask a Sandlapper to complete the phrase, "a mess o' ____," he will unhesitatingly reply, "greens!"

A bunch—or mess—of greens is usually about 8 plants, weighing about 5 pounds. As our soil is very sandy here, the greens often need careful washing—though not nearly so much if picked during a dry spell, when there has been no rain to splash the sand up in the plants. To clean greens, rinse them thoroughly under running water, discarding any yellowish or wilted leaves and tearing or cutting out any thick pieces of the stalks from larger greens such as collards. Then cover the greens with water and continue filling the sink with as much water as it will hold. Shake the greens gently around in the water so that any dirt sinks and repeat the process as many times as necessary until the greens are free of grit.

It is true that greens are traditionally cooked with salted or smoked pork, but Erlene Davis of Walterboro, South Carolina, says that meats, both cured and fresh, are specific to the greens. For example, for mustard greens she uses a smoked hock; for collards, smoked neck bones; and with turnips, a piece of fresh pork. Salted fatback, "sliced thin and fried out a little," is used with fresh peas and beans.

To cook a mess o' greens, follow the general guidelines for collards.

COLLARD GREENS

SERVES 10 TO 12

1 gallon water
½ pound smoked pork neck bones
1 bunch (about 8 plants, or 5 pounds uncleaned) greens
1 dried hot pepper (optional)

Put the water and smoked pork in a pot and boil, uncovered, for about 30 minutes, until the water is pleasantly flavored. In the meantime, clean the collards as described in the preceding section on greens. You will end up with only about 3 pounds of greens since the stems of collards are very tough and must be discarded.

Tear the greens into pieces about the size of your palm and add them to the water, with the hot pepper if desired. Simmer the greens, uncovered, until they are very soft, or to taste. Collards can take as long as 2 hours. Other greens will cook in much less time. Serve with hot pepper vinegar.

Leftover greens are delicious reheated in a frying pan with roasted peanuts and crushed red peppers—a dish at once African, Southeast Asian, and Lowcountry in flavor and spirit.

TURNIPS

Purple-tinged turnip roots appear at roadside stands and farmers' markets in the Lowcountry with the first cool weather in October. Buy small to medium turnips with bright greens still attached. Pare the turnips, being sure to cut away any tough or woody areas. Quarter small turnips; cut larger ones into 1-inch chunks. Wash the greens as described on page 191.

SERVES 4

¼ pound sidemeat (salt pork)
2 medium bunches turnips, each with about 8 young turnip plants,
    with greens
    salt and freshly ground black pepper to taste
2 cups water

In a large Dutch oven, brown the sidemeat. Pour off the fat and add the cleaned greens and salt and pepper. Add the water, bring to a boil, immediately reduce the heat, and simmer, uncovered, for 15 minutes. Add the washed, pared, and cut-up roots, cover the pot, and simmer for another 15 minutes or until the roots are tender. Serve with hot pepper vinegar.

SPINACH AND BACON

As Verta Grosvenor noted in *Vibration Cooking*, "Greens contrary to popular belief don't have to be cooked all day." The recipe for spinach in cream in *Charleston Receipts* warns, "Boil 3 minutes—no longer."

Cook this side dish of spinach at the last moment, to accompany virtually any main course. The quantity of spinach may at first seem large, but it will wilt in cooking to a fourth of its volume. You can accomplish the sautéing in a skillet, but a large Dutch oven will allow you to cook the whole lot very quickly, stirring briskly for a few minutes until all the spinach is just wilted.

SERVES 4

 2 slices bacon
1½ pounds spinach leaves, cleaned
    juice of ½ lemon
    freshly ground black pepper to taste

In a frying pan or Dutch oven, fry the bacon until crisp and remove the strips to drain. Just before serving the spinach, throw all of it into the same pot and, over high heat, quickly stir-fry the greens. Squeeze the lemon juice over the spinach and remove from the heat as soon as all of it is wilted. Season with freshly ground black pepper and crumble the reserved bacon over the greens if desired.

SORREL SOUP

In a minuscule backyard in downtown Charleston, I keep two sorrel plants to provide me with a sour treat about once a month. Some years the plants make it through our winters; seldom are they completely killed. Growing up in the Lowcountry, I loved to chew on the wild "sourgrass" that grew in open fields and along roadsides, but it wasn't until I lived in France that I learned about the cultivated French variety of *Rumex* that used to be a part of every Charleston kitchen garden.

In this particularly rich version of the classic French soup, both egg yolks and cream are added. I prefer it cold, but it may be served hot, and the simple puree need not be thickened with the dairy products at all.

SERVES 4

---

1 quart duck, chicken, or vegetable stock (pages 33–37)
2 cups (¼ pound) picked sorrel leaves, washed and stemmed
1 leek, the white and light green parts only, thinly sliced
4 large egg yolks
1 cup cream
  salt and freshly ground black pepper to taste
4 small sorrel leaves for garnish

Bring the stock, sorrel, and leeks to a boil in a saucepan, reduce the heat, and simmer, uncovered, for 10 to 15 minutes. Puree in a blender or food processor in batches. Mix the yolks with the cream and add spoonfuls of the hot puree to the cream mixture a little at a time. Then add the cream to the soup, correct the seasoning, and serve either hot or cold. Garnish each serving with a small fresh sorrel leaf and serve with cheese pigs (page 42).

SORREL OMELET

Omelets were well established in the kitchens of both the English and the French by the time South Carolina was settled. Early versions in the Low-country often included sorrel, spinach, and tansy—a recipe unchanged since the Middle Ages. The omelets were, in fact, often called "tanseys." Tansy has disappeared from Lowcountry tables, but it is still thought to have abortive properties among old root doctors. Tansy is very bitter and aro-matic, and I use it sparingly in combination with other potherbs. A classic French sorrel omelet is more to my liking—a perfect light summer supper with a glass of fruity white wine. If you want the flavor, but not the bite, of the garlic, don't mince it; instead, impale the clove on the tines of a fork and beat the eggs with the fork.

SERVES 1

3 large eggs
    salt and freshly ground black pepper to taste
    a handful of young fresh sorrel leaves, washed, dried, deribbed, and
        cut into small strips (about 1 cup loosely packed, weighing
        about 1 ounce)
1 small garlic clove, finely minced (see note above)
2 tablespoons unsalted butter
    chopped fresh chervil, chives, or parsley for garnish

Beat the eggs with salt and pepper. Over medium-high heat (preferably in an omelet pan), melt the butter while you beat the egg mixture with the sorrel and garlic. The butter will sputter and hiss for a minute. Swirl the butter around in the pan to coat the sides, then just at the moment that it stops hissing, pour the egg mixture into the pan all at once.

Let the eggs set partially, then, using a wooden spatula, pull the omelet away from the edges of the pan toward the center and let some of the raw egg trickle out toward the edges so that it is more evenly cooked. Fold the outer third of the omelet over the center, then fold the entire omelet over again. Turn off the heat and let the omelet rest in the pan for a moment or 2; it should puff up a little. Slide the omelet out onto a warm plate and top with herbs (chervil is traditional). The sorrel inside the omelet will be partially cooked, and its tartness will nicely balance fresh fruit or a fruity wine.

MUSHROOMS: CHANTERELLES

When Henry William Ravenel published his findings on the fungi and lichens of South Carolina in the 1850s, it was the first written treatise on American mushrooms. But early manuscripts and published works found in the papers of Lowcountry families had long referred to cooking mushrooms—stewed, pickled, put up in catsups, and dried. The earthy flavors of fungi, esteemed in both France and England whence came so many Carolina settlers, married well with the poultry and rice dishes of the area and complemented the game of the plantations. Sarah Rutledge included a "German receipt" for a mushroom soup in her 1847 *Carolina Housewife,* as well as a white fricassee of the fungi. In the Lowcountry mushrooms often mean chanterelles.

When the rains of August and September come to the Lowcountry, coupled with the longer, cooler nights, chanterelles pop up under stately oaks, dotting lawns with splashes of their bright apricot color. Hampton Park is the former site of the South Carolina Interstate and West Indian Exposition that took place in 1901–02 to attract tourism and business to the state by showing off its peculiar resources. Built north of the city on the site of a private horse track, the exposition—really a "world's fair"—was meant to inject some spark into an economy still crippled from the Civil War and Reconstruction. The *Carolina Rice Cook Book* of 1901 was a favored souvenir. The park, which is filled with chanterelles, is now surrounded by an inner-city suburb, with houses built in the first half of the century. In no neighborhood in America is racial integration more prevalent and long-standing. Hampton Park has provided several fanatics such as me with plenty of the distinctive fungi for years.

If you take mushrooms from the wild, please be responsible when you do so. In many areas sources have been depleted by the greedy. A pocket or paring knife or a pair of very sharp scissors should be used to snip the mushrooms off at ground level so that genetic information is left behind for next year's crop. Leave the smaller mushrooms and extremely dirty ones behind. And take only what you yourself will use. In South Carolina it is illegal to sell natural items from the wild without a license, and with good reason. If local chanterelles were sold in restaurants, our local supplies would quickly be depleted, with the millions of tourists that come to Charleston each year.

Given our sandy soil, it is hard to find local chanterelles that are not without grit; but no mushroom benefits from coming in contact with water. On the old plantations along Lowcountry rivers, chanterelles grow on the vast lawns that spread out under the towering old live oak trees. Mushrooms that crop up through thick grass will not be sandy. If your chanterelles are dirty, try brushing the gill-like crevices with a pastry or mushroom brush to remove any dirt; or place the mushrooms on a screen outdoors and spray them with the finest mist from your garden hose. As a last resort, wash them quickly under running water, being sure to let them drain from a rack, and lightly pat them dry before using them.

Other edible species of mushrooms such as field mushrooms (an agaric not unlike the cultivated variety at every American grocery store), puffballs, and morels grow in the Lowcountry and have graced the tables of the knowing for more than 200 years, but their growth is too sporadic and unpredictable for them to be considered real Lowcountry fare. When the field mushrooms would crop up in our yard, my mother would send me out to pick the large, fully opened ones for our table. They were invariably simply prepared—sautéed in butter and added to an omelet or sliced raw and added to a spinach and bacon salad, then topped with a soft-boiled egg.

Though chanterelles are almost unmistakable, unless you are absolutely sure of their identity (or of any wild mushroom), of course you should not eat them.

SAUTEED CHANTERELLES

The delicate, fruity flavor of chanterelles deserves to be featured by itself. Sauté some onions in butter until they just begin to become transparent, then add the whole chanterelles (or cut up the larger ones), with the tiniest bit of salt and plenty of freshly ground black pepper. Cook them fairly slowly, but thoroughly, until almost all of their liquid has evaporated. Serve them up on toast or add them to scrambled eggs or an omelet at breakfast. They make a good appetizer, on toast or in a pastry shell. Or top a main dish of poultry or veal with the delicate, attractive fungi. You may add some cream or a little sherry to the mushrooms if you wish—or port when coupled with game—but the simpler preparation is traditional in the Low-country.

CHANTERELLE BUTTER

If the mushrooms you gather are too gritty to be sautéed and served simply, grind them thoroughly in a food processor and put them in a heavy pot over low heat to extract the liquid. Add sticks of butter to the mushrooms as you would for a shellfish butter, cooking the fungi very slowly so that the flavor is infused into the butter. When all of the liquid has cooked out of the mushrooms, drain the mixture through a fine sieve, pushing to release the flavorful last bits of juice. Refrigerate the mixture overnight, then remove the congealed mushroom butter from the surface of the mixture the next day. A little spoonful of mushroom butter added to a sauce for meats or pasta can be stunning. (See the recipe for steaks on page 122.) Wrap well what you don't plan to use within the week and freeze it for later use.

OKRA

I love okra—fried, boiled, sautéed, stewed, pickled, in soups, in pilau, and steamed. Okra and tomatoes over rice. In gumbo as the thickener. I even love the slimy quality, though it can be cooked so that it isn't that way at all. Buy okra no longer than your finger—bright green, unblemished, and all uniform in size. Trim the caps from the okra pods as closely as possible without cutting into the pod itself so that the pod remains whole in cooking. Try the following recipe that teams okra with a little white wine.

SERVES 6

- ¼ cup olive oil
- 2 cups chopped onion
- 1 teaspoon Herbal Mix (page 31), *herbes de Provence,* or Italian seasoning
- 1½ pounds trimmed okra (2 pounds before trimming)
- 1 cup dry white wine or clear stock such as chicken (page 34)

Heat the olive oil in a large frying pan over medium-high heat, add the onions, and sauté until they just begin to become transparent, 3 to 5 minutes. Sprinkle the herbal mix over the onions and add the okra. Cook over medium heat for about 10 minutes, stirring occasionally, until the mixture begins to dry out and threatens to scorch. Add the wine and cook until the okra is tender, about another 10 minutes or until most of the wine has evaporated. You may cover the dish and vary the heat as you cook the vegetables if you need to time them to coincide with the main dish you are serving, but do *not* overcook the okra—it should be tender but still bright green.

OKRA AND TOMATOES

This simple dish of stewed tomatoes and okra is pure Lowcountry Creole and is served over rice alongside pork, poultry, and seafood. Don't salt the stew; the bacon will impart its salty smokiness to the vegetables.

SERVES 6 TO 8

8 thick slices hickory-smoked bacon
1 medium onion, chopped (about ¾ cup)
1 pound fresh okra, trimmed
5 vine-ripened tomatoes, peeled and quartered, *or* 1 1½-pound can
      whole peeled tomatoes, quartered, with their juice
1 fresh hot pepper *or* cayenne pepper to taste
   dry white wine or chicken stock (page 34)
   chopped fresh herbs of your choice for garnish

Cook the bacon in a cast-iron skillet over medium heat until it is uniformly crisp. Remove from the skillet and set aside to drain. Add the onion to the bacon grease and cook until the onion begins to become transparent, about 5 minutes. Add the okra and continue cooking until the okra begins to glisten with moisture. Add the tomatoes and pepper and lower the heat. Simmer, uncovered, until the okra and tomatoes are stewed evenly, stirring occasionally and adding wine or stock to the pan if necessary to keep the mixture soupy. Serve over white rice steamed in chicken stock and garnish with the chopped fresh herb of your choice and the reserved bacon, crumbled.

FRIED OKRA, GUINEA SQUASH, AND GREEN TOMATOES

Ask many people if they know or like the flavor of okra, eggplant, or green tomatoes, and they are likely to answer, "I'll eat them fried." Southerners are well known for their artful frying. (See About Frying, page 171.) Perfectly fried and drained foods are never greasy.

Slice okra, eggplant (or Guinea squash, as it is called in the Lowcountry), and green tomatoes and put them into ice water for about 30 minutes before frying. (A splash of lemon juice in the water will prevent the eggplant from discoloring.) Drain the vegetables well, dust them in cornflour seasoned to taste, and fry in deep fat, preferably lard, at 370° until golden, about 3 or 4 minutes. Drain the vegetables on wire racks before serving.

STEAMED OKRA

Okra is also delicious steamed. Trim the okra pods just where the stem begins, but do not cut into the pods. Put a tiny amount of water into a pan, add the okra, and cover tightly. Steam over medium-high heat for about 10 minutes or until all of the water evaporates. Open the lid and dress the okra with a bit of butter and salt and pepper to taste.

OKRA SOUP

This soup is an old Charleston favorite. Nothing fancy, it is cooked all day and served at night with the ever-present pot of steaming hot white rice. Some cooks throw a "soup bunch" into the pot while the shank boils. Sold in predominately black neighborhood grocery stores, the bunch is an elaborate *bouquet garni* of mixed vegetables and aromatics for the soup pot. A typical soup bunch includes a carrot, celery, thyme, cabbage, and turnips with their greens. It is usually cooked with a shank for several hours, then thyme, turnips, and potatoes are added to finish the hearty winter soup.

MAKES ABOUT 10 SERVINGS

1 large, meaty beef shank bone
3 quarts water
3 pounds okra, trimmed and cut into small pieces
3 pounds fresh or canned tomatoes, peeled and chopped
1 large onion, chopped (about 1½ cups)
1 bay leaf
1 fresh thyme sprig *or* ½ teaspoon dried
   salt to taste

Place the shank in a large stockpot and cover with the water. Bring to a boil, reduce the heat, and simmer, uncovered, for 2 hours or until the meat is tender. Add the okra, tomatoes, onion, herbs, and salt; cook for another 2 hours. Fresh, hot green bird's eye peppers are traditionally picked just before the soup is served. The pepper is mashed in the bowl before the soup is added. Rice and corn bread (page 219) accompany the meal.

ENGLISH PEAS AND LETTUCE

This is classic French country cooking, and it is delicious. Five pounds of green pea pods yield approximately 2 pounds of peas. One pound of pods yields about a cup.

> The common method of cooking this delicious vegetable, by boiling in water, is nearly destructive to its flavour, at least so says a lady who has sent us the following method of preparing them for the table, which, after experience, we must add, is a great improvement: "Place in the bottom of your sauce-pan, or boiler, several of the outside leaves of lettuce; put your peas in the dish with two ounces of butter in proportion to half a peck of peas; cover the pan or boiler close, and place over the fire; in thirty minutes they are ready for the table. They can be seasoned in the pan or taken out. Water extracts nearly all the delicious quality of the green pea, and is as fatal to their flavour as it is destructive to a mad dog."
>
> Phineas Thornton, *Southern Gardener and Receipt Book*, 1839

SERVES 4

- 4 pounds fresh unshelled English peas
- 10 ounces pearl onions
- ¼ pound (1 stick) unsalted butter
- 1 tablespoon chopped fresh herbs of your choice, especially thyme
- 1 medium head leaf lettuce
  salt and freshly ground black pepper to taste

Shell the peas. You should have about 4 cups. Drop the whole onions into boiling water for 2 or 3 minutes, drain, and rinse in cold water. Drain again. Slice the base off each onion and pop it out of its skin.

Heat the butter in a heavy, straight-sided sauté pan. Add the herbs and about half the lettuce leaves, lining the bottom of the pan. Add the onions. Add the shelled peas, season with salt and pepper, and cover with the rest of the lettuce leaves. Cover the pot tightly and simmer over low heat for 30 minutes. Uncover the pot and taste the peas. Depending on their size, they may need a little more time.

POTATOES—WHITE AND SWEET

Because the word *potato* was used interchangeably for both the white, or so-called "Irish," and the sweet potato in the Lowcountry for nearly 200 years, it is difficult to know in many old recipes which tuber the cook meant. Indeed, in many bread recipes from the latter part of the 19th century, next to the word *potato* is the explanatory note "either Irish or sweet." One of my favorite accompaniments to winter meat dishes is mashed potatoes—half white and half sweet.

Both white potatoes and sweet potatoes entered European kitchens at about the same time, from South America; their histories have often been confused. Adding to the confusion is the fact that yams, native to the tropics, appeared in the colonies at that time. They have always been mistaken as sweet potatoes; when the Lowcountry was settled by people who had first lived in the West Indies, they called sweet potatoes "yams," even though true yams were not and are not part of the local cuisine.

As for white potatoes, I usually buy locally grown boiling potatoes, new and red-skinned, small to medium-sized. I scrub them well, boil them with their jackets on until they are about half cooked, then roughly cut them and fry them in hot oil or lard, heavily seasoned with Herbal Mix and freshly ground black pepper, until they are golden brown all over. And, as with all fried foods, I drain them on a rack rather than letting them sit on a piece of paper, so that they do not absorb grease.

Sweet potatoes are another story. They appear in crab soup with coconut (page 104), in orange shells, and in breads, but not all Lowcountry cooks love them as I do. Lucille Grant, one of the best Lowcountry cooks, won't eat sweet potatoes. Having grown up poor, the daughter of a fisherman on Bulls Bay, she tells of having only sweet potatoes to eat in the afternoons after school. It was not proper to eat before one's elders, and her father could return in his small boat only with the incoming tide, which might be very late at night. Lucille and her sisters would go get potatoes from the "bank," a mound of earth filled with dirt and straw where potatoes are stored from November to May, toss them in the glowing embers of the hearth, and, after 30 minutes, pull the perfectly roasted sweet potatoes out and eat them, with a little butter if it was available. Lucille swore to herself she would never eat sweet potatoes again.

We do not have root cellars in the Lowcountry because the land is at sea level; when we dig, we hit water. Aboveground potato banks serve the same purpose as the cellar; they are still common sights on the barrier islands. If you stop at any of the small vegetable stands in the winter months, you will probably see a mound of earth not far from the dizzying display of greens and root vegetables. You will also probably be confronted by several varieties of sweet potatoes—I've seen as many as a dozen at one stand. Ask the vendor which are the *least* recently dug, as they will be the sweetest. There are potatoes for baking, others for boiling. Some will cook quickly in a stir-fry, and some are very woody, like true yams. My favorite way to eat sweet potatoes is baked twice in their jackets and served with butter. (Bake them whole in a 425° oven until they give to the touch, about 45 minutes. Then reheat them in a hot oven until they are warm.) The Porto Rico is a nonhybrid baking variety that has a rust-colored jacket and deep, reddish orange very sweet flesh. It is a favorite in the Lowcountry. Most recipes call for potatoes that have been parboiled.

SWEET POTATO PIE IN ORANGE SHELLS

Charleston Recollections and Receipts: Rose P. Ravenel's Cookbook is a beguiling collection of recipes and memoirs compiled by a Charleston lady during her long life, which spanned 100 years from the mid–19th to the mid–20th century. Her potato pie in orange shells is a favorite for the fall holidays. I have reduced the amount of eggs and replaced the sugar with molasses. "Pies" in the Lowcountry are often crustless; the word is used as a general term, in the same way that the British use the term *pudding* to mean dessert.

SERVES 6

---

6 to 10 oranges, depending on size
    1 pound sweet potatoes, boiled, peeled, and mashed
    ¼ pound (1 stick) unsalted butter at room temperature
    3 large eggs
    1 cup milk
       grated zest and juice of 1 lemon
    2 tablespoons (⅛ cup) molasses

Preheat the oven to 350°. Cut the top fourth off each orange, then hollow it with a grapefruit spoon or a melon baller. Blend the remaining ingredients together well, then fill each orange shell with the mixture. Bake for 20 minutes or until juice begins to run from the oranges.

SWEET POTATOES CARIBBEAN STYLE

This is another of those country recipes that sing of the Lowcountry and the West Indian influences here. It is to be played with, not taken seriously, served with dinner or afterward with whipped cream, and enjoyed in the laid-back style of the subtropics. A similar recipe, without the banana, is called "Likker Pudding" in the 1950 *Charleston Receipts.*

SERVES 6

  2 sweet potatoes, about 1¼ pounds, cooked, peeled, and sieved
  4 large eggs
  2 cups loosely packed grated fresh coconut
     a pinch of salt
  1 tablespoon unbleached all-purpose flour
 ¼ cup molasses
  1 ripe banana, riced
 ¼ cup dark rum or bourbon
  1 tablespoon grated fresh ginger
     spices to taste

Preheat the oven to 350°. Mix all of the ingredients together and bake for about 45 minutes, until the pudding is set.

CANDIED YAMS

We all know that sweet potatoes aren't yams, but the name remains. During the holidays, when I serve a big meal of country ham with spiced peaches, I save the pickle juice to make this traditional southern dish. The idea is one of many I have learned from the second printing of *Orangeburg's Choice Recipes,* sponsored by the city's PTA in 1948. Many of the recipes are Lowcountry classics that were repeated in the Junior League of Charleston's *Charleston Receipts* of 1950.

SERVES 6

3 medium sweet potatoes
1 cup syrup from spiced peaches (page 313)
2 tablespoons unsalted butter
2 tablespoons (⅛ cup) light or dark brown sugar

Boil the potatoes until nearly done. Preheat the oven to 400°. Peel and slice the potatoes lengthwise. Lay them in a shallow ovenproof glass or earthenware pan, pour the syrup over them, and dot with butter. Sprinkle with brown sugar. Bake for 30 minutes, then brown under the broiler.

MINTED SQUASH CASSEROLE

Zucchini, bright yellow crookneck, and cymling, or pattypan, squash are local favorites. These summer, or soft-shelled, squashes are often steamed with onions or sautéed with tomatoes. Many Lowcountry cooks stuff them or put them in casseroles. Every recipe I've seen for a squash casserole tells you to parboil the squash, but I never do.

The mint is a delicious addition to this southern classic.

SERVES 6 TO 8

½ cup loosely packed fresh mint leaves
1 large egg
⅔ cup milk
3 tablespoons unsalted butter
3 medium onions, thinly sliced (2 to 3 cups)
  salt and freshly ground black pepper to taste
1 pound young, tender fresh summer squash, cut into ¼-inch slices
1 cup dry bread crumbs

Preheat the oven to 350°. Put the mint leaves in a food processor fitted with the metal blade and chop finely. Add the egg and milk and blend.

In a saucepan, melt the butter over medium heat. Add the sliced onions, season with salt and pepper, and continue cooking over medium heat until they are evenly heated through and have just begun to become translucent.

Line the bottom of a 1½-quart casserole dish with a single layer of the squash. Cover the squash with a layer of the buttered onions, then a layer of bread crumbs. Drizzle some of the egg and milk mixture over the layer, then continue making similar layers to use all the ingredients, ending with a sprinkling of bread crumbs. Bake for 45 minutes.

FRIED SQUASH BLOSSOMS

A quick dip of freshly picked zucchini or summer squash blossoms into a tempura batter, then into hot lard, makes a delightful summer appetizer. If the blossoms come from unsprayed plants and are picked early in the morning, you should not have to wash them. The blossoms of other squash, pumpkin, and melon plants—as well as sliced vegetables and shrimp—can be used in this tempura batter.

SERVES 6 TO 8

lard for frying (see page 25)
2 dozen squash blossoms with 2-inch stems attached
1 large egg yolk
1 cup ice water
1 cup unbleached all-purpose flour
salt to taste

Heat 2 inches of lard in a Dutch oven or deep skillet to 365°. Preheat the oven to 200°. Check the blossoms for bugs and dirt. Wash and pat dry if necessary. In a wide bowl, mix the egg yolk well into the ice water, using a wooden spoon; then dump the flour into the liquid all at once, stirring quickly. The batter will be lumpy. Holding the blossoms by the stem, drag them through the batter and drop into the hot fat, frying each one for about 30 seconds on one side, then flipping it over and frying for about 10 to 20 seconds on the other side, until it has begun to brown. Remove each blossom as it is cooked to a wire rack placed on top of a sheet pan and keep in the warm oven until all the blossoms are fried. Salt lightly and serve immediately.

Tomatoes

Tomatoes are integral to Lowcountry cuisine. Many soups, stews, and vegetable dishes owe their distinctive qualities to the humble tomato and its miraculous saucing abilities. With our subtropical climate, 2 crops per year are normal. It is a waste *not* to have a few tomato plants here, if only on a balcony: nothing matches the flavor of juicy vine-ripened ones. In their absence I often use canned tomatoes in cooked dishes calling for tomatoes; they are invariably better than store-bought and out of season. When the harvest is in, though, I do make my own catsup and sun-dried tomatoes (pages 326 and 324) using very old Carolina receipts.

During the 6 months of the Lowcountry tomato season, nearly every meal at my house includes sliced ruby-red ripe tomatoes, sprinkled with good olive oil and salt and pepper. If you grow your own tomatoes, or if you live near a tomato farm, you can enjoy the distinct flavor of the green fruit. Pick rock-hard, unblemished, very round fruits with no sign of red. Slice them thickly, salt and pepper them, brush with oil, and place them on a grill for a few minutes on each side; or dust them with seasoned corn or wheat flour and fry them (page 201). A recipe for green tomato relish, a popular Lowcountry condiment, is on page 325.

TOMATO ASPIC

Salads are of three types: simple, composed, and molded. Carême (1784–1833), the great French chef famous for his architectural creations, was fond of jellied dishes. Savory aspics have long been held in esteem by the French and in the Lowcountry, where they are as varied as souse (page 133) and this congealed tomato salad. *Two Hundred Years of Charleston Cooking* (1930) includes four recipes. Serve this salad in the spring and early summer when the weather is hot but tomatoes have not yet appeared on the vine. It is a cool harbinger of summer fruits to come.

Tomato aspic is often served in the Lowcountry as the first course at a formal luncheon. Other vegetables such as asparagus or seafood such as crabmeat or shrimp may be added to the dish if desired. It is served on crisp salad greens with a rich homemade mayonnaise (pages 309 and 310).

SERVES 12

½ cup boiling water
2 tablespoons (2 envelopes) unflavored gelatin
4 to 5 cups tomato juice or puree (see *Note*)
2 celery ribs, very finely diced (½ cup)
½ small onion, grated (1 tablespoon)
1 teaspoon salt
¼ teaspoon cayenne pepper
3 tablespoons sherry vinegar

Pour the boiling water over the gelatin in a mixing bowl and stir vigorously so that all of the gelatin dissolves. Add the remaining ingredients and mix well. Pour into a 1½-quart mold or twelve ½-cup individual ramekins rinsed in cold water. Refrigerate to set and chill. To unmold, dip in hot water for a few seconds, then invert.

Note: To make puree, I use a 28-ounce can of crushed tomatoes with basil *plus* a 16-ounce can.

11
BREADS

The breads of the Lowcountry have changed dramatically in the past hundred years. A piggin (a small wooden pail) of fresh yeast made from homegrown hops was commonly kept in the cool storage area under the "big house" on plantations. As baking powder became available to the homemaker, yeast breads gradually disappeared in the aftermath of the Civil War. Rice continued to be grown locally up until the 1920s; it was cheaper than wheat and was often added to bread made with wheat flour, extending its shelf life. Fresh breads made with rice and rice flour were common; *The Carolina Housewife* (1847) includes thirty recipes. Rice bread was the daily bread of the Lowcountry, but no one I have ever met remembers it. A rice-enriched yeast bread is the first recipe in *The Carolina Housewife* after directions are given for making yeast at home. It has become my daily bread—my favorite bread from my favorite book.

But I love the muffins and baps we owe to our British heritage and the quick breads that grace today's Lowcountry tables. Corn breads are served with fish and seafood; biscuits are served at breakfast. And while I have found no evidence of the Huguenots having brought a classic French bread recipe with them to the area, we do prefer yeast rolls with our red meats. The biscuits we serve with slivers of country ham include both yeast and baking powder. They are often called "angel biscuits" for their heavenly texture or "bride's biscuits," possibly because they are so often served at weddings.

Making your own bread takes little actual working time. Even yeast doughs require only about ten minutes of mixing, then ten minutes or so of kneading. Plan to make yeast breads when you're going to be home anyway. The half hour of work is relaxing and satisfying, and the bread is nourishing for days after the baking. Baking staples are described on pages 26–27.

I've never tried to freeze the dough. Well-wrapped, the breads don't suffer too badly in freezing.

CAROLINA RICE BREAD

This bread is easy to make, it keeps well, and it makes the most delicious toast you have ever eaten.

Of the 30 recipes for rice breads included in Sarah Rutledge's 1847 *The Carolina Housewife,* this, the first of them, is one of the best:

"Simmer one pound of rice in two quarts of water until it is quite soft; when it is cool enough, mix it well with four pounds of flour, yeast and salt as for other bread; of yeast four large spoonfuls. Let it rise before the fire. Some of the flour should be reserved to make the loaves. If the rice swells greatly, and requires more water, add as much as you think proper."

There are artesian wells in and around Charleston where people of all races, classes, ages, and ethnic backgrounds meet to fill their jugs. Though too sulfurous for some, the water loses its sulfur taste in boiling. Well water can be a clean and safe alternative to tap water for bread baking, as the chlorine and other chemicals that Charleston and other cities add to their municipal water supplies can kill yeast.

The yeast should be fresh, not dried (see page 27). Make sure it is fresh: it should have a sweet, not sour, aroma of yeast, and it should be moist and uniformly smooth. The salt that you use should be free of yeast-destroying chemicals. Use a pure salt such as kosher, pickling, or sea salt; check the labels for additives.

The first time you make this recipe, I advise using high-gluten (bread) flour and long-grain white rice. You may wish to add some whole-wheat flour or wheat germ to the dough or use a different rice. The more flavorful the rice you use, the more flavorful your bread will be. If you use a brown rice, increase the amount of water accordingly, as it will absorb nearly twice as much water as white rice.

Follow this recipe very carefully and respond to your own batch of dough as it demands. (This is a recipe for which you must weigh ingredients; volumes will be too variable.) Every dough, every quart of well water, the humidity of each day and each oven is different. But don't be discouraged; you should have an excellent-tasting bread that makes wonderful toast, even if you judge the rising incorrectly or bake it at the wrong temperature.

This recipe makes 3 loaves in standard bread pans. Half of the recipe makes a big round loaf that you can bake on a baking stone or under a big overturned flowerpot, as Karen Hess suggests, to imitate the brick ovens that produce nice crusts. It will weigh about 4 pounds. You can make a smaller batch than called for in the recipe, but I don't recommend a larger one, simply because it is too big to handle. You will need a very large bowl, about the size of an antique wash basin. Weigh the rice, the yeast, and the flour before beginning.

MAKES 3 LOAVES

1 pound rice
3 tablespoons pure salt
2 quarts well or spring water (or more if you're using brown rice)
2 ounces fresh compressed yeast
4 pounds unbleached bread flour

Add the rice and salt to the water and boil in a large pot, uncovered, until all the liquid is absorbed and the rice is quite soft, about 20 to 30 minutes. Place the rice in a very large bowl. Set aside to cool.

When the rice is cool enough to handle, it should be about right for the yeast (below 120°). Add the yeast and mix into the rice, then work in the flour, kneading and folding it all together in the bowl until you have a smooth, elastic loaf. It will take very nearly all the flour and about 10 minutes of time. (Note: you will get out of a loaf of bread only what you put into it. Put on a favorite record and get into a good mood while you knead the loaf. If you try instead to take out your anger on the dough, you will end up with a knotty, uneven bread.)

Wipe the rim of the bowl clean, then cover the entire bowl tightly with plastic wrap. If your bowl is not large enough to allow the bread to double in size, you may want to lightly brush the top of the dough with oil or butter to keep it from sticking to the plastic. Now cover the entire bowl with a towel or blanket and set in a warm, draft-free place to rise. It may take a couple of hours, or it may take all day or night ("warm" is relative), depending on many factors; but it is usually ready in my kitchen—which stays very warm, even in winter—in about 2 hours.

Grease 3 bread loaf pans and set aside. When the dough has doubled, punch it down, knead it lightly so that it is evenly textured again, divide it into 3 parts, and roll each part into a log that fits nicely into the pan, with all edges on the bottom and only the smooth top showing. Cover the 3 pans with the plastic and the towel or blanket again and place on top of the stove while the oven preheats to 450°. The loaves need rise only halfway this time—say, to the tops of the pans. Check them at about 30 minutes. I find that they are often ready then, and the oven should be well heated.

Bake the loaves in a classic "falling" oven, simulating the gradually falling temperatures of a wood-fired stove: 15 minutes at 450°, then turn the oven down to 400° and bake for another 15 minutes. (You might peek to see that the loaves are baking evenly. Sometimes ovens have "hot spots": if so, rotate the loaves.) After 30 minutes (total) of baking, take the loaves out of the pans and return them naked to the oven. If, at this point, the loaves seem to be browning too quickly, turn the oven down to 350°; otherwise, leave it at 400°.

From this point you must watch them, turning them on their sides so that they brown evenly all over and waiting for that special moment when a thump on the bottom of the loaves gives a reassuring, resounding report that they are done. A dull thud sends them back to cook more. Do not, however, be so constantly in the oven that it stays fired—it should be hovering at the lower temperature at this point. It will take anywhere from 15 to 25 minutes for the loaves to finish cooking. When they are done, remove them to racks to cool and resist the temptation to cut them while they are hot.

PHILPY

Philpy was one of the quick rice breads common in the Lowcountry in the 18th and 19th centuries. It is apparently unique to the area, but it's just a journey, or johnny, cake enriched with an egg. *Charleston Receipts* and other modern cookbooks give recipes for philpy enriched with butter and made with wheat flour, but I prefer the old-fashioned kind, served with delicate sorrel or she-crab soup (page 195 or 51). The following recipe, from *Two Hundred Years of Charleston Cooking* (1930), follows the 1847 original, from *The Carolina Housewife*, exactly:

MAKES 8 SLICES

---

bacon grease
½ cup soft-cooked long-grain white rice, cooled
6 tablespoons water
½ cup rice flour
1 large egg, lightly beaten
¼ teaspoon salt (optional)

Thoroughly grease an 8-inch pie plate or small cast-iron skillet with bacon grease. Place in a cold oven and preheat to 425°. Rub the rice through a sieve. Mix the water and rice flour into a smooth paste, then add to the rice. Add the egg and mix all together. If the rice was cooked with salt, add none to the batter. Otherwise, add ¼ teaspoon salt to the recipe. Fold the batter into the hot pan. Bake for about 30 minutes or until golden. Cut into slices, butter, and serve at once.

SKILLET CORN BREAD

This recipe appears across the South, but people are always amazed when they eat it, swearing it's the *best* corn bread. It is typically southern, with no sugar or wheat flour. It is the way both of my grandmothers, from opposite ends of Tennessee, made corn bread, and it is now the way everyone I know in the Lowcountry makes it. I have given the recipe out literally hundreds of times, much to the chagrin of my family. To reproduce this corn bread, you will need a 9- or 10-inch well-seasoned, never-washed cast-iron skillet to obtain a golden brown crust. Serve with fish stews, pilaus, gumbos, and greens. My family reaches for the sorghum syrup when corn bread is served.

    1   large egg
    2   cups buttermilk
    1¾ cups cornmeal
1½ to 2 teaspoons strained bacon grease
    1   scant teaspoon baking powder
    1   scant teaspoon salt
    1   scant teaspoon baking soda

Mix the egg into the buttermilk, then add the cornmeal and beat it well into the batter, which should be thin. Put enough bacon grease in the skillet to coat the bottom and sides with a thin film, then put it in a cold oven and begin preheating the oven to 450°. When the oven has reached 450°, the bacon grease should be just at the point of smoking. Add the baking powder, salt, and soda to the batter, beat in well, and pour the batter all at once into the hot pan. Return to the oven to bake for 15 to 20 minutes or until the top just begins to brown. Turn the loaf out on a plate and serve with lots of the freshest butter you can get your hands on.

SQUASHPUPPIES/SWEET POTATO HUSHPUPPIES

Traditional hushpuppies are served almost exclusively at outdoor fish fries. They are made by adding seasoned cornflour (a finely ground corn meal— page 27) and chopped onion to the preceding skillet corn bread batter. This variation, however, goes with a variety of foods as a side dish that is more spoon bread than vegetable. You can deep-fry or panfry these.

MAKES 8 PUPS

---

lard for frying
½ cup (about ½ pound) cooked squash or sweet potatoes
2 large eggs
¼ cup cornmeal
¼ cup unbleached all-purpose flour
¼ teaspoon salt
¼ teaspoon ground cinnamon
cayenne pepper and freshly ground black pepper to taste
2 tablespoons (⅛ cup) chopped onion (optional)

Preheat lard to 385° in a deep skillet or Dutch oven. Thoroughly mix the remaining ingredients and drop by the tablespoon into the hot lard. If you're frying in deep fat, the pups should take only about 2 minutes. In a shallow pan, you may have to cook them a little longer and turn them so that each side is browned evenly. The exterior should be crisp and the inside moist and mousselike.

BISCUITS

No bread is more misunderstood than the lowly southern biscuit. Fast-food restaurants across America have made biscuits an everyday word throughout the country, but they have been taken so far out of context that even respectable southern restaurants are now serving biscuits at dinner, with steaks or fried fish, when yeast rolls and corn bread would be appropriate.

The text and recipes in Bill Neal's books are excellent, and both Elizabeth David and Karen Hess have tackled the history of chemical leavenings and quick breads. But the perfect biscuit? It's largely in the choice of flour. If you don't live in the South, try to find a soft southern flour to make biscuits. Several companies such as White Lily distribute their flours nationally. And handle the dough as little as possible.

Biscuits are the classic quick breakfast bread throughout the South, chemically leavened with baking powder, which is a mixture of an acid and a base. Make your own with a little cream of tartar and baking soda (page 27) to avoid the metallic taste of aluminum sulfate in the commercial brands. These are my favorite biscuits, perfect for topping with sour cream and fig preserves or served alongside fried quail and gravy. The humidity of the day always affects baked goods, so be sure to weigh the flour (which can absorb moisture and make biscuits tough).

MAKES 10 BISCUITS

¾ **pound (about 3 cups) soft southern flour (page 27), plus a little
      extra for dusting**
1 **teaspoon baking soda**
1 **teaspoon cream of tartar**
1 **teaspoon salt**
3 **ounces (½ cup) chilled lard**
¾ **cup buttermilk**

Preheat the oven to 425°. Sift the flour, soda, cream of tartar, and salt together into a large mixing bowl. Cut in the lard with a pastry blender or 2 knives until it is uniformly incorporated into the flour and there are no large clumps. Working swiftly, fold in the buttermilk a little at a time with a rubber spatula until it is just blended in smoothly.

(continued)

Dust a countertop lightly with some flour and scoop up the dough onto the countertop with the spatula. *Lightly* work the dough, working only with the fingertips, until it is evenly blended. Roll it out about ½-inch thick and cut into ten 2-inch biscuits, using a clean metal biscuit cutter dipped in flour and a quick, clean motion. Do not twist the biscuit cutter; you should be punching the biscuits out of the dough. Place the biscuits close to each other on a baking sheet and bake for 12 to 15 minutes, until the tops are lightly golden brown. Serve immediately with butter or sour cream, sorghum, or homemade preserves.

HAM BISCUITS

There is hardly a wedding or garden party in the Lowcountry without these yeast biscuits. They are small, only about an inch in diameter, and they are split to hold slivers of salty country ham tempered with dollops of chutney or mustard. One ham provides enough meat for 200 to 250 biscuits.

These doubly lightened breads—really yeast rolls—are also called "angel biscuits" and "bride's biscuits." Bill Neal has suggested that the "bride" is the inexperienced cook who needs the insurance policy of the double leavening.

MAKES ABOUT 40 BISCUITS

1 pound (about 4 cups) unbleached all-purpose flour, plus a little extra for dusting
1 teaspoon cream of tartar
1 teaspoon baking soda
1 teaspoon pure salt
3 ounces (about ½ cup) chilled lard
½ ounce fresh compressed yeast
1¼ cups buttermilk at room temperature

Sift the dry ingredients together into a warmed mixing bowl. Cut the lard into the flour mixture with a pastry blender or 2 knives until it is evenly distributed. In a separate bowl, stir the yeast into the buttermilk until it is well blended, pour the liquid into the flour mixture, and stir until blended.

Turn the dough out onto a floured surface and work lightly until the mixture is smooth and evenly textured. Roll out to about ½-inch thick, then cut 1-inch biscuits with a clean, floured metal biscuit cutter. Place the biscuits on an ungreased sheet pan, cover with a dish towel, and allow to rise for a while. In the meantime, preheat the oven to 400°. When the biscuits have risen by about a fourth, bake them for about 15 minutes or until the tops are lightly browned.

SWEET POTATO BISCUITS

Breads made with root vegetables are common in the Caribbean, home to so many of the early Lowcountry settlers. This rich and doughy biscuit adds color, texture, and flavor to the dinner plate; this is not a breakfast bread.

MAKES 10 BISCUITS

1 teaspoon baking soda
1 teaspoon cream of tartar
½ teaspoon salt
2 cups soft southern all-purpose flour, plus a little extra for dusting
¾ cup cold mashed cooked sweet potatoes
⅔ cup buttermilk
4 tablespoons (¼ cup) unsalted butter, melted

Preheat the oven to 425°. Sift the dry ingredients together into a mixing bowl. In another bowl, combine the sweet potatoes, buttermilk, and butter. Add the wet ingredients to the dry and mix with a rubber spatula until all of the ingredients are combined.

Dust a work surface with flour and turn the dough out onto it. Lightly work the dough with the fingertips only until it is evenly blended. Roll out the dough about ½-inch thick and cut into ten 2-inch biscuits using a clean metal biscuit cutter dipped in flour and a quick, clean motion. Do not reroll the scraps, as this is a very dense dough that becomes rubbery as it is worked. Place the biscuits on an ungreased cookie sheet and bake for 12 to 15 minutes, until the tops just begin to brown lightly. Serve immediately.

SCOTTISH BREAKFAST BREAD, OR BAPS

The first year I moved to Charleston, I roomed with Archibald MacLeish Martin, a member of the St. Andrews Society with deep roots in the Lowcountry. Some 20 years later he asked me for a good recipe for short-bread; the family had misplaced his grandmother's. If they should find her yellowed papers, they might well find among them a copy of Meg Dods's *The Cook and Housewife's Manual,* which appears regularly in the inventories of 19th-century Charleston libraries. First published in 1826, the book helped the Scots who settled along the Cooper River maintain traditional kitchens in the Lowcountry, where more than a fourth of the white pop-ulation had roots in the British Isles.

Baps, the breakfast rolls of Scotland, appear in several Lowcountry recipe collections, including Harriott Pinckney Horry's from the 1770s. By the time her cousin published *The Carolina Housewife* in 1847, baps in the Lowcountry, and elsewhere in the South, included eggs and other enrich-ments. The following traditional recipe comes from Marian McNeill's *The Scots Kitchen* of 1929, and she notes, "Baps appear exclusively on the breakfast-table, and should be eaten warm from the oven."

MAKES 10 TO 12 BAPS

———

1 **pound (about 4 cups) unbleached all-purpose flour, plus a little**
   extra for dusting
1 **teaspoon pure salt**
2 **ounces (about ⅓ cup) lard**
1 **ounce fresh compressed yeast**
1 **teaspoon sugar**
1 **cup tepid milk, plus milk for glaze**

Sift the flour and salt into a warm bowl. Rub the lard into the flour with the fingertips, until it is evenly distributed. In another bowl, stir the yeast and sugar together with a wooden spoon until they are liquid. Add the milk to the yeast, stir, then strain the mixture into the flour. Stir it all together to form a soft dough, cover the bowl, and set to rise in a warm, draft-free place until about doubled in size—about an hour.

(continued)

Punch down the dough and turn it out onto a floured surface. Knead it lightly, then divide it into pieces of equal size to form oval shapes about 3 inches long and 2 inches wide. Brush with milk or water to give them a glaze and, if "floury baps" are desired, dust them with flour just after brushing them.

Place the baps on a lightly greased and floured sheet pan and set again in a warm place to rise for about 20 minutes. In the meantime, preheat the oven to 425°. To prevent blisters, press a finger into the center of each before placing them in the oven. Bake for about 20 minutes or until they are lightly browned. Serve warm with butter and jam.

CREAM MUFFINS

What we call cream muffins in the Lowcountry are really popovers. These airy foils for butter and jam are also called Yorkshire pudding. In York, in northern England, they appear at the breakfast table as well as being the classic accompaniment to roast beef. I am always surprised to hear British cooking maligned by Americans; so many of our best dishes, especially in the South, are absolutely English.

Serve these marvelous breads with lots of butter and homemade preserves and big cups of café au lait to begin a lazy Sunday breakfast. You will need to make the batter at least an hour in advance of baking. I like to make it the night before, tuck it into the refrigerator, then surprise my friends the next morning with hot cream muffins.

Popovers are very easy to make. I have made this recipe with as few as 3 and as many as 6 eggs, in both preheated and cold baking pans. However, to prevent the popovers from falling, you must not open the oven door during the first 20 minutes of baking—and little thereafter. There are several popover pans on the market, but I bake them in well-greased heavy porcelain custard cups.

MAKES 10 TO 12 POPOVERS

2 cups sifted unbleached all-purpose flour
½ teaspoon salt
4 large eggs
2 cups milk
2 tablespoons unsalted butter, melted, plus butter for greasing the
   cups

Mix the flour and salt in a bowl. Beat the eggs lightly. Mix the milk and butter together, then pour the mixture into the eggs and stir well. Slowly add the wet ingredients to the dry, stirring constantly. Do not overbeat. Cover the batter and allow to rest for at least an hour. If you refrigerate it overnight, be sure to allow it to warm up for a while before you begin baking.

When you're ready to bake, preheat the oven to 400°. Grease a dozen 3-ounce ovenproof custard cups. If the batter is lumpy, strain it. I pour it into a pitcher, then pour the batter into the greased cups, filling them no fuller than ½ inch from the tops. Set the cups on a baking sheet and bake for about 40 minutes. This recipe makes cream muffins that are moist on the inside and crispy brown on the dome. For a drier popover, bake them at a lower temperature (350°–375°), prick them with a knife after 50 minutes, and let them bake for another 5 minutes. Turn out of the cups and serve immediately.

PERSIMMON BREAD

Before Hurricane Hugo roared into Charleston on September 21, 1989, a native persimmon tree said to be the oldest in the country (indeed, in the world, since native persimmons grow only in the New World) gracefully shadowed the lawn of Peter Hanahan's old house in Ansonborough, a few blocks north of my home and bookstore. It was over 80 feet tall before the storm ripped it in half. Experts had guessed it to be between 400 and 700 years old.

Reaching out over the corner lot, the tree dumped 5 pounds of ripe fruit each day for 2 months each fall. Peter always lets me take what I want of the fresh, ripe fruit. I've made persimmon pies and tarts and wine and beer, breads and cookies and salsas and ice cream. But the simplest and most traditional preparations are the best.

It's said that persimmons shouldn't be eaten until there has been a frost, but that's not true; in the Lowcountry there *is* no frost until well after the trees have shed all their fruit. It is true, though, that you must wait until the fruits are very, very ripe. They must be very soft—downright mushy to the touch—or they will be so astringent they'll pucker your mouth. Ripe native American persimmons are one of the most intensely flavored fruits of the world, aromatic on the palate—flowery, like the finest muscat grapes. You can substitute the Japanese variety in recipes calling for " 'simmons"; but the flavor of the American variety is altogether different.

Persimmons do not take well to cooking, as they become mealy upon heating. Only in recipes in which the pureed fruit is used as a cookie or tart topping, or in which the flavor is extracted, such as in wine, or in which the texture is rounded by the addition of flour—as in this bread— is the native American persimmon shown off at its best.

The fruits are only 1 or 2 inches in diameter and have several large, flat seeds that half-fill the fruit. To use, simply push the pulp of extremely ripe persimmons through a colander with the palm of your hand, discarding the seeds and skins that do not pass through. This pulp may be frozen.

If you look at a map of the range of native persimmons in the United States, you will see what is essentially the states of the Confederacy, though they do grow along roadsides in the southern reaches of Illinois, Indiana, Ohio, Pennsylvania, and New York. The easiest way I know to find a persimmon tree is to travel on unlit back roads at night in October and look for the reflections of the eyes of 'possums and 'coons in the trees along the road. The trees are common along the banks of old rice fields, and the rice banks at Turnbridge Plantation down near the Savannah River are filled with them. You will be hard-pressed, however, to beat the wildlife to the ripe persimmons in the wild. Trees in inner cities are better sources.

Recipes for persimmon pudding abound, all similar. But I opt for a dense, moist batter bread without the usual spices that hide the distinctive persimmon flavor.

MAKES 2 LOAVES

½ pound (2 sticks) unsalted butter, plus butter for greasing pans
2 cups sugar
1½ teaspoons baking soda
½ teaspoon cream of tartar
4 cups unbleached all-purpose flour
3 cups ripe persimmon pulp
¾ cup chopped black walnuts

Grease 2 loaf pans and preheat the oven to 350°. Cream the butter and sugar together in a mixing bowl. Sift the soda, cream of tartar, and 2 cups of the flour together, then resift with the rest of the flour. Blend into the creamed butter and sugar, then fold in the persimmon pulp and nuts. Pour the batter into the prepared pans and bake for 1 hour.

HUGUENOT WAFFLES

I named these waffles after the famous Charleston dessert, the Huguenot Torte (page 268), because they are filled with the same nuts and apples that distinguish the cake.

MAKES 8 WAFFLES

2 large eggs, separated
2 cups unbleached all-purpose flour
½ teaspoon baking soda
1 teaspoon cream of tartar
1 tablespoon sugar
½ teaspoon salt
2 cups buttermilk
7 tablespoons unsalted butter, melted
¼ cup Nut Mix (page 25), finely ground
¼ cup finely minced apple

Preheat the waffle iron. Beat the egg whites until they form soft peaks and set aside. Sift the dry ingredients together into a mixing bowl, then make a well in the center of the mixture. Beat the egg yolks into the buttermilk, then add the melted butter and mix in thoroughly. Pour the mixture into the well in the dry ingredients, mixing them in quickly with a wooden spoon. Do not mix the batter too thoroughly; it should have some small lumps, like a muffin batter. Fold in the egg whites. Sprinkle the ground nuts and minced apple over the batter and fold in lightly. Cook according to the manufacturer's instructions on your waffle iron, until the waffles are very crisp. Serve immediately with warmed syrup.

12
DESSERTS

The ridiculously sweet tooth of southerners has historical roots in Charleston harbor. Sugar and dried fruits, chocolate and bonbons, and fresh fruits from the Caribbean have been imported into the "Holy City," as it's called, for well over two hundred years. It's hard to classify many Lowcountry sweets: sweet potato pie might accompany a meal or follow as dessert; tea fare shows up at the breakfast table. Some pickles, such as watermelon rind preserves, are very nearly candy. There are Mediterranean and African influences, though most of our desserts can be described as typically country French and English.

On the other hand, the very best Lowcountry desserts are simply fresh fruit. Cantaloupes are splashed with port and dusted with black pepper; figs are anointed with ratifia. Watermelon, native to Africa, is grown all over the Lowcountry; it is often the dessert at summer picnics and beach weekends. When the weather is suffocatingly hot, fresh berries suffice. And no Christmas stocking is without fresh oranges from points south and apples from the mountains. Ambrosia, made with fresh coconuts, is truly heavenly; a child can make campfire cobbler.

Some very old recipes, like gingerbread, have not changed in centuries; just as many, such as the loquat tart, are brand-new. There are simple custards and delicate tortes; foods from Africa as well as the courts of Europe. And pies, like the English pudding, at every meal.

There are cakes and cookies and puddings and candies, as well as sweet yeast breads, chocolate, and mint. Orangeburg, on the Edisto River, was settled by Swiss and Germans. Its cookbooks brim with cookie recipes. In Charleston, with its great port, eighteenth-century receipts feature coconuts and bananas fresh from Cuba. The Lowcountry kitchen is justly famed for its custards, creams, and ice creams; its pies and cobblers; its cakes and cookies; its candies; and its fresh fruit. These are some of our most delicious foods.

CUSTARDS, CREAMS, AND ICE CREAMS

Southern desserts, especially in the Lowcountry, nearly all once called for a creamy sauce of eggs and milk. The holiday fruitcake is tempered with a Bavarian; angel food cake is merely a foil for a custard sauce and fruit. Baked and "boiled" custard are enjoyed alone; stale cake becomes trifle with the addition of sherry and custard. A little gelatin firms the Bavarian; surrounded by ladyfingers, it becomes Charlotte Russe. Some of the old receipts call for isinglass, a form of gelatin derived from the bladders of sturgeon. Manuscript receipt books from old Lowcountry families are filled with recipes for Italian, Spanish, coffee, orange, St. Julien, lemon, and almond creams, all derived from their distant relative, the *blanc manger*. Charleston's ties to aristocratic England, very real in the minds of Charlestonians, kept these dishes in favor in the Lowcountry long after they had disappeared from the courts of England and Europe. They are both centerpiece and starting point for a number of delectables. Every ice cream recipe included is custard-based.

Old Receipts from Old St. Johns (c. 1919) includes the following, from Numertia Plantation:

CZARINA CREAM

Whisk 1½ pints of cream to a strong froth. Add 14 ounces fine sugar (powdered), a wine glass of Maraschino, ½ glass of Kummel, 16 drops of concentrated essence of vanilla and 1½ ounces Ising glass dissolved in boiling rosewater. Have ready a glass of spinach juice, color the cream therewith. Beat the mixture thoroughly and drop into it some shredded pistachios and almonds. Pour into a mould and place into a pail of crushed ice and salt to freeze. Serve with iced Champaigne sauce and vanilla Gaufres.

BOILED CUSTARD

Boiled Custard must *never* be allowed to boil. This is the custard sauce—*crème anglaise*—that accompanies cake slices and fresh fruit. Chilled in cups, it is offered as "morning custard." One of the first kitchen chores I was assigned as a child was stirring the custard in the double boiler. The sauce is served warm or chilled. If chilled, be sure to stir it occasionally to prevent a skin from forming on the surface. The richness of the sauce can be altered by varying the number of egg yolks.

MAKES ABOUT 3 CUPS

6 large egg yolks
1 cup sugar
   pinch of salt
2 cups milk, scalded
1 teaspoon rum, amontillado sherry, or bourbon; ½ teaspoon grated
      lemon or orange zest; *or* ¼ teaspoon vanilla seeds (scraped from
      a vanilla bean) (optional)

In a very heavy saucepan, in the top of a double boiler, or in a stainless-steel mixing bowl that will fit snugly over a pot, beat the egg yolks, sugar, and salt together until they are smooth and form a ribbon as they fall from the spoon or whisk. Gradually add the scalded milk, stirring constantly. Place the heavy pot over very low heat or place the double boiler insert or mixing bowl over a pot of simmering water. Stir constantly until the mixture begins to thicken. If desired, add the flavoring of your choice. If there are any lumps in the custard, pass it through a fine sieve.

Bavarian Cream

I am always surprised by the indiscriminate use of flavorings, particularly vanilla extract, in modern dessert recipes. I love the taste of vanilla, but I find that it loses both itself and other flavors when used without discretion. It marries well with chocolate and complements most fruits, but it has no business in banana or Persimmon Bread. It is best when it's the featured flavor. With her recipe for Bavarian Cream, Sarah Rutledge noted:

"When to be flavored with vanilla, break up two fresh beans in a pint of water, and simmer down to half the quantity in a covered vessel; strain it, and mix it with the isinglass [gelatin] and sugar, before they are added to the cream."

The Carolina Housewife, 1847

It is said that the great French chef Carême commemorated his service to the court of Alexander I with Charlotte Russe. Henry Middleton (1770–1846), an early president of the Continental Congress, was minister to Russia shortly after Carême had left, perhaps explaining why the recipe is so prevalent in 19th-century Lowcountry recipe collections. This is speculation on my part; still, Sarah Rutledge gave two recipes for Charlotte Russe in 1847, just 14 years after the publication of Carême's masterpiece—evidence that the finest Parisian pastries of the time were being attempted in home kitchens in Charleston.

(continued)

1 recipe Boiled Custard (page 234)
¼ teaspoon fresh vanilla seeds *or* 1 teaspoon vanilla extract
¼ cup water
1 tablespoon (1 envelope) unflavored gelatin
1½ cups heavy cream

Begin with the preceding recipe for boiled custard and flavor with ¼ teaspoon of fresh vanilla seeds or 1 teaspoon vanilla extract.

As the custard cools, pour the water over the gelatin and wait for it to be absorbed. Stir it well into the custard, then cool the custard, stirring occasionally so that the gelatin does not set on the bowl. When the custard is cool to the touch, whip the cream to soft peaks, then fold it into the custard. Pour the Bavarian into sherbert glasses and allow to chill for several hours before serving. Thin, crisp cookies and rich coffee are perfect accompaniments.

Note: The Charlotte Russe is made by lining a mold with ladyfingers, sprinkling them with liqueur, and filling with Bavarian Cream. It is chilled, turned out of the mold, and served with architectural garnishes of whipped cream, in the style of Carême.

RICE PUDDING WITH CRANBERRY-ORANGE PUREE

As the rice industry gradually fell apart in the Lowcountry after the Civil War, cooks began preparing more and more nontraditional rice dishes, such as sweets. At the South Carolina and West Indian Exposition in Charleston in 1901, the *Carolina Rice Cook Book* compiled by Mrs. Samuel G. Stoney was a favored 25-cent souvenir. It included some two dozen recipes for rice pudding.

I serve individual rice puddings chilled, with a cranberry-orange puree, which is not only delicious but a delight to the eye as well. Prepare both the pudding and the sauce several hours in advance of serving. It's essential to use fresh oranges in this recipe.

SERVES 6 TO 8

FOR THE SAUCE AND GARNISH:
- ¾ pound (about 3 cups) fresh cranberries
- 2 or 3 large juicy oranges
- 1 cup sugar

FOR THE PUDDINGS:
- ½ cup long-grain white rice
- ½ teaspoon salt
- 1 quart milk, or more if needed
- 1 tablespoon unsalted butter, plus butter for greasing cups
- 4 large eggs
- ¾ cup sugar
- 1 teaspoon grated orange zest

Reserve a few cranberries to roughly chop for the garnish. Cut strips of zest from the oranges for the garnish, grate a teaspoon of zest to flavor the puddings, and set aside. Squeeze a cup of orange juice and add to the cranberries and sugar in a heavy-bottomed saucepan. Bring to a rapid boil, stirring constantly. When all of the cranberries have popped and split open and the liquid has reduced by about a fourth, remove the pan from the heat and press the mixture through a fine sieve. Allow to cool at room temperature.

To make the pudding, in a heavy-bottomed saucepan, simmer the rice, salt, and milk, uncovered, until the rice is soft and the milk has reduced by one fourth, about 15 minutes. You should still have 3 cups of liquid; if not, add more milk. While the rice is cooking, grease eight 4-ounce ramekins or six 5-ounce custard cups with butter. Refrigerate the custard cups to chill the butter, then grease again.

Preheat the oven to 325°. In a separate bowl, beat together the eggs, sugar, 1 tablespoon butter, and orange zest, then stir into the rice and milk mixture. Pour into the greased cups and bake for 30 to 45 minutes, until the custard sets, stirring the custards once after about 15 minutes so that the rice does not all fall to the bottom of the cups. Remove from the oven when the custards are set, set aside to cool, then chill until serving.

To serve, dip the custard cups into very hot water; it will melt the butter and loosen the puddings. On each dessert plate, spoon a pool of the sauce, then invert the individual puddings onto each plate. Garnish with a sprinkling of cranberries that have been roughly chopped (a couple of quick bursts in a food processor is ideal) and orange zest.

POTS DE CRÈME

In the Lowcountry as in Paris and New York, lovely little sets of porcelain chocolate pots (*pots au crème*) have come in and out of vogue every 20 years or so. *Pots au crème* come with their own tight-fitting lids and are smaller than custard cups. You will need 8 of them or about 6 custard cups with lids made of aluminum foil.

This is a sinfully rich dessert that is the final coup, topping off a long, leisurely, sumptuous dinner with your dearest friends. *Pots de crème* are surprisingly easy to make. Use only the finest chocolate and cream you can find.

SERVES 6 TO 8

½ pound semisweet chocolate, broken into small pieces
2 cups cream
6 tablespoons sugar
2 large eggs
3 large egg yolks
2 tablespoons (⅛ cup) coffee-flavored liqueur, such as Kahlúa

Preheat the oven to 350° and set a pot of water to boil. Melt the chocolate in the cream in a heavy-bottomed saucepan over very low heat, stirring occasionally. Stir in the sugar. In a mixing bowl, whisk the eggs and egg yolks together until just blended, then pour in the chocolate and cream, stirring constantly until well blended. Stir in the coffee-flavored liqueur. Now fill the cups, pouring slowly and carefully, and remove any little bubbles on the surface of the custard with a demitasse spoon. Place the lids on the pots or cover each custard cup tightly with aluminum foil.

Set the cups in a baking pan and pour the boiling water about three fourths of the way up the sides of the pots. Bake for about 20 minutes. Do not let the water come to a boil. The custards are done when a silver knife inserted in the middle comes out clean. Cool, chill, and serve in the pots with freshly brewed hot coffee.

MINT-CHOCOLATE CHIP ICE CREAM

Late in the summer I make fresh mint ice cream. The flavor of the mint cooked in custard is so intense, it tastes salty to me. Charleston's master confectioner, Mark Gray, tells me the high sodium content of fresh mint accounts for that. I balance out the intensity of the mint by adding roughly cut bits of bittersweet chocolate to the ice cream.

MAKES 1 QUART

1   cup loosely packed fresh mint leaves
1   quart milk
6   large egg yolks
2   cups sugar
¼   pound roughly chopped bittersweet chocolate (Merckens if
      possible; page 30)

Add the mint leaves to the milk and scald the milk. In a large stainless-steel mixing bowl that will fit over a boiling water bath—or in the top of a stainless-steel double boiler, beat the egg yolks and sugar until well mixed and lightly colored. Gradually add the hot milk and mint and cook over hot water, stirring frequently, until a custard is formed—until the mixture thickly coats the back of a spoon (about 20 minutes). Cool, then chill.

When the custard is cold, strain out the mint leaves and any solids through a fine sieve, then freeze it in an ice cream freezer according to the manufacturer's instructions. When the mixture is softly frozen, fold in the chocolate, then pack the ice cream to freeze for about 2 hours.

BENNE BRITTLE ICE CREAM IN A BENNE COOKIE CUP

This nontraditional sesame ice cream is made like a classic French *glace* flavored with praline (brittle) powder. Don't try this recipe on a humid day, however, or you will end up with a soggy cookie and rubbery brittle.

BENNE BRITTLE

1 cup sugar
1 cup benne (sesame seeds), toasted (page 28)
½ teaspoon vanilla extract

Slowly melt the sugar in a heavy skillet, then add the toasted benne and vanilla extract. Stir quickly together, then pour out onto a greased marble slab or into a greased cake pan to cool.

When the candy is thoroughly cooled, break it up with a mallet or a rolling pin and grind a cup of the brittle into a powder in a blender, a spice mill, or a food processor. Leave the rest of the brittle in bite-size chunks to garnish the ice cream.

BENNE COOKIE CUPS

This recipe is made like a French wafer or *tuile*, sesame seeds replacing the ground almonds. You will need a half-dozen inverted custard cups or glasses on which to mold the cookies into cups. The recipe should make 18 cookie cups, but it is a very tricky recipe that varies greatly with the flours and ovens used and the humidity of the day. You may wish to bake the cookies slowly, at 350°, for about 10 minutes, or allow them to cool on the baking sheet for a moment before molding them. Mix a batch of dough according to the following recipe, then try one panful. If the cookies are cooking too quickly, try the recipe at the lower temperature.

4 tablespoons unsalted butter at room temperature
½ cup sugar
2 large egg whites at room temperature
5 tablespoons unbleached all-purpose flour
⅓ cup benne (sesame seeds)

Preheat the oven to 425°. Beat the butter and sugar in an electric mixer bowl at medium-high speed until very light and fluffy. Gradually add the egg whites a little at a time and continue beating until they are well incorporated into the butter and sugar. Sift the flour into the batter, continue beating at a lower speed, then fold in the benne with a spatula. Using a heaped tablespoon for each, make mounds of the batter 3 inches apart on a greased baking sheet. Spread each mound out evenly into a 3-inch circle. Do not crowd the cookies; they will spread.

Bake for 4 to 6 minutes or until they have browned on the edges about ½ inch in but with the centers still creamy white. Remove from the oven. With a spatula, remove the cookies from the baking sheet while they are still pliable and place them on the inverted cups to cool, gently pressing them into the desired shape. The cookies can be served unmolded as well.

BENNE BRITTLE ICE CREAM

This recipe is very simple to make and will become one of your favorites.

MAKES 1 QUART

---

2 cups milk
6 large egg yolks
¾ cup sugar
1 cup cream
1 cup benne brittle, ground to a fine powder

To make the custard, scald the milk in a saucepan and remove from the heat. Beat the egg yolks in the bowl of an electric mixer until they are very light-colored. Add the sugar and continue beating until doubled in volume. Gradually add some of the scalded milk to the egg mixture, then pour the eggs into the milk in the saucepan and cook over medium-low heat, stirring constantly, until the custard coats the back of a spoon, about 8 to 10 minutes.

Add the cream to the custard, cool, and chill. When thoroughly chilled, add the benne praline powder to the custard and freeze in an ice cream maker according to the manufacturer's instructions.

Serve the benne brittle ice cream in a benne cookie cup and garnish each serving with a sprinkling of benne brittle broken into morsels.

FRESH PEACH ICE CREAM

*T*he *Carolina Housewife* (1847) includes a recipe for "Matrimony," calling for two dozen common-sized peaches, sugar, and a quart of cream "or a very rich custard." Peaches have grown in size since then, but I wonder if we will ever know how the old cultivars tasted. My peach ice cream marries the custard and some cream and calls for the almondlike kernels from within the peach pits. The real magic of the recipe is in letting the peaches sit overnight to become very sugary, so ice crystals do not form in the ice cream. The recipe is best begun the day before.

SERVES 6

8 to 10 **very ripe large freestone peaches**
juice of ½ lemon or lime
1 **cup sugar**
2 **cups milk**
6 **large egg yolks**
1 **cup cream, well chilled**

In the bottom of a double boiler, bring several inches of water to a boil. Drop the peaches in for a few seconds, remove them, peel them, and stone them, reserving the pits. Leave the water to simmer.

Place the peach pulp in a bowl, crushing it with your hands so that there are no large clumps, but do not puree it.

Remove the kernels from the pits by tapping them with a hammer one at a time. I put the pits in a towel or a paper grocery bag before I strike them so that pieces of the pits do not fly up in my face.

Chop the kernels finely (a nut mill or a food processor can do this easily for you) and add them to the peach pulp along with the lemon or lime juice and ¼ cup of the sugar. Chill thoroughly, preferably overnight.

Place the milk on the stove to scald, but do not let it boil. In the top of a double boiler, off the heat, or in a wide stainless-steel bowl that will fit snugly on top of the hot water bath, begin whisking the egg yolks and the remaining ¾ cup of sugar together. Continue until the eggs and sugar are well mixed and lightly colored, then, a little at a time, strain the scalded milk into the egg mixture, stirring constantly.

(continued)

Place the mixture above the hot water bath and cook until the custard thickly coats the back of a wooden spoon (about 20 minutes), stirring all the while. Remove the custard from the heat and chill thoroughly.

The next day, or when all of the ingredients are well chilled, mix all of the ingredients together and freeze them in an ice cream maker according to the manufacturer's instructions. I use a hand-cranked model with 3 parts ice to 1 part salt. When the ice cream is softly frozen, remove the dasher, stir the ice cream all together once, then pack it in 4 parts ice and 1 part salt for another 2 hours to ripen before eating.

COCONUTS

When I lived in the Caribbean, I was often awakened by street noises shortly after sunrise. I would hurry down the hill, half asleep, to buy meat "pâtés" (spicy turnovers). A local woman made two or three dozen of these as well as coconut-filled ones each morning, which she sold briskly as soon as they came out of the oven. Pâté in hand, I would stroll over to the harbor, where down-island boats along the waterfront displayed mounds of fresh green coconuts for sale—the rest of my island breakfast.

Wielding a machete, the boatman would chop through the outer, green husk, slicing off the end of the coconut with the flourish of a Japanese steak house chef. Through this hole I could drink its soothing juice, cheaper than bottled water. The boatman then cut away all the outer husk, spinning the coconut in one hand and whacking away at it with the machete until the luscious, soft interior pulp was revealed, glistening in the already bright morning sun. The smooth, gelatinous texture of the green coconut always reminded me of custards I ate as a child here in the Lowcountry, and, indeed, green coconuts lend themselves well to custards. Often the custards are baked in the shells, not only in the Caribbean, home of the early settlers of Carolina, but also in Indochina and Indonesia, where the coconut palm originated.

Cocos nucifera now flourishes throughout the tropical world and is a major source of food for a third of the world's population. Though green coconuts are seldom available outside the tropics, the mature brown seeds of these drupes are available year-round in most parts of the country. We Sandlappers, with a long history of involvement in the spice and slave trades (and, hence, with strong African and Asian influences in our cuisine), have taken more readily to coconuts than have Europeans, who tend to use them as almond substitutes. I have eaten the gelatinous pulp of unripe, green almonds in Italy, but never have I seen a coconut in a market there, and I lived in the great port city of Genoa.

The rich interior of the mature nut has the most intense flavor. More than 200 years ago Eliza Lucas Pinckney, who had been raised in the West Indies, wrote down her receipt for "cocoanut torte," which was really delicious macaroons (page 265) to be made from these tropical nuts. But even today coconuts stay out of the European tradition. With its great harbor and Caribbean connection, Charleston led the way for coconut cookery.

Verta Grosvenor is a South Carolinian granddaughter of a slave. In *Vibration Cooking* she tells of two ways black people here have used coconut—in a custard pie and with sweet potatoes. The recipes are flawless, and I have prepared them many times, but I have adapted her ideas to my own taste, using fresh coconut.

I have found that I can still use the grated coconut from which the milk has been squeezed in recipes calling for shredded coconut with no loss of quality and often more flavor than store-bought.

Canned coconut milk is certainly readily obtainable today, with our increasing Asian populations, but it is so much fun making your own, I wonder why more people don't do it. Most of these recipes come from the Caribbean-American sweet tradition, but coconuts lend themselves well to rice and chicken dishes, and also to seafood and meats, as any Southeast Asian or Brazilian cook knows. Fresh peach and coconut chutney (page 314), though stylistically Lowcountry, is a cross-cultural inspiration.

When you're buying fresh coconuts (fall and winter are the best seasons), look for dark-skinned ones with shiny, clean "eyes" (3 dots on one end). They should be heavy and full of coconut water (not to be confused with coconut milk; recipe follows). Puncture two of the three eyes and drain the water into a container. You should at least taste the water, if not drink it, to be sure that the coconut is fresh. The water should taste sweet and clean, not musty or sour. To get at the meat, crack the shell. Some people prefer to place the nut in a 350° oven for 20 minutes, but I simply tap it around its equator with a hammer until it cracks into two pieces. (If you have a patio or sidewalk nearby, you can also throw it against the ground, monkey-style, but be careful of flying fragments of shell.) Then pry the meat away from the shell, unless you have a rotary coconut grater from India, available in Asian markets, which grates the meat while it is still in the shell. The thin brown skin can be pared off with a vegetable peeler, but it is not necessary to remove it if the meat is to be used only for making coconut milk or cream.

An average coconut will yield 4 to 6 cups of grated meat.

COCONUT MILK

There are several methods for making coconut milk, but I opt for the method calling for cow's milk, because I use it most often in custards, and homemade coconut milk made with water tends to be a bit too thin for that purpose. The following results in a thick, reliable coconut milk that will behave much like whole cow's milk.

MAKES 2 CUPS

1 coconut
   about 1½ cups milk

Drain the coconut water, strain it through muslin or several thicknesses of cheesecloth, and reserve.

Crack open the coconut and grate all interior white flesh with a hand grater, with an Indian rotary grater, or in a food processor (follow the manufacturer's instructions).

Add milk to the coconut water to make a pint of liquid. Bring this liquid to a boil and pour it over the grated coconut. Set aside to cool.

Strain the liquid from the coconut by twisting it tightly in a piece of muslin, squeezing all the liquid from the meat. Save the meat to use in recipes calling for shredded coconut.

Store the milk in the refrigerator and use within a week. The cream that rises to the surface can be scooped off and used to make coconut butter.

FRESH COCONUT ICE CREAM

The basic formula for this ice cream comes from the great French pastry chef, Gaston Lenôtre. When Verta Grosvenor tasted it at my house, she proclaimed it "the best ice cream in the world."

SERVES 6 (SLIGHTLY MORE THAN A QUART)

2 cups milk
1 cup sugar
1 cup firmly packed freshly grated coconut (pages 245–46)
6 large egg yolks
1 cup *crème fraîche,* homemade *crème fraîche* (page 24), or cream
    (preferably not ultrapasteurized) plus 1 tablespoon buttermilk

Heat the milk, half the sugar, and the coconut in a saucepan until it boils. Remove from the heat and set aside to cool for 10 minutes.

Beat the egg yolks with the remaining sugar until they are light-colored and begin to form a ribbon.

When the milk mixture has cooled, spoon a little of it at a time into the egg yolks, beating constantly. When all of the milk mixture has been added to the egg yolks, pour it back into the saucepan, over low heat, and cook, stirring constantly, until a thick custard is formed—about 20 minutes, or until a candy thermometer registers 185°.

Fold the *crème fraîche* into the mixture, chill, and freeze in an ice cream maker according to the manufacturer's instructions.

Note: What distinguishes this ice cream is the fresh coconut in combination with the tartness of the *crème fraîche* or buttermilk. It is true that you cannot make real *crème fraîche,* but there are several tricks to improve store-bought cream. Without *crème fraîche* or the homemade version described on page 24, however, buttermilk itself can add that tartness to counteract the sweetness of the coconuts. Add up to ¼ cup to the recipe.

PIES AND COBBLERS

COCONUT CUSTARD PIE

Inspired by Verta Grosvenor's coconut custard pie, this recipe is more authentically Lowcountry with its use of fresh coconut and its lack of a crust.

MAKES 12 4-OUNCE CUPS

1 quart milk
  grated meat of 1 large *or* 2 small (about 6 cups loosely packed)
    fresh coconuts (pages 245–46)
5 large eggs
½ cup sugar
½ teaspoon almond extract
½ teaspoon vanilla extract
1 teaspoon grated orange zest
  pinch of salt

Preheat the oven to 350°. Pour the milk over the coconut in a saucepan and bring just to the boiling point.

Beat the eggs well in a mixing bowl, add the sugar, and continue beating until they are light-colored.

Gradually add some of the hot milk to the egg mixture and beat in, then add the eggs to the milk and coconut.

Add the remaining ingredients, blend, and pour into a 2-quart porcelain dish or into a dozen 4-ounce cups.

Place the custard in a hot water bath and bake until a silver knife poked into the custard comes out clean, about 30 to 35 minutes. Set aside to cool. Serve chilled or at room temperature.

GRAPE PIE

This is my favorite pie, though many people have never heard of it. It is a Lowcountry classic. It can be made with any of the native American grapes (page 303). Some people use cornstarch or instant tapioca to thicken fruit pies—or, worse, wheat flour. Rice flour is tasteless and disappears, utterly transparently, into the fruit juices.

It was the pastry chef Kelly Bugden who taught me how to make perfect piecrust. Alas, I am never satisfied with my results unless I use lard (see page 25). You may use butter or another solid shortening—or a combination. Be sure to have everything as cold as possible and to maintain the ratio of 4:1 (in weight) for flour to shortening. And avoid touching the dough with your hands, which will toughen it.

FOR THE CRUST:
    1 pound (about 4 cups) unbleached all-purpose flour
      pinch of salt
    1 tablespoon sugar
    ½ cup water, plus ice cubes
    ¼ pound (about ⅔ cup) chilled lard (or any combination of chilled
        lard, shortening, and butter)

FOR THE FILLING:
    4 cups (about 1¾ pounds) slip-skin grapes such as muscadine,
        scuppernong, or Concord
    ¾ cup sugar
    ½ tablespoon rice flour
      grated citrus zest and lemon juice (optional)

FOR THE PIE:
      reserved pastry dough and filling
      milk or half-and-half
      sugar

To make the crust, sift the flour with the salt and sugar into a large stainless-steel mixing bowl. Add a few ice cubes to the measured water and set aside. Cut the lard into the flour with a pastry blender, a large fork, or 2 knives, until the mixture is uniform and, as the old cookbooks say, resembles small peas. Do not touch the dough with your hands. Place a wet towel under the bowl so that it will not slide around on the counter. Working deftly, scoop up large spoonfuls of the mixture from the bottom of the bowl with a large metal slotted spoon while sprinkling water into the mixture a little at a time. Work quickly as you "lift in" the water, stopping before all the water is in. You should stop the second you feel the dough will hold together without more water. Now grab the entire mass of dough in your hands and push it all together into a ball. If the pie filling is ready, wrap the dough in some wax paper or plastic wrap and put it in the freezer for 10 minutes; otherwise, put the wrapped dough in the refrigerator to chill while you prepare the fruit.

To make the filling, pulp the grapes by squeezing them over a nonreactive pot. Reserve the skins. Cook the pulp over medium-high heat for about 5 minutes, just enough to loosen the seeds. Press the pulp through a colander to remove the seeds. Combine the pulp with the skins, sugar, and rice flour. If the grapes are very sweet, such as ripe Concords, you may add a little citrus peel and juice for flavor. The skins of scuppernongs, however, are very tart on their own.

Preheat the oven to 450°. To assemble the pie, remove the pastry dough from the freezer or refrigerator and place on a large lightly floured surface. Try not to touch it with your hands. Roll it out evenly to a thickness of ⅛ inch. Place a 9-inch pie plate on top of the dough and, with a blunt knife, cut across the dough so that an area large enough to fill the pie plate is marked off as one large piece. Set the pie plate off to the side. Place the rolling pin on one edge of this large piece of dough, and gently roll it up off the surface and onto the pin. Lay the dough down in the pie plate, allowing it to roll off the pin, always avoiding handling the dough. Press it lightly into place, allowing any excess dough to hang over the sides. Fill with the fruit.

Cut the remaining dough into long strips and gently make a lattice top on the pie. Run a sharp knife blade at an angle around the rim of the pie plate, trimming off excess dough. Brush the top of the piecrust lightly with milk or half-and-half, then crimp the edge of the piecrust down with a large fork. Sprinkle the pie lightly all over with a little sugar, place in the middle of the oven, and bake for 10 minutes. Lower the heat to 350° and bake for another 20 or 30 minutes or until the crust is nicely browned all over. Be sure to bake the pie well so that the crust will not be soggy. If you have clear glass pie plates, you can leave the pie in until the bottom has begun to brown. Don't worry about the timing. All ovens and batches of flour bake differently. Bake the pie until it is a rich golden brown, and it will be delicious. Allow the pie to cool to lukewarm before serving. Do *not* serve this pie with cream, or you will mask the distinctive grape flavor.

MILE-HIGH APPLE PIE

This overstuffed apple pie is topped with a glorious dome of a crust made with duck fat. The crust is pushed down with the palm of the hand before being sliced.

MAKES 8 TO 10 LARGE SLICES, FULL OF FRUIT

FOR THE CRUST:

1½ recipes piecrust dough for Grape Pie (page 249), using chilled duck fat (page 160) instead of lard

FOR THE FILLING:

8 to 10 large tart baking apples

½ cup sugar

grated zest of 1 lemon

freshly grated nutmeg to taste

1 tablespoon rice flour

FOR THE PIE:

2 tablespoons unsalted butter, chilled and cut into small pieces

milk

sugar

Make the crust exactly like the crust for the grape pie (preceding recipe), but be sure that all of the ingredients and utensils are chilled—duck fat melts at a lower temperature than lard. Make 1½ times the recipe given for the lattice-topped grape pie and use chilled duck fat, rendered as described on page 160. Fill a 10-inch pie plate with half the crust, allowing it to fall over the edges of the pan. Wrap the other half of the dough in plastic wrap and chill both the filled pie plate and the wrapped dough in the refrigerator while you prepare the filling.

Peel, core, and slice the apples. (I use an apple corer that simultaneously cores and sections the fruit into 8 perfect slices.) In a bowl, sprinkle them with the sugar, lemon zest, nutmeg, and rice flour. Toss so that all the ingredients are evenly mixed.

Preheat the oven to 400°. Remove the chilled pie shell from the refrigerator and begin filling it with the apples, evenly distributing the butter pieces throughout. Pile the apples high in a mound. They will come above the top of the pie plate, several inches above in the center. Set the filled pie aside.

Roll out the remaining half of the dough, then gently lift it up on the rolling pin and center it on the filled pie, allowing the excess dough to fall over the edges. Gently pat the top crust into place on top of the apples, then run a sharp knife point around the rim just inside the lower crust so that the top crust is cut off just where it meets the lower. Set the excess dough aside. Then, working deftly and lightly, lift up the bottom crust that is hanging over the sides of the pie plate and fold it over the rim, tucking in and sealing the top to the bottom crust and crimping the rim between thumb and forefinger to create an attractive edge.

With a thin, sharp blade cut several steam vents in the crust, brush it lightly with milk, and sprinkle it with sugar. Place in the middle of the oven and bake for about an hour or until the crust is an even golden brown. Allow to cool partially before slicing, pushing the golden dome down lightly to meet the fruit, which will have settled somewhat. Serve with *crème fraîche*, whipped cream, or vanilla ice cream.

COBBLERS

Throughout the South you are likely to be served a variety of deep-dish fruit pies, some made with a rich, sweet biscuit dough topping the fruit, others with a cakelike batter. In older cookbooks from the Lowcountry, recipes for fruit-filled desserts are more likely to be boiled puddings in the English manner or custardy creations not unlike the *clafoutis* of France's

Limousin. Either of these recipes may be made with soft summer fruits such as berries, with fall apples, or with "put-up" fruit, such as peaches. You can flavor the fruit with sugar, rum, spices, or lemon juice and zest if you like. Or you can add more fruit. These recipes are not written in stone, and they always work. The first one is often called "campfire cobbler" because of its utter simplicity. The second is a classic French dessert, possibly brought to the Lowcountry by the Huguenots.

CAMPFIRE COBBLER

SERVES 8

¼ pound (1 stick) unsalted butter
2 to 4 cups fruit and its juices
1 cup sugar
2 teaspoons baking powder
1 cup unbleached all-purpose flour
1 cup milk

Put the butter in a deep casserole at least 9 inches in diameter, put it in a cold oven, and preheat to 350°. If the fruit is not juicy, sprinkle it with some of the sugar and set aside for a while.

Sift the baking powder and flour into a mixing bowl, add the sugar and milk, and mix until evenly blended. The batter will be thin. When the butter has melted and the oven has reached 350°, pour the batter all at once into the dish, then pour the fruit and juices into the center of the batter. Return to the oven and bake for about an hour or until the top is golden brown and a cake tester poked into the batter comes out clean. Serve hot, warm, or at room temperature with or without cream, *crème fraîche,* or ice cream. Hard sauce (page 308) is served on hot cobbler.

CLAFOUTIS

This fruited custard is very similar to the preceding cobbler, with eggs replacing the baking powder. The classic French version is made with cherries, but I am partial to big, juicy Johns Island blackberries.

SERVES 8

3 to 4 cups blackberries, cherries, or blueberries
⅓ cup sugar
4 large eggs
1 vanilla bean and 1 tablespoon rum *or* 1 tablespoon vanilla
      extract
   pinch of salt
1½ cups unbleached all-purpose flour
1½ cups milk

If the fruit is not sweet and juicy, sprinkle it with a little sugar and set aside for the juices to draw. Butter a large glass pie plate and preheat the oven to 350°.

Beat the eggs and sugar until the mixture is foamy, then add the seeds from the vanilla bean and the rum (or the vanilla extract) and the salt and beat well. Sift the flour into the mixture and continue to beat well, being sure to incorporate all the ingredients evenly. Beat in the milk. Pour about a third of the batter into the buttered dish, distribute the fruit evenly in it, then add the remaining batter. Bake for about an hour or until the top is golden brown and a toothpick stuck into the batter comes out clean. If the clafoutis is done and the top is not brown, you may brown it under the broiler. Serve hot or warm.

TEA FARE: CAKES AND COOKIES

The tea table remains a strong tradition in the Lowcountry, if only in training young ladies in comportment and etiquette. As late as 1934, when the *Charleston City Directory* listed only eight hotels in downtown Charleston, there were as many "Tea Rooms." Recipes for sugar cookies, gingerbread, and old plantation favorites such as wigs, jumbles, and marvels are passed down through the generations like the family silver. The recipes have changed little in Charleston's three-hundred-year history. Bill Neal, describing one such recipe in his book on southern baking, commented, "Recipes for the Queen of Puddings are remarkably consistent all over the South. Even the proportions are constant." The recipe he gives for the meringue-topped tea cake is identical to those I have seen in several manuscript receipt books in the private collections of several old Charleston families.

If truth be told, practically anything can be served at tea, which is just a scaled-down version of dinner. In the Lowcountry a bridge game often provides the occasion for tea fare. Coffee is the common drink; sweets are served. The following "tea cakes" are traditional. Those heirloom receipt books invariably offer at least two recipes for each type of cookie: one will be crisp, the other soft. Three cake recipes follow the cookies; they are thoroughly modern, but based in Lowcountry tradition.

RUSKS

The first of these recipes is Anne Sinkler Fishburne's "rusk as defies modern shortcuts" (c. 1919). These sweet rolls were split, buttered, baked a second time, then served at tea on the plantations along the Cooper River north of Charleston, where so many Scots had settled. The second recipe, also from Mrs. Fishburne's collection, is a modern muffin-like sweet bread which she classifies as a dessert.

Ophir Plantation was the country seat of the Porcher family, French Huguenots who first spent time in London before moving to the Lowcountry in the 1680s. Robert Wilson, a surgeon and Episcopal priest, wrote of the area in *Lippincott's Magazine* in January 1876: "To understand the home and life of the wealthy Carolina planter we must remember that he was the most contented man in the world. . . . [He had] no expensive tastes except for rare old Madeira and racing stock." At Ophir there were stables for those horses, domesticated ducks and geese, and houses for the chickens, turkeys, dogs, and hogs. In the storeroom, a basement held flour, sugar, and salt by the barrel; the meat room was filled with hams, sausage, and liver pudding.

Ophir, famous 150 years for its breads, was lost to the floodwaters in the late 1930s when the massive Santee-Cooper hydro-electric project was completed. Baking with fresh yeast had all but disappeared throughout most of the area, however, long before the dam was constructed. Fresh yeast made from home-grown hops was kept in a piggin, or small wooden pail. A gill, or half-cup, of yeast was a common measurement for home-baked breads. As Fleischman's two-ounce, compressed yeast cakes became readily available, we see the gill of liquid yeast being replaced by this soft, compressed product or by "yeast powder," which is just homemade baking powder. Mrs. Fishburne gives the following formula: ½ pound cream of tartar, ¼ pound soda, and ¼ pound flour, all sifted together. She notes that "One gill yeast is equivalent to ½ Fleischman's yeast cake or 1 teaspoon baking powder." Baking powder may cause the breads to puff up, but it will never replace the natural richness of yeast.

OPHIR PLANTATION RUSK

At 2 p.m. make a leaven with ½ yeast cake dissolved in a gill of water, mixed with enough flour to beat easily with a spoon. Beat into the leaven a light spoonful of lard and butter evenly divided, 2 eggs, ½ pint sugar and 1 gill of sweet milk. Knead in flour enough to make a stiff dough. In the morning, knead again. Make into rolls, set to rise in a warm place (in winter). When risen, bake in a hot oven.

QUICK RUSK

Two eggs, froth the whites, stir spoonful butter and a cup of sugar and then add the yolks, then whites of eggs. Put one teaspoon yeast powder in a pint of flour and stir in with a cup of milk. Bake immediately.

Old Receipts from Old St. Johns

SHORTBREAD

This is an old recipe for traditional Scottish shortbread that was easily made in the Lowcountry with its rice mills. I keep lightly salted butter on hand just for shortbread. Butter was always salted for storage purposes both in Scotland and in the Lowcountry, and directions in the old recipes invariably call for "squeezing all the water from the butter." I opt for salted butter for authentic flavor, and in my oven of a kitchen I use an electric mixer to cream chilled butter and sugar and almost never allow my hands to touch the flour, which toughens the dough. This is a sandy, delicious, easy-to-make cookie—and the secret to the best bourbon balls (page 275). Note that the flours are weighed (volume measures are also given).

(continued)

¼ pound (1 stick) lightly salted butter, chilled
¼ pound (½ cup) superfine sugar or well-sifted granulated sugar
¼ pound (1 cup) unbleached all-purpose flour, dried in a low oven
    and well sifted
2 ounces (⅓ cup) rice flour

Turn on the electric mixer and drop pieces of the chilled butter into the large bowl one or two at a time, occasionally scraping down the sides of the bowl if necessary. When the butter is creamed, add the sugar and continue beating until the butter and sugar are creamed together. Turn off the motor.

Sift the flours into the bowl through a fine sieve. Turn the motor back on and, working quickly, mix it all together until just blended. It will be very crumbly but will come together into a ball in your hands. Form a ball of the dough, trying to handle it as little as possible, then press the dough evenly into an 8-inch cake pan (see *Note*). With the tines of a fork, press a pattern around the edge of the dough. Refrigerate. Preheat the oven to 325°.

When the oven has preheated, remove the pan from the refrigerator and bake until the shortbread just begins to blush with color. This may take anywhere from 15 to 30 minutes. Remove from the oven, score into 8 wedges as for a pie while still warm, and allow to cool in the pan.

Note: This recipe can also be made in an 8-inch *square* cake pan. The shortbread will be slightly thinner, but it is spread with 1 recipe of Lemon Curd (recipe follows) to make sixteen 2-inch old-fashioned lemon squares, to be eaten immediately.

LEMON CURD

Variously called lemon curd, lemon cheese, lemon jelly, and lemon filling, this delicious custard appears at the breakfast table on toast, between the layers of cakes, and on top of lemon squares, a favorite Lowcountry cookie originally made with shortbread. It is a staple of the traditional kitchen here, a favored gift at Christmas. In antebellum days, lemon and orange trees were grown on many of the plantations, with orangeries built to house the frost-sensitive plants in winter.

MAKES 1²/₃ CUPS

juice (⅓ cup) and grated zest of 2 lemons
5 large egg yolks
¾ cup sugar
¼ pound (1 stick) unsalted butter at room temperature, cut into
   pieces

Measure the juice from 2 average lemons. If you don't have ⅓ cup, squeeze more juice from another lemon. In the top of a double boiler or in a wide stainless-steel mixing bowl that will fit snugly on top of a saucepan, beat the egg yolks with the sugar and the lemon juice and zest with a wire whisk. Put the bowl on top of a simmering water bath and continue to whisk until the mixture is very thick and light-colored, about 7 minutes. Remove from the fire and gradually whisk in the butter, a little bit at a time. The mixture should be bright yellow and very silky. Store covered in the refrigerator. Keeps up to a month, but you'll eat it more quickly than that.

GINGERBREAD

This recipe is adapted from the vintage soft gingerbread recipe that appears in *Old Receipts from Old St. Johns;* it is attributed to Northampton Plantation. Gone now, the plantation on the lower Santee River was home to an illustrious line of owners, among them General William Moultrie. Born in Charleston to Scottish parents, Moultrie became a Revolutionary War hero and an admired friend of George Washington. In the mid–nineteenth century the noted botanist Dr. Henry Ravenel lived at Northampton and assembled his mycological collection, which would provide the basis for his treatise on mushrooms in America—the first book of its kind. After Ravenel the plantation passed back into the hands of Lowcountry Scots, whose recipes for gingerbreads are varied.

This is a fine-crumbed, old-fashioned, cakelike gingerbread. Serve with *crème fraîche* (page 24) or boiled custard (page 234).

SERVES 12

½ pound (2 sticks) unsalted butter
2 cups loosely packed light or dark brown sugar
3 large eggs at room temperature (page 27)
½ cup molasses
½ cup whiskey
1 pound (about 4 cups) unbleached all-purpose flour
1 tablespoon ground ginger
1 teaspoon baking soda
1 cup milk

Grease an 11- by 15-inch baking pan and set aside. Preheat the oven to 350°. In the work bowl of an electric mixer, cream the butter and brown sugar together until light. Add the eggs one at a time, beating well after each addition. Lower the speed of the mixer and add the molasses and whiskey. Sift in the flour and ginger and blend well. Stir the soda into the milk and add to the batter, mixing well. Turn the batter out into the greased pan and bake until "it leaves the tin," about 45 minutes—or until a straw inserted into the center of the dough comes out clean. Serve warm or at room temperature.

GINGERSNAPS

MAKES 3 TO 4 DOZEN COOKIES

———

¼ pound (1 stick) unsalted butter
⅔ cup light or dark brown sugar
¼ cup molasses
2½ cups cake flour, plus flour for dusting
½ teaspoon salt
¼ teaspoon baking soda
 2 teaspoons ground ginger
⅓ cup milk

In the large mixing bowl of an electric mixer, cream the butter and brown sugar together. Add the molasses and blend well, then sift the dry ingredients over the mixture, continuing to beat at a lower speed until evenly blended. Add the milk and blend well, then chill the dough in the refrigerator for 1 hour.

Grease a cookie sheet. Preheat the oven to 350°. Remove the dough from the refrigerator. Heavily dust the work surface and rolling pin with sifted cake flour. Roll the gingersnaps as thinly as possible. The thinner they are, the crisper and spicier they will be. Cut cookies out with a cookie or biscuit cutter, then carefully lift them onto the greased sheet. They will be soft. Bake for 10 minutes, then remove the snaps from the sheet while still warm. Cool on wire racks.

JUMBLES

Martha Washington's Booke of Cookery contains several recipes for this twisted, coiled cookie from the 16th century. *Old Receipts from Old St. Johns*, collected by Anne Sinkler Fishburne in the early part of this century, contains two. Emily Whaley, Mrs. Fishburne's daughter, helped her mother assemble the book when she was a child. "Jumbles were sweet cookies which were always served after lunch," she recently explained. Both of the recipes call for "peach water" as flavoring (the extract is available through specialty food distributors). Walworth Plantation, always in the Porcher family, donated this recipe. Mrs. Porcher added the directions—usually ne-glected—for shaping the cookies: "The jumbles were always shaped in finger lengths by hand and joined so as to make a circle."

MAKES ABOUT 3 DOZEN JUMBLES

----

  2 large egg whites
¼ pound (1 stick) unsalted butter
¼ pound (½ cup plus 1 tablespoon) sugar
½ pound (2 cups) unbleached all-purpose flour
  1 teaspoon freshly grated nutmeg
¼ cup peach or rose water
     confectioners' sugar
     cinnamon sugar (optional)

Place a baking sheet in a cold oven, then preheat to 400°. After a few minutes, remove the warmed sheet, grease it well, and set it aside where it will stay warm.

In the small bowl of an electric mixer, beat the egg whites to soft peaks. Set aside. In the large bowl of the mixer, beat the butter until very light, then beat in the sugar and mix until well creamed. Lower the speed and add the egg whites, beating until the mixture is smooth. Sift the flour and nutmeg over the mixture and continue to beat on low. Add the rose or peach water and beat until the mixture is well blended. Refrigerate the dough until it is firm, at least an hour. Dust your work surface heavily with confectioners' sugar. Pinch off small handfuls of the dough and roll it into finger lengths, then form circles or the more traditional pretzel twists.

The cookies can be rolled in cinnamon sugar, as a recipe from a neighboring plantation suggests, before baking, if desired. Place the cookies on the warm greased sheet and bake for about 8 minutes or until lightly browned. Remove to racks to cool. Store in airtight tins.

MARVELS

Marvels are deep-fried pastries peculiar to the Lowcountry, like *les oreilles de cochon* of northwest Louisiana. *Larousse Gastronomique* offers a *merveille* recipe similar to these of 19th-century Charleston.

MAKES SEVERAL DOZEN, DEPENDING ON THICKNESS

¾ pound (about 2¾ cups) unbleached all-purpose flour
¼ pound (1 stick) unsalted butter
1 tablespoon sugar
3 large eggs
  confectioners' sugar or cinnamon sugar for garnish

Sift the flour into a large mixing bowl. Cut in the butter with a pastry blender or 2 knives until it is incorporated evenly. Lightly beat the sugar into the eggs, then add the eggs to the flour mixture and blend well. If the mixture appears crumbly and dry, use your hands to press it all together, but do not knead it or the marvels will become tough. Cover the dough and refrigerate for an hour.

After an hour, roll the dough out as thinly as possible and cut into various shapes with cookie or biscuit cutters. Fry in hot lard at 370° for 2 to 5 minutes, or until golden brown. Drain on wire racks and dust with confectioners' sugar or cinnamon sugar. These are delicious for breakfast with café au lait.

SUGAR COOKIES

My mother called these "old-fashioned southern tea cakes," but when rolled thin, they are the Christmas cookies that we iced with colored sugar glazes, sprinkles, and nonpareils. Children love to make these simple, delicious cookies.

MAKES 1 TO 3 DOZEN, DEPENDING ON THICKNESS

2¼ cups sifted unbleached all-purpose flour, plus flour for dusting
¼ teaspoon salt
1 teaspoon cream of tartar
½ teaspoon baking soda
¼ pound (1 stick) unsalted butter
1 cup sugar
2 large eggs, beaten
½ teaspoon vanilla extract
1 tablespoon milk

Preheat the oven to 375°. Sift the flour a second time with the salt, cream of tartar, and baking soda. Cream the butter and sugar in a large mixing bowl. Add the eggs, vanilla, and milk and beat in well. Add the sifted ingredients and blend well. Refrigerate for 1 hour. Place the dough on a lightly floured surface, sprinkle a little flour on it, and roll it out ¼ inch thick (or thinner). Cut with cookie cutters, place on cookie sheets, and bake for 12 to 15 minutes or until lightly browned. Transfer to racks to cool. Stored in airtight containers, the cookies will keep several weeks.

COCONUT MACAROONS

When Harriott Pinckney Horry copied her mother's old recipes in 1770, she often changed them to suit her own palate. Her mother's "torte" more appropriately became "Cocoa Nut Puffs":

"Take a Cocoa Nut and dry it well before the fire, then grate it and add to it a good spoonfull of Butter, sugar to your tast, six Eggs with half the white and 2 spoonfulls of rose water. Mix them all together and they must be well beat before they are put in the Oven."

Modern recipes for these macaroons are little changed from Eliza Lucas Pinckney's version of 200 years ago, but seldom is the prudent advice to dry the coconut included. To dry a freshly grated coconut, spread the shreds out on a baking sheet and place in a preheated 300° oven for about 25 minutes, tossing them every 5 minutes or so and not allowing them to brown. Allow the coconut to cool before adding it to recipes.

This recipe makes a delicious macaroon, slightly crunchy on the exterior and rich and moist inside.

MAKES ABOUT 30 MACAROONS

3 cups grated fresh coconut (page 245), dried
1½ cups sugar
3 large egg whites, beaten until foamy

Grease a baking sheet and set aside. Preheat the oven to 325°. Mix the coconut and sugar together well, then mix in the egg whites. Using a tablespoon, scoop up heaped spoonfuls of the mixture. Press each scoop of coconut tightly into the spoon to hold it together, then place each spoonful onto the sheet, with an inch between them. Bake for 10 to 12 minutes or until they just begin to brown. Transfer to racks to cool, then store in airtight containers. They don't keep long.

FRESH COCONUT CAKE

Homemade cakes filled with chewy shreds of fresh coconut are a southern tradition. Most modern recipes call for coconut in the icing alone. The following recipe should help revive a grand old Lowcountry favorite.

Before you begin, open a coconut and grate the meat (page 245). You should have 4 to 6 cups. Save what you don't use in the cake to make macaroons (preceding recipe).

SERVES 8

FOR THE CAKE:

    4 large eggs at room temperature (page 27)
    1 large egg yolk at room temperature
    1 cup sugar
    1 cup soft southern flour (page 27) or cake flour
    1 cup grated fresh coconut (page 245)

FOR THE ICING:

    1⅓ cups cream
    1 large egg white
    1 cup grated fresh coconut
      confectioners' sugar (optional)

Grease two 9-inch cake pans, line with parchment or wax paper, and grease the paper. Dust the insides of the pans with flour. Preheat the oven to 350° and set the oven rack in the lower third of the oven.

Warm a mixer bowl, then add the eggs and the yolk (save the egg white for the icing). Beat until doubled in volume. Add the sugar and beat until tripled in volume. Sift the flour over the mixture and fold in. Fold in the coconut. Pour into the prepared pans and bake for 25 to 30 minutes or until a cake tester inserted in the center of the cakes comes out clean. Set aside on racks to cool.

To make the icing, beat the cream and the egg white together until stiff peaks form. Fold in the coconut and sweeten to taste with confectioners' sugar.

Just before serving, turn the cakes out of the pans, remove the paper, then invert them. Place one of the cakes on a serving plate and put a mound of icing on top of it. Spread it out evenly over the cake, then place the second cake on top of it. Ice the top of the cake, then the sides.

HOLIDAY FRUITCAKE

Fruitcakes sporting day-glo cherries and dyed pineapple chunks are anathema to most, and understandably so. But I love a good fruitcake, drenched in bourbon or rum. In place of the glacé cherries and pineapple I use sundried fruits such as figs, dates, and cherries soaked overnight in spirits. This holiday fruitcake can be eaten immediately; it is delicious. Or, you can make a fruitcake at Thanksgiving, then drown it in liquor and put it inside a plastic bag in a cool, dark place, turning it about once a week so that the entire cake is evenly soaked in booze by the time Christmas arrives.

Scots with a rich heritage of baking and tea fare settled in the Lowcountry, bringing with them recipes for their near-black Dundee cake. Traditional ingredients are flour, butter, sugar, currants, raisins, sultanas, candied citrus peel, almonds, and eggs. The citron that is called for in older fruitcake recipes was not the Mediterranean citrus rind used today but the pickled peel of a melon known by the same name. Any dark fruitcake recipe will give you proportions; use whatever dried fruits and nuts you desire and replace the candied citron with the Watermelon Rind Preserves on page 327. This recipe is typical.

1½ pounds (about 3 cups) mixed dried or candied fruits, including
    some candied citrus peel, diced
¾ cup bourbon or dark rum
1 cup shelled nuts (pecans, walnuts, black walnuts and/or almonds
    in any combination) or pecan halves
¼ pound (about 1 cup) unbleached all-purpose flour
¼ pound (1 stick) unsalted butter, softened, plus butter for greasing
    the pans
½ cup sugar
3 large eggs at room temperature (page 27)
    pinch of salt

Soak the fruits in the liquor overnight.

The next day, grease a standard loaf pan with butter, line it with parchment paper, then grease it again.

Preheat the oven to 350°. In a large mixing bowl, toss the fruit and nuts in about ¼ cup of the flour. Cream together the butter and the sugar with an electric mixer. Add the eggs one at a time, beating well after each addition, until the mixture is fluffy. Sift the salt and remaining flour over the fruit and nuts, tossing all together. Fold the mixture into the butter and eggs, then turn the batter into the prepared loaf pan. Bake for 1½ hours or until a straw inserted in the center of the cake comes out clean. The top should be browned and the edges should be just pulling away from the sides.

Set the cake in its pan on a rack and allow to cool for 20 minutes. Turn the cake out on a plate, and, if desired, sprinkle liberally with the liquor of your choice. Fruitcakes keep very well. Store for a month or more in a plastic bag in a cool, dark place (see above), or wrapped in liquor-soaked cheesecloth in an airtight container, before serving. Keeps for several months.

HUGUENOT TORTE

Charleston's most famous dessert is its misbegotten "Huguenot Torte," an apple and nut cake that first appeared in print in *Charleston Receipts.* In researching the recipe I finally tracked down the author, Evelyn Florance, who confirmed my suspicions that the cake was not local. She told me that it was adapted from a recipe for Ozark pudding from the Mississippi River delta (where pecans are indigenous). Mrs. Florance used to make the dessert for the Huguenot Tavern in the 1940s in the heart of old Charleston, one of the last public dining places where you could eat Lowcountry food.

The recipe is neither a torte nor Huguenot. Leavened with five (!) teaspoons of baking powder, it is a 20th-century conceit with no French antecedent. Pecans or walnuts are specified. I prefer a combination of two or even three nuts for flavor. Black walnuts, the South's other native nut, are too unctuous, overpowering, and expensive by themselves—however delicious.

In the version that follows, the baking powder, salt, and vanilla have been eliminated from the original recipe. All of the favorable and most familiar characteristics of this "modern classic" have been retained—that is, the lightness of the sponge cake, the richness of the nuts, the crunchy exterior, and the presentation with whipped cream.

Ozark pudding, the real antecedent of this dish, is one of those regional specialties that have gone the way of cooter pie and rice bread. It rarely appears in Arkansas cookbooks, though it seems to have originated in northwest Arkansas and southwest Missouri, according to John Egerton. The oldest recipe we have found is Mrs. S. R. Dull's "apple pudding" in her 1928 *Southern Cooking*.

Ozark pudding was purportedly a favorite dish of President Truman. It was served to Winston Churchill when he visited the Trumans in Fulton, Missouri, and made his famous "Iron Curtain" speech. Clementine Paddleford, hailing Mrs. Florance's Huguenot Torte in the *New York Herald Tribune* in the 1950s, might have recognized it as a dish fit for a president, but she did not know any more than we do about the reclusive inhabitants of the Ozarks. Recipes for the two dishes are identical. This recipe is a real torte.

SERVES 16 (2 CAKES, 8 SLICES EACH)

FOR THE CAKE:

  2 cups nut mix (page 25)
    about 2 good-size apples, peeled
  4 large eggs at room temperature (page 27)
  1 large egg yolk at room temperature
1¾ cups sugar
 ¾ cup unbleached all-purpose flour

TO SERVE THE CAKE:

16 perfect pecan halves
    sugar
 ⅔ cup cream

Prepare two 9-inch cake pans by lightly greasing them, lining them with wax paper or parchment, greasing the paper, and lightly dusting with flour.

Preheat the oven to 375° and put a pan of water in the bottom of the oven.

(continued)

Finely grind the nuts in a nut grinder, blender, or food processor, proceeding in small batches. (Blending too long will render the nuts oily.)

Very finely chop the apples with a knife or in a series of quick bursts in a food processor. You should have 1¾ cups.

In a warmed electric mixer bowl, beat the eggs and egg yolk on high speed until doubled in volume. It may take 10 minutes or more. Slowly add the sugar while beating and continue beating until the volume is tripled. The eggs should be very thick and light in color. Don't be afraid of over-beating.

Sift the flour over the egg mixture. Sprinkle the ground nuts over all, followed by the apples. With a large spatula, fold the mixture together rapidly but gently, being certain to bring all the elements from the bottom of the bowl up into the mixture.

Divide the batter between 2 cake pans and bake in the middle of the oven for about 25 to 30 minutes, until the top is golden brown and the sides have begun to pull away. Do not push on the meringuelike top, or it may cave in.

Place on a rack in a draft-free place and let cool completely.

Lightly toast the pecan halves (page 50) while the cakes are in the oven. While the pecans are hot, quickly dip them in water and then roll them in granulated sugar until they are lightly coated. Let them dry on a rack.

The cakes must be perfectly cool, or the heat will melt the cream. Invert the pans to remove the cakes, discarding the paper liners, and turn the cakes back over again so that the crusty top surface is in its original position. Place each cake on a serving platter.

Whip the cream until stiff and pipe 8 rosettes or place 8 dollops of the cream evenly around each cake. Garnish each bit of cream with a sugared pecan and serve immediately or chilled. Serve with a shot glass of bourbon neat.

CANDY

Downtown Charleston has nearly always had at least one successful confectioner. Menus from eighteenth- and nineteenth-century dinner parties include "an immense quantity of bonbons." (See Mrs. Charles Alston's menu in Chapter 1, page 12.) For the first half of the twentieth century street vendors were renowned for the quality of their groundnut cakes (always flavored with orange peel) and "monkey meat" (a molasses and coconut praline). And today Charleston is home to Mark Gray, one of the finest confectioners in America. His candies at Cacao's (344 King St., Charleston, SC 29401, 1-800-441-2402) are made fresh daily from his own recipes, using the finest ingredients and no preservatives. Mark's instructions for tempering chocolate and a few of his recipes follow.

TEMPERING CHOCOLATE

Perfect chocolate candies and glazes are accomplished by tempering—heating and cooling the chocolate to precise temperatures. A pure chocolate (which may include cocoa butter, cocoa mass, milk, sugar, lecithin, vanilla or vanillin) should never be subjected to temperatures above 120°.

Over a simmering *bain-marie* (do *not* allow the water to boil), place a stainless-steel bowl containing a small amount of chocolate. Begin to stir immediately. Continue to add the rest of the chocolate to be tempered. When all of the chocolate is smoothly melted, remove the bowl from the *bain-marie*. Wipe any water off the bottom of the bowl before you approach your clean work surface—marble, a sheet tray free of any grease or water, or an enameled countertop. Pour half to three quarters of the chocolate onto the surface. Spread out with a spatula, occasionally bringing some chocolate up on the spatula to touch your lower lip, to test the temperature. When the chocolate first feels cool against your lip, it's ready to be tempered. When first out of the bowl, it should be between 110° and 120°.

Cooling—or tempering—the chocolate does not take long. When the chocolate on the counter has cooled (to about 85°), scoop it up off the counter and combine with the remainder in the bowl. Stir well and scrape down the chocolate on the sides of the bowl, mixing all the chocolate well together. Using a candy thermometer, test the chocolate frequently for cooling. It is perfectly tempered at 86°, but 85–88° is acceptable. Tempered chocolate should be shiny, with a velvety texture. It will have changed from "chocolate brown" to a nearly jet black, and it will seem to have changed in both volume and weight, feeling tighter and heavier. When it passes all of these tests, it is perfectly tempered and ready to glaze cakes and candies. After 10 to 15 minutes the chocolate will become thick. Simply reheat, add freshly shaved chocolate, and repeat the process.

MARK GRAY'S TRUFFLES

MAKES ABOUT 7 DOZEN

1 cup heavy cream
1 pound chopped or premelted dark chocolate (not unsweetened)
½ cup your favorite liqueur

Bring the cream to a violent boil, reduce the heat, and add the chopped or melted chocolate. Stir until smooth and remove from heat. While warm, add the liqueur. Allow the mixture to reach room temperature, 8 to 24 hours. Do not refrigerate.

Line a sheet pan with parchment paper. When the chocolate is ready, pipe truffles out through a pastry bag fitted with a no. 7 straight tube, holding the bag ½–1 inch from the pan. Allow the mixture to flow out. It should form a sphere (between a nickel and a dime in diameter) as it hits the surface. Stop the flow with a slight upward twist of the pastry bag.

After filling the tray, place in the refrigerator for 10 to 20 minutes until firm. (Mark notes that most home refrigerators are set for 40° and warns not to leave the chocolate in for longer periods, or condensation will form on the candies.) Remove from the refrigerator and roll the ganache into ¾-inch balls. Place back in the refrigerator while you temper chocolate for coating the truffles (see preceding page). Dip the balls into the tempered chocolate by hand and place them on a lined sheet tray to dry. Store at room temperature as refrigeration destroys truffles' delicate flavor, but be warned that they don't keep well.

POMONA

Reminiscent of Victorian "sugarplums," this candy of mixed fruits and nuts is very popular in Charleston. It is excellent for tea. It's necessary to weigh the ingredients, or the recipe simply won't work. You will need an accurate candy thermometer (test your thermometer in boiling water—212°—and adjust accordingly). The recipe is Mark Gray's.

MAKES 120 1¼- by ½-INCH PIECES

- 1 pound (4 sticks) unsalted butter
- ½ pound honey
- ½ pound maple syrup
- ¼ pound light corn syrup
- ¾ pound light or dark brown sugar
- 2 ounces granulated sugar
- 6 ounces dried apricots, chopped
- 6 ounces pitted dates, chopped
- ¼ pound light or dark raisins
- 2 ounces orange peel or orange chunk marmalade
- 2 ounces rolled oats
- 2 ounces dried peaches, chopped
- ¼ pound whole almonds, roasted
- ¼ pound pecans, roasted
- ¼ pound English walnuts
- ¼ pound hazelnuts (filberts), blanched and roasted

In a heavy saucepan over medium heat, combine the butter, honey, maple syrup, light corn syrup, brown sugar, and granulated sugar, stirring only in the beginning stages of cooking. Heat to 249–250°.

Add the remaining ingredients and mix in well, then place in a parchment-lined sheet pan (an inch-deep 12- by 17-inch pan) and allow to seize for 8 hours or overnight. Cut into little squares. Store in airtight containers with wax paper between layers. Keeps for a month or more.

TURKISH FUDGE

Dried figs and other dried fruits are used in this simple recipe for a spicy sugarplum. Alice B. Toklas's notorious "haschich fudge" (which contained neither hash nor chocolate) is a similar concoction. These are not nearly so strong, however, as those you might encounter in the Mediterranean. Use whatever dried fruits and nuts you have on hand. If you find this recipe too spicy for your palate, reduce the spice. Add the corn syrup a teaspoon at a time as the last step until the mixture forms a uniform ball in the food processor.

MAKES 1½ DOZEN 1-INCH SUGARPLUMS

½ cup chopped pitted dates
½ cup chopped dried figs
½ cup dried apples
¼ cup light or dark raisins
¼ cup whole shelled almonds
¼ cup unsalted dry-roasted peanuts
2 teaspoons *Quatre-Épices* (page 32)
1 tablespoon light corn syrup

Put the dried fruit, nuts, and spices in a food processor and grind until well blended. Add the corn syrup and blend until the mixture forms a ball. Pinch off small pieces of the fudge and roll into 1-inch balls. Store in wax paper–lined airtight containers. Keeps for a month or more.

BOURBON BALLS

This "candy" is simplicity itself to make, and it appears in every Christmas cookbook and at every holiday party south of the Mason-Dixon line. Most recipes call for using store-bought vanilla wafers as a base for the confection, but my mother's recipe calls for shortbread.

MAKES 3 TO 4 DOZEN BALLS

2 cups crushed shortbread (page 257)
¾ cup confectioners' sugar, plus ⅓ cup for dredging
1¼ cups chopped pecans
¼ cup unsweetened cocoa powder
¼ cup light corn syrup
⅓ cup bourbon or sour mash whiskey (or dark rum if you prefer)

Put all of the ingredients except the sugar for dredging in a food processor and process until blended together. Roll into ¾- to 1-inch balls, roll in the powdered sugar, and store in wax paper–lined tins. They will keep for about a month.

PEACH LEATHER

One of my fondest memories of Charleston is coming to her confectioners when I was a child. Although I'm not crazy about candy, I have always been a fool for dried fruit. Peach leather is one of the easiest sweets to make, and it lasts a long time—or until your friends, young and old, find your jar. This is an excellent recipe to share with a child.

MAKES ABOUT 16 PIECES

5 or 6 peaches, not too ripe
    sugar or honey
    flavorless vegetable oil

Drop the peaches into boiling water and leave them for 2 minutes. This will make them easy to peel and will set the color. Remove them from the water, peel them, halve them, remove the stones, and puree them in a food processor, a blender, or a food mill. Taste the puree and sweeten to your taste, remembering that the sweetness will be concentrated when the peaches are dried. For 2½ cups of puree, which will fill an average cookie sheet, a tablespoon or two of honey is usually plenty.

Preheat the oven to its lowest temperature (140–160°). Brush a cookie sheet lightly with oil, then pour the puree onto the sheet so that it is evenly distributed. Place the cookie sheet in the oven and leave until the puree is no longer tacky to the touch but is soft and pliable. It may take as long as 24 hours.

Roll it up while it is still warm, then cut the leather into 3- and 4-inch strips and wrap each strip in plastic wrap. You may sprinkle the leather with sugar or ground nuts or shredded coconut before rolling it up if you like, or you may add spices to the puree before you dry it; but I prefer the pure flavor of ripe peaches.

ORANGE WALNUTS

At Christmas we exchange all sorts of confections and condiments, some of them put up in summer and some of them made just for the holidays. Libby Demetree was born into dual old Lowcountry families—the Scottish Frasers of Georgetown and the French Hugers (pronounced "U.G.") of Charleston, both renowned for their cooking skills. Her aunt Bessie Fraser Betancourt makes wonderful preserves and candies, among them these orange-flavored, sugared nuts, which Libby brings to me. Of these favored treats, Bessie says, "Very easy and very nice." I'll say!

MAKES ABOUT 3 CUPS

---

1 large juicy orange
1½ cups sugar
3 cups walnut halves

Taking care not to dig into the white part, zest the orange rind and set aside. Squeeze the juice of the orange into a measuring cup; you should have ½ cup (if not, add enough water to make ½ cup). Boil the sugar with the orange juice until a thermometer reads 234° or a small quantity of the mixture dropped into cold water forms a soft ball. Remove from the heat and add the orange zest and walnuts. Stir until the mixture looks cloudy. When it begins to sugar, dump it all out onto wax paper or a greased cookie sheet or marble slab. If it hardens before it is dropped, scrape the entire contents of the pot onto the paper or greased surface. Separate into bite-size morsels about half the size of a walnut.

FRESH FRUIT

Loquats are the first fruits to ripen in the Lowcountry. Mulberries, black-berries, and blueberries follow closely behind. In May, Sea Island melons begin to appear on the vines, and clingstone peaches arrive at the Charles-ton Farmers Market from the orchards an hour inland. Pomegranates, best enjoyed out of hand, are popular courtyard trees in Charleston. Summer meals in the Lowcountry are often just fresh vegetables; dessert is fruit.

Watermelons, native to Africa, are an important crop in the Low-country. The Charleston Gray is a national favorite. I have seen that variety grow nearly 3 feet long. When we were children (and local waters were unpolluted), our parents would send us out on the beach with long slices of watermelon as dessert after a meal of sliced tomatoes, cucumbers, corn on the cob, crowder peas, and rice. We would take the slices with us into the surf, beyond the breakers, where we would alternately swim and eat, letting the melons float in the salty water. To this day, I prefer desserts that feature fresh, local fruits. I never turn down a slice of melon.

LOQUAT OR APRICOT TART

The loquat, usually called "Japanese plum" in Charleston, is a common tree of dooryards and gardens in the Lowcountry. Most of the trees have been cultivated from unimproved seedlings in this century as ornamentals; the fruits are undersized and full of the large seeds. The juicy, firm texture of the fruits, which resemble apricots, makes them a local favorite, partic-ularly eaten out of hand.

The season for the ripe fruit (and it must, indeed, be ripe to softness to be edible) is brief; it is the first summer fruit to arrive. Some years the fruits ripen in early April; other years they are still on the trees when the Spoleto Festival USA ends in early June. Neighborhood children love to climb the trees; they go from door to door offering the fruits for sale. The following recipe is from Joann Yaeger, a local chef.

Apricots, another exotic fruit favored for Charleston courtyards, can be substituted here. If you have neither fresh apricots nor loquats, use dried apricots soaked in water overnight. (Instructions follow the recipe).

SERVES 8 TO 10

3 ounces (about ½ cup) sugar

½ pound (2 sticks) unsalted butter

½ teaspoon vanilla or almond extract

½ cup milk

1½ cups unbleached all-purpose flour, plus flour for dusting

¼ cup apricot jam

2 cups seeded loquats, apricots, or rehydrated dried apricots (see Note)

½ cup chopped pecans

Grease a 9- or 10-inch tart pan and set aside. In the large bowl of an electric mixer, add the sugar (minus 1 tablespoon) to the butter and beat well. Add the extract and milk and continue to beat until well blended. Turn the mixer to low speed and sift the flour into the mixture a little at a time until it is all incorporated into the dough. Preheat the oven to 350°.

Turn the dough onto a floured surface and roll out about ½-inch thick. Score off a section of the dough big enough to fill the pan. Roll that section up onto the rolling pin, then unroll it into the tart pan. Lightly press into place. Brush a layer of jam onto the tart, then add the fruit, interspersing it with little pinches of the remaining dough. Sprinkle with the nuts, then sprinkle the entire tart with sugar. Bake for about 45 minutes or until the dough is browned evenly. Serve warm or at room temperature.

Note: For 2 cups of rehydrated apricots, fill a 2-cup measuring cup loosely with dried apricots. Fill with water to barely above the 2-cup mark. Pour the water into a small saucepan and bring to a boil. Add the apricots, stir well, remove from the heat, and cover. Let stand overnight.

AMBROSIA

In my family we serve a big bowl of ambrosia at our Christmas meal, which begins early in the morning with fresh pastries. We take turns preparing the food in the kitchen and opening and eating raw oysters outdoors. Ambrosia is often found on the dessert table in the South, heavily laced with liquor; but it is also a perfect foil for our rich holiday brunch of fried quail, grits, and biscuits. No one in my family is a lover of cold weather; we rejoice, however, in the delicious oysters and citrus that winter brings.

SERVES 12 TO 14

2 large grapefruits
6 large seedless oranges
1 pineapple
1 small coconut

Over a large serving bowl, section the grapefruits and oranges as described on page 187, squeezing the extra juice into another container. Pare and core the pineapple and cut into small chunks, adding them to the citrus. Crack the coconut and grate the interior white flesh as described on page 245. Add the grated coconut to the fruits and toss the ambrosia to mix well. Drink the excess citrus juice while it is fresh.

13

BEVERAGES

Charleston's history of imbibing is legend. Robert Rosen's *A Short History of Charleston* includes a half-dozen entries about the city's drinking habits; *Charleston! Charleston!* by Walter J. Fraser, Jr., is a social history of the city that portrays a hedonistic upper class and a debauched citizenry. Rosen quotes the historian Carl Bridenbaugh: "The importation of liquors at Charles Town in 1743 staggers the imagination—1500 dozen empty bottles, among other items, to be used for 'six months' supply' of 1219 hogsheads, 188 tierces, and 58 barrels of rum."

> **"Punch Houses"** like the Two Brewers on Church Street and The Pig and the Whistle on Tradd Street served common laborers and sailors, while a few slightly more respectable public taverns catered to merchants, artisans, and planters. Here they were served salted fish, wild game, and rice-flour puddings with rum-based "slings," "flipps," and "toddies," wine, or molasses and persimmon beer to slake their thirst. For amusements the taverns offered cockfights, raffles, and other entertainments.
>
> *Charleston! Charleston!*

Drinking, however, was by no means restricted to the taverns. When Josiah Quincy, a gentleman from Massachusetts, dined at the elegant home of Miles Brewton, he had "By odds the richest wine I ever tasted." Eliza Lucas Pinckney, a lady planter, recorded in her receipt book of 1756 the recipe for the ratifia that follows, as well as one called the Duke of Norfolk Punch. Punch recipes have been passed down for generations: *Charleston Receipts* begins with twenty pages of drink recipes, many of them for punches that serve hundreds.

Fine old Madeira, sherry, and port, as well as the ubiquitous claret, fill eighteenth- and nineteenth-century Charleston estate inventories. At Middleburg, the oldest house in South Carolina, arrows written in chalk on

the wall in the wine closet point to the house store of "Port 1830" and
"Madeira 1832." The house was home to descendants of Benjamin Simons
for more than two hundred years. A Champagne bottle dating to the 1870s
was unearthed under the kitchen building; by then the family owned all
the property on that side of the Cooper River north of Charleston.

Henry Laurens was a Charleston merchant and planter who served as
president of the Continental Congress while Washington was at Valley
Forge. He was, like Thomas Jefferson, an avid gardener, a gastronome, and
a wine connoisseur. His correspondence with a London wine merchant with
Oporto connections reveals much about the consumption of spirits in
Charleston in the 1760s:

> *You could scarcely have fallen upon a more unlikely article for the Carolina
> Market than Wine. This is almost always the case as many Gentlemen on
> your side the Water can witness, but it is rather worse now than I have
> known it (I mean the Market) to be for 15 or 20 Years past. We have lately
> had no less than 1,250 pipes of Madera & Canary Wines fairly imported
> besides no small quantity from Lisbon, & Ca., which supplies the demand
> of purchasers tho it makes no appearance at the Custom House. Some
> hundred pipes of Madera, Vidonia, & low Claret have been from day to day
> selling at public Auction. . . .*

This is an admission not only (as the editors of Laurens's papers noted)
that some wines were smuggled into Charleston, but also that Charlestonians were risking punishment to obtain the spirits they wanted at the best
price. Wine was forever available on the black market. After a century of
trying to temper the Charleston drinker with laws, Rosen notes, "In the
1970s the state of South Carolina gave up and passed a 'mini-bottle' law
that allows the rest of the state to do what Charlestonians had been doing
all along—drinking in bars and restaurants."

Laurens was no dilettante; he knew good beer and wine. Of a shipment
of nineteen cases of bottled ale and three of claret that he received in 1764
from a Glasgow shipper, he wrote, "The former is very good & I cou'd have
sold it ere now if I wou'd have taken less than 60/ per dozen which people
do not care to give at this time of Year. The Claret is by no means approved
of or I shou'd have sold it upon tryal & I know not what to do with it."
Laurens also knew grape cultivation, and tried his hand at winemaking:
"This vine of mine has given Spirits to our New French incomers; 'tis said
by many Gentelmen to be as fine as any they have seen in Lisbon or Spain
& the French cry out, *C'est beau et bon.*"

When John Bartram, the naturalist, visited Laurens a year later, he measured "A fine grape vine seven inches & half Circumferenc[e.] Bore 216 clusters, one of which measured eleven inches in length & sixteen & A quarter in circumference." The vines, like the olive trees Laurens had cultivated, however, would not continue to produce; it is said the soil is too rich.

Iced tea surely must be the most common drink in the Lowcountry; nearly everyone drinks it, several glasses at a time. Still, very few restaurants know how to make it properly. A recipe follows.

Like the early gastronomes of the Lowcountry, I prefer my meals with red wine. But what is most important is to please your own palate. While I recommend wine with most food, the typical Lowcountry liquor cabinet contains spirits of all sorts; refrigerators always hold some beer. The drinks that follow the iced tea and lemonade are all for special occasions.

ICED TEA

We say "ice' tea," and we drink it by the gallon. In local barbecue houses and cafeterias, where you find some inklings of Lowcountry food, pitchers of iced tea are placed on the tables. On Wadmalaw Island, just south of Charleston, tea is cultivated; it is the only tea grown in America. In 1773 Charleston shared sentiments with Boston over the Tea Act; with strong allegiance to the Crown, however, Charlestonians would eventually allow the tea (stored in the basement of the Exchange Building) into their homes. Eighteenth-century visitors to the city remarked on its ridiculous British airs; it does seem ludicrous that they wore heavy woolens and drank hot tea in the steamy subtropical afternoons. If that British ritual has disappeared, it is perhaps for the better; better still that we now ice our tea.

To make a pitcher of southern iced tea, use only orange pekoe tea, either in tea bags or loose—1 bag or 1 teaspoon of loose tea per glass. Use fresh cold water; bring it to a boil in a nonreactive pot. Pour the water over the tea and let the tea steep, covered, for 5 minutes, or to desired strength. Strain out the loose tea; squeeze the tea bags. Sweeten the tea to taste and pour over ice in tall glasses. Serve with lemon wedges and, if available, freshly snipped sprigs of mint.

To make "sun tea," fill a clear glass gallon container with cold water and add 6 or 8 tea bags or teaspoons of loose tea. Leave the container to stand at room temperature overnight or in the hot sunshine for 3 or 4 hours.

LEMONADE

Good homemade lemonade is remarkably refreshing. This recipe comes from Sunny Davis, who grew up in her family's Pine Crest Restaurant on U.S. Highway 15 in Walterboro. Before the construction of interstate highways, the Pine Crest was a favored stop on the north–south highway. It was one of the last restaurants to serve genuine Lowcountry food.

SERVES 8

6 fresh lemons
1 cup sugar, plus sugar to taste
6 cups water
   fresh mint sprigs (optional)

The lemons should be free of oil or wax coatings. To be sure, scrub them with a little soapy water and rinse them well. Halve the lemons and put them in a 2-quart heat-resistant pitcher. Add the cup of sugar to the pitcher.

Bring the 6 cups of water to a boil and pour over the lemons, filling the pitcher. Stir to dissolve the sugar, then set aside to cool. When the lemons are cool enough to handle, after about 30 or 40 minutes, squeeze the juice out of them into the pitcher. Discard the lemons. Sweeten the lemonade to taste.

Pour the lemonade over ice in tall glasses, garnishing with sprigs of mint if desired.

MINT JULEPS

Much to the chagrin of Kentuckians, Charlestonians claim both the first jockey club and the first mint julep. I offer no proof for the julep, but it is true that no Lowcountry dooryard or garden is without its mint plants. I have friends over for a ritual mint julep once a year, usually in early May. Pound ice in a towel against bricks, then make a simple sugar syrup by mashing several fresh mint leaves in a teaspoon of sugar with the back of a spoon in each silver mint julep cup. Add, a little at a time, some bourbon or sour mash whiskey and a little of the finely crushed ice to each glass, stirring all the while and alternating the liquor and the ice until the julep cup is filled and heavily frosted on the outside. Garnish each julep with a sprig of fresh mint and serve with a white cloth napkin folded around the base of the cup.

EGGNOG

Several historical collections in South Carolina have eggnog recipes that antedate Sarah Rutledge's of 1847. Milk drinks were spiked with wine in England prior to the colonial era. Brandy was the popular spirit for about 100 years; then rye appears to have become the favorite. Bourbon is king in the Lowcountry today, though many eggnog enthusiasts prefer blended Canadian whiskeys. The real secret to perfect nog is to dribble the spirits into the mixture, drop by drop. This is a very old-fashioned type of eggnog, with sweetened, stiffly whipped egg whites whipped into the cool custard. It is very light on the palate, so the amount of liquor is reduced from other recipes, because you will find you and your guests drinking more than you had planned. Some versions leave out the whites. If you do, double the amount of cream.

SERVES 8

6 large eggs, separated, at room temperature
⅔ cup sugar
2 cups milk
2 cups cream
1 cup bourbon or spirit of your choice
    freshly grated nutmeg

Beat the egg yolks with half the sugar until they are well mixed and light-colored. Stir the milk and cream into the yolk mixture. Chill thoroughly. When ready to serve, beat the egg whites until very stiff, gradually adding the remaining sugar, and set aside. Dribble the spirits into the chilled milk mixture, stirring constantly, then fold in the beaten egg whites. Top with freshly grated nutmeg.

RATIFIA

Ratifia ("ra-ti-FEE-a"), an almond-scented wine fortified with sweet wine and sugar, spans Charleston's three centuries of imbibing. Although it's all but vanished from Lowcountry tables, the Charleston Museum has a bottle of ratifia that was made in the 1880s and rebottled and corked in the 1950s.

This version of ratifia (also called ratafia or *noyau*) is flavored with the kernels of peaches; it comes from my earliest Carolina source, Eliza Lucas Pinckney, who recorded it in her mid–eighteenth century diary. The older spelling persists in Charleston.

Escoffier splashes ratifia over freshly sliced fig halves for a perfect summer dessert. I add a few drops to custards, especially for peach ice cream, or drink it chilled, like sherry bolo, on a sultry afternoon. It is also added to Champagne punches, as follows.

MAKES ABOUT 1 QUART

75 (about 2 ounces) peach kernels (about ½ bushel peaches; see
    page 243 to remove kernels)
2 cups brandy
½ cup sweet wine, preferably a muscat
½ cup orange flower water
½ cup sugar

Mix all the ingredients together in a covered quart jar and leave in the sun for 6 weeks, shaking the jar every day. Strain and rebottle.

CHAMPAGNE PUNCH

Charleston's winter social season is no less festive than it was 200 years ago, when balls were given nearly every night in January and February. Today the season runs from Thanksgiving to New Year's, but the social-izing—and drinking—are still legend in the port city. Most people opt for glasses of white wine or cocktails these days, but I love to serve a big bowl of punch once a year. Many of the beverages in *Charleston Receipts* are Champagne- and tea-based punches. This tea is not the orange pekoe tea drunk cold at dinner, but green, uncured tea. A good formula includes a quart of green tea, a pint of brandy, a pint of ratifia (or a flavored brandy of your choice), thin slices of a half-dozen lemons and a half-dozen oranges, a quart of dark rum, and, just before serving, 4 quarts of Champagne and 4 quarts of seltzer. *Charleston Receipts* advises, "And never forget that punch stock should be poured over a block of ice and served cold, cold, cold!" Cut the top out of a gallon plastic milk or water jug and fill with water to make a block of ice that is the perfect size for a 5-gallon punch bowl.

MAKES 3 GALLONS

PEACH FUZZIES

Long before "*il miracolo del boom*" (caused largely by the Spoleto Festival USA) brought yuppies, fancy bars, and peach schnapps to Charleston, we were drinking a truly fuzzy peach drink, a frozen daiquiri made with unskinned fresh peaches. Some people make them with frozen pink lemonade, which is fine (grape juice is used as coloring in the better brands), but I prefer the more subtle flavor of lime as a backup to the fresh peach flavor.

SERVES 1

¼ cup or 1 jigger light rum
   juice of ½ lime
1 tablespoon superfine sugar (or granulated sugar put in the blender
      for a few seconds until finely ground)
1 ripe fresh peach, pitted but unpeeled
2 cups crushed ice (or several ice cubes put in the blender and
      crushed)

Place all of the ingredients in a blender and blend until uniformly smooth and frozen, adding ice if desired.

CHERRY BOUNCE

The recipe for this cherry cordial that appears in *Charleston Receipts* tells us to "Go to Old Market in June and get a quart of wild cherries." The cherries are the fruits of the black cherry tree, *Prunus serotina*, native to all of the eastern states and to New Mexico. About every four years, usually following a very wet spring, the trees, which grow best in moist, sandy soil, produce a bumper crop, their limbs heavy with fruit hanging down over country roads. These cherries have the distinctive wild cherry flavor most of us know only from cough drops.

MAKES ABOUT 1 QUART

1 **quart wild cherries**
1 **cup sugar**
3 **cups bourbon or rye, more or less**

Wash the cherries, drain them well, then put them in a wide-mouth quart jar. Add the sugar and gently shake the jar until the sugar is dispersed evenly. Set the jar, uncovered, aside in a cool place for the juice to draw, several days.

Add the whiskey to the jar, being sure to cover the cherries. Lightly cover the jar and allow to steep for 10 days. Strain the Cherry Bounce into a nice decanter and serve over ice cream or as an after-dinner liqueur.

MULBERRY WINE

Mulberry trees grow all over the Lowcountry; in downtown Charleston they dump gallons of berries on sidewalks and parked cars for two months each summer. The grackles love them, but the trees are really a sort of curse on the neighborhoods where they grow. Some years I'll purposely prune trees back at the wrong time of year so that they don't bear the next year; some years I make mulberry wine. This wine is awfully sweet, but it can be used as a cordial. It improves with age, and by its third year it resembles port. Before the wine is ready to drink, during the fall deer season,

I open a bottle and marinate a haunch of venison in it before roasting. The rest of the wine will clear in about a year, indicating that it is ready to be drunk. Turn the bottle upright about a month before pulling its cork so that any sediment settles to the bottom of the bottle. Like a late bottled vintage port, it continues to mature in the bottle; it must be decanted.

This is a country wine, the recipe for which you can find on any British or European farm. You will need several items not found in the everyday kitchen to make it. If there is a wine-making supply store where you live, it may stock the hard-to-find items. A jelly bag is used to extract the juice of the fruit. One can be made simply by tightly stitching a piece of muslin into a funnel shape; a bleached country ham bag is perfect; a clean, heavy cotton pillowcase will also work. Wine bottles must be sterilized; the recipe will fill 4 to 5. Corks and bottle corkers haven't changed much in several hundred years. Buy an inexpensive plastic corker and the best corks you can find. The wine ferments in a 3-gallon glazed crock, often available at garden stores.

MAKES 4 TO 5 BOTTLES

2 pounds mulberries
2 quarts boiling water
2 pounds sugar
½ ounce fresh compressed yeast

Using a nonreactive container, crush the berries and pour the boiling water over them. Leave them to soak for 24 hours. The next day, let the liquid drip through a jelly bag, muslin, or a clean heavy pillowcase hung from a hook over a 3-gallon container. Do not squeeze or force the mixture through, or the wine will have too much sediment and will never clear. Bring the liquid just to a boil and add the sugar, stirring until it is completely dissolved. Allow the sweetened juice to cool to below 120°. Crumble the yeast on top and stir in. Pour into a glazed crock, cover with a clean towel, and allow to ferment for 2 weeks before transferring to sterilized wine bottles. Cork the bottles and store them on their sides in a cool, dark place until the liquid clears, about a year. Improves with age.

14

CONDIMENTS: PICKLES, RELISHES, PRESERVES, AND SAUCES

A vast array of condiments adds harmonies of color, flavor, and texture to Lowcountry meals—scuppernong jam, dilled green beans, home-made mayonnaise, spiced peaches, pickled watermelon rind, fig conserve, pear chutney, and various mixed pickles and relishes such as achar and chow chow. Older recipes for pickles, relishes, and preserves sometimes call for huge quantities of Jerusalem artichokes or peaches. Look at the Indian, Caribbean, and Mediterranean influences in this chapter, attesting to the colony's long involvement with the slave and spice trades as well as to the diversity of its settlers.

Preserving really isn't difficult, and the rewards—shelves full of the harvest's bounty—are deeply satisfying. Read through these recipes well before beginning. Remember that for many of these recipes you will need special equipment. I recommend a kitchen scale; weight measurements are given. If you don't weigh ingredients, chances are the recipe simply won't work. You will also need a large open kettle canner with a rack. Jars must be sterilized before they can be filled. Most of these recipes need only ten or fifteen minutes of processing.

To process, always begin with new metal lids for screw-type jars (such as Ball and Mason brands) and new rubber rings for clamp lids. Sterilize all equipment, including jars, lids, and funnels, by placing them in a boiling water bath in the canning kettle. Make sure the water returns to a boil to ensure sterilization. Turn off the heat, but leave the jars in the hot water until the ingredients are ready to be canned. Remove the jars and lids from the hot water, draining out the water as you remove them. Make sure all jars are free of chips and cracks. Return the water to a boil.

Fill the jars with the prepared recipes to within a half inch of the tops, then run a thin spatula down around the inside of the jars to dispel any air bubbles. Wipe the top of the jar with a clean cloth. Place the lids on the jars (with the rubber ring in place on clamp lids and the screw band loosely tightened on the metal lids). If your kettle's rack can be raised and hooked onto the edge of the pot, raise it and be careful while placing the jars on the rack, two at a time, opposite each other, so that one side of the rack does not slip down into the kettle, splashing boiling water up on you. Lower the rack carefully into the water, making sure the jars are covered by at least 1 inch of water, cover the pot, and bring to a boil. Process, or allow to boil, according to the recipe. The self-sealing metal lids are sucked down by a sealing vacuum. If some of the lids do not seal, simply store the condiments in the refrigerator and use them within two or three weeks.

Traditionally, the very sweet Lowcountry preserves were not processed in a boiling water bath. Forget tradition in this case. Go ahead and process the recipes for pickles and preserves. Nothing is more disheartening than finding a spoiled jar of preserves that you spent hours preparing. Only the spiced peaches (page 313) lack this extra step.

And, finally, in an effort to *preserve* your preserves, use only clean utensils to remove condiments from their containers. A finger in a jar of pickles or a buttered knife in the jam invites early spoilage.

ARTICHOKE RELISH

Jerusalem artichokes are one of the few native American foods that remain unchanged through hybridization. Indigenous to the Lowcountry, they appear most often in pickles and relishes. I know Lowcountry cooks who still walk along roadsides and make notes of the flowers blooming, only to come dig up the tubers in the fall. Mary Clare Ulmer, from Hell Hole Community, is one of the area's great country cooks. She insists on artichokes from the wild, even though they are difficult to clean. Some people put the 'chokes in their washing machines to clean them, but Mrs. Ulmer says, "I don't want sand in my washing machine any more than I want it in my pickles." Happily for all of us, the water chestnut–like tubers are now cultivated and are readily available, sand-free, in grocery stores across the country. Jerusalem artichokes are delicious raw in salads, roasted, and pureed in soups.

A plate of rice, a pork chop, and Sieva beans become a Lowcountry supper with the addition of a spoonful of this tart and crunchy relish.

MAKES 5 PINTS

1 cup pure salt
1 gallon water
2 pounds Jerusalem artichokes, scrubbed and minced, ground, or thinly sliced
2 cups minced or ground green and red bell peppers
2 cups minced or ground onion
¼ cup mustard seeds
1 tablespoon ground turmeric
2 cups sugar
1 quart white vinegar
cayenne pepper to taste (optional)

Mix the salt and water. Soak the vegetables in the brine for 24 hours.

The next day, drain the vegetables well, rinsing them briefly under cold running water. Squeeze out all the excess moisture. Sprinkle the mustard and turmeric over the vegetables and mix thoroughly. In a nonreactive pot, dissolve the sugar in the vinegar, bring to a boil, and pour over the vegetables. Fill sterilized jars, add a dash of cayenne to the jars if desired, seal, and process in a boiling water bath for 15 minutes.

ATS JAAR, OR ACHAR

Mixed pickles in the Indian manner have graced Lowcountry tables for centuries. In my childhood Charleston restaurants set tables with a tray of the bright ochre vegetables, cured in a bath of salt, turmeric, and vinegar. All sorts of vegetables not included here may be added, including asparagus and bell peppers. Some cucumbers, if too ripe, will become soft in the mixture, but when served as a condiment alongside complex rice dishes such as Country Captain (page 153) they are delightful nonetheless. This recipe must be begun at least one day ahead.

MAKES 6 QUARTS

FOR THE VEGETABLES:

    1 **cup pure salt**

    1 **gallon cold water**

    ½ **pound fresh young green beans, trimmed**

    1 **pound (about ½ head) green cabbage, cut into small pieces**

 1½ **pounds small cucumbers, cut into 1-inch slices**

    1 **head cauliflower, about 2 pounds, broken into small flowerets**

    ½ **pound peeled carrots, cut into 2-inch pieces**

    1 **pound (about 7 ribs) celery, cut into 2-inch pieces**

    ½ **pound radishes, cut into ½-inch dice**

    1 **pound small (about 8 egg-sized) onions, peeled and halved or left whole if smaller**

    ½ **pound (about 5 heads) garlic cloves, peeled**

FOR THE PICKLING SOLUTION:

    ¼ **pound (about 5 inches) fresh ginger, peeled and thinly sliced**

    1 **tablespoon ground turmeric**

    3 **tablespoons mustard seeds**

3 or 4 **fresh or pickled chili peppers (1 for every other jar)**

    ½ **gallon white vinegar**

To prepare the vegetables, dissolve the salt in the water, then pour over the prepared vegetables in a nonreactive pot (unchipped enamel, glazed crockery, or stainless steel). Let stand overnight, at least 12 hours.

The next day, drain the vegetables well, then pack into hot sterile jars. Bring the pickling solution to a boil and pour over the vegetables to ¼ inch from the top of the jars. Seal and process in a boiling water bath for 10 minutes or refrigerate for a few days before eating.

BLACKBERRY VINEGAR

As recently as 1988, food writers were saying that blackberries will not grow in sandy soil, yet South Carolina has at least six species that I know of, and I am no botanist. Some summers there is not much rain in the Lowcountry, and the wild varieties are small, hard, and bitter. But on Johns Island, just outside Charleston, farmers are growing cultivars that are large, sweet, and juicy even in drought. They are delicious in cobblers, simply splashed with cream, or infused into vinegar.

The recipe for this heavily sweetened vinegar comes from *Old Receipts from Old St. Johns*, written just outside Charleston at the turn of the century. Though the cookbook lists it as a beverage, I would drink it straight only as a sore throat remedy. Instead, pour a dollop or two over iced soda or seltzer water for a refreshing summertime drink or into a glass of low-acid wine, as for a *kir*. It is also delicious when splashed onto fruit salads, and it marries well with the pan juices from duck breasts or venison steaks when used to deglaze the pan.

In a nonreactive pot, cover ripe berries with white vinegar and let stand for 24 hours. The next day, scald the mixture by bringing it just to the point of boiling. Strain the liquid from the pulp, then add a pound of sugar to each pint of juice. Return the juice to the pot and boil for 20 minutes.

Strain the mixture again into sterilized wine bottles and cork.

CHOW CHOW

Chow chow is such a culinary oddity—a British interpretation of an Indian relish that appears in all southern states in various forms. More often than not it includes cabbages and green tomatoes boiled in a pickle thickened with flour. Recipes invariably call for salting the vegetables "overnight," but I prefer to begin the process in the morning before work, then do the canning at night before I go to bed. This recipe makes exactly seven pints, which fill a small canning kettle. I count off the pings of the lids sealing as I fall off to sleep.

MAKES 7 PINTS

FOR THE VEGETABLES:

    1 small firm head of green cabbage, finely chopped (4 cups)
    8 cups chopped (about 8 average) green tomatoes
    4 large green bell peppers, chopped (4 cups)
    4 cups chopped (about 4 large) onions
    1 cup pure salt
    3 quarts boiling water

FOR THE PICKLING SOLUTION:

    ½ cup prepared mustard *or* 3 tablespoons dry
    ½ cup unbleached all-purpose flour
    1 tablespoon ground turmeric
    1 quart white vinegar
    2 cups sugar
    2 tablespoons celery seeds
    3 tablespoons unsalted butter

To prepare the vegetables, put them in a large nonreactive bowl or pot. Dissolve the salt in the boiling water and immediately pour it over the vegetables. Allow them to sit uncovered for 12 hours.

Line a large colander with a double thickness of cheesecloth or muslin and dump the vegetables into it to drain, squeezing as much of the liquid out of the vegetables as possible.

(continued)

To make the pickle, mix the mustard, flour, and turmeric into a paste in a little of the vinegar, then add to the rest of the ingredients and bring to a boil. Add the vegetables and boil for 10 minutes, stirring so that the mixture does not scorch. Pour into sterilized jars and process in a boiling water bath for 10 minutes.

CORN RELISH

This corn relish is very vinegary. I never add the sugar often called for in corn relishes because I use not only sweet modern varieties of corn, but local Wadmalaw Sweet onions (see page 29) as well. Use the sweetest corn and onions you can find to make this relish and make a small batch the first time around. Small batches not only are easier to handle but also are easier to season to taste.

Serve this condiment with poultry, tossed into salads, or with beans and rice.

MAKES ABOUT 6½ PINTS

———

1 red bell pepper, chopped (about 1½ cups)
1 green bell pepper, chopped (about 1½ cups)
1 very large sweet onion, such as a Wadmalaw or Vidalia, chopped
   (about 2 cups)
2 cups chopped celery
½ cup chopped fresh chili peppers, such as jalapeño
3 cups white vinegar
½ cup fresh lemon juice
1 teaspoon celery seeds
1 teaspoon dry mustard
½ teaspoon ground turmeric
6 cups sweet corn kernels (about 12 ears, the kernels cut, not
   scraped, from the cob)

Put everything but the mustard, turmeric, and corn in a nonreactive pot and simmer for about 5 minutes. Put the mustard and turmeric in a small bowl or teacup and mix together with some of the hot liquid from the pot, then add the mixture to the pot along with the corn. Bring to a boil, then reduce the heat and simmer for another 5 minutes.

Pack the mixture into sterilized jars, seal, and process in a boiling water bath for 10 minutes.

CREOLE SAUCE

When I lived in the Caribbean, the natives steamed the fishy coral-dwelling fish such as oldwife and triggerfish in the same Creole sauce that we serve here with fried fish. It's the famous *salsa criolla cruda* of all Latin America.

MAKES ABOUT 1½ CUPS

1 onion, chopped (about ¾ cup)
1 large tomato, peeled, seeded, and chopped (about ⅔ cup)
1 hot pepper, such as jalapeño, seeded and chopped
2 garlic cloves, finely minced
  salt and freshly ground black pepper to taste
  juice of 1 lime
½ to ¾ cup olive oil
  fresh parsley or cilantro leaves, chopped, to taste
1 tablespoon anchovy paste (optional)

Mix all of the ingredients and allow to stand at room temperature for about an hour. Serve raw with fried fish and boiled seafood such as shrimp or cover a fish with it and steam it.

DILLY BEANS

With locally grown green beans available as many as ten months out of the year in the Lowcountry, it seems foolish not to have a jar of some pickled ones in the refrigerator. I can't think of a simpler pickle to make.

MAKES 6 PINTS

---

  3 pounds tender young green beans, trimmed at the stem end
  6 garlic cloves, peeled
  6 bunches, or heads, of fresh dill
1½ teaspoons hot red pepper flakes
3¾ cups white vinegar
3¾ cups water
⅜ cup pure salt

Sterilize 6 pint jars and keep them hot. Taste the beans to see if they feel furry in the mouth. If so, blanch them for a moment or two. Pack them into the hot sterilized jars, adding a garlic clove and a bunch of dill to each jar. Combine the remaining ingredients, bring to a boil, and pour hot over the beans, leaving ¼ inch of space at the top of the jars. Run a plastic spatula handle around the inside of the jars to remove air bubbles. Add caps and seal. Process the jars in a boiling water bath for 10 minutes or simply store in the refrigerator. They will be cured in about 2 weeks.

FIGS

Nothing so spells summer in South Carolina to me as the fresh figs of July and August. There are trees 20 feet tall, covered with figs, in postage-stamp-size Charleston courtyards. My father once planted a fig cutting at his home in Beaufort, expecting to wait the seven years everyone had told him it would take to bear. The following summer he had a fig! The second summer, three. And the third year, we harvested a quart a day for six weeks from his 10-foot "cutting."

Figs quickly established themselves in the Lowcountry after the Spaniards brought them here in the 16th century; unlike peaches, they are hardy right up to the ocean's edge. The best way to eat them is raw, but I include two ways to preserve them.

Harvest figs in the early morning before the birds get them and always pick them with stems attached.

FIG CONSERVE

This variation on one of my mother's recipes is typical of the vast array of condiments we southerners pride ourselves on. I use it as a marmalade on toasted hearty bread or like chutney alongside game. I usually put several whole peppercorns in every other jar of preserves, but some years I just add a tablespoon or so to the entire batch while it is cooking.

MAKES ABOUT 5 PINTS

2 pounds ripe fresh figs
1 cup chopped fresh pineapple
2 medium lemons, unpeeled, cut into small pieces
½ teaspoon pure salt
  sugar
1 cup roughly chopped nuts (optional; see *Note*)
  black peppercorns to taste (optional)

Wash the figs and cut them into small pieces. Mix the pineapple and lemons, then fold them into the figs with the salt. Add an equal weight of sugar. Put the entire mixture in a heavy nonreactive pot and bring to a boil over medium-high heat. Reduce the heat and simmer gently, uncovered, until it thickens but is still a little runny. It will take an hour or two.

Add the nuts and peppercorns, if desired, put in hot sterilized jars, and screw down the lids. Process for 15 minutes in a boiling water bath.

Note: Mother always used pecans, but I like to use walnuts or walnuts mixed with pecans and/or black walnuts (for proportions, see page 25).

FIG PRESERVES

Although figs are common in Lowcountry backyards, they are not produced commercially here. If you have access to a productive tree, you may have a plethora of fruit during the ephemeral season. Ripe figs fade rapidly and must be eaten the day they are picked. I usually preserve them with their stems on, so that they maintain their shape, but you may pluck the stems or crush the fruit. The pickling lime called for in the recipe firms the fruit. It is available in 1- and 2-pound bags from grocers. It is calcium hydroxide, a weak base. Also known as hydrated or slaked lime, it is available from pharmacies as well.

Old Receipts from Old St. Johns (c. 1919) includes three fig preserve recipes among its dozen jams and jellies. Each produces a distinctive preserve, affected even more by choice of figs. This is one of those recipes that defy modern instructions: preserve what you have, using the following formulas:

> **figs**
> **pickling lime (see above)**
> ⅔ **pound sugar for each pound of figs**
> 1 **pint jar for each pound of figs**

In a nonreactive pot, cover the figs in lime water (1 tablespoon of pickling lime to each quart of water) and soak for 10 minutes. Rinse the figs thoroughly in cold water.

Add sugar to the figs in a preserving kettle and cook at a low boil until the figs are transparent, about 1 hour. Pour into hot sterile jars at once and screw down the lids. Process in a boiling water bath for 15 minutes or simply put the preserves in the refrigerator and use within a couple of weeks.

WILD GRAPES

The summer after my grandfather died, when I was 12, I went to spend some time with my grandmother, who lived in western Tennessee, 600 miles from the Lowcountry. I learned more about food in those few weeks than I would learn in many years to come. It was Grandma's approach to living more than her recipes, however, that so influenced me, and I am forever grateful for that one time alone with a real homemaker and her garden. There was much solace for her in her daily chores, and I too learned to enjoy hanging clothes on the line (which I still do), watching for cracks in the soil around the potato plants, and drying apples in the sun.

We removed all the window screens from her house, scrubbed and hosed them clean, and set them in the sun to dry. We then gathered green summer apples from the trees that bordered the garden, and she showed me how to pare, core, and slice them. We placed the slices on the screens that were stacked on concrete blocks in the sun. Every night we carried them into the garage, away from the dew, then back out into the sun each day until, after about a week, the apple slices were perfectly—and naturally—dried. But the real treat of the summer came when the grapes were ripe.

More species of *Vitis*, the grapevine, grow wild in the United States than in all the rest of the world combined. And second to apples, grapes are our most widely cultivated fruit. At Grandma's, there were both wild muscadines trailing up over the trees beyond her property and cultivated American Concords, whose flavor is what most Americans think of as "grape" and wine connoisseurs as "foxy." The muscadines, which grow only in the Deep South, are the sweetest of the American native varieties. They grow in bunches, not clusters, on vines that often climb into the highest reaches of hardwood forests.

On the border of the woods beyond my grandmother's garden, vines of wild purple muscadines and tawny scuppernongs—each a variety of native *Vitis rotundifolia*—could be found trailing up into the trees, entwined with reddish catawbas, a variety of *Vitis labrusca*, which probably escaped from 19th-century cultivation there. We would spread old sheets beneath the vines to catch falling grapes as we pulled vines down through the limbs. We didn't worry that the birds left us just a few grapes, because she had Concords trained along the fence and on an arbor.

Making grape preserves that summer with my grandmother remains one of my favorite memories, and I look forward each year to the brief season, which varies from state to state, when I can buy these native American "slip-skin" grapes at farmers' markets and roadside stands. My waste-not-want-not grandmother would be proud that I know wonderful uses for those vines we would pull down and for the grape leaves as well.

Early English accounts of the Carolina coast speak of vines so fragrant that sailors could smell them days before the boats reached land. Nowadays, agricultural spraying that coincides with the vines' blooming often prevents the fruit from setting. Fortunately, in the Lowcountry, both scuppernongs and muscadines have taken well to cultivation and are widely available in late August and early September. Roger Larsson's Lowcountry Winery on James Island just south of Charleston produces a delightful sweet muscadine wine, Carolina Rosé. It is naturally fermented but has an alcohol content of about 13 percent, more like fortified wines and spirits, and is served as an apéritif.

Greeks were among the earliest of the settlers in the Lowcountry, and many culinary traditions thought of as purely southern—such as watermelon rind preserves—have long histories in the Mediterranean. Charleston's Greek Ladies Philoptochos Society first published its excellent *Popular Greek Recipes* in 1958, including instructions for canning grapevine leaves. Leaves are best gathered in the spring and early summer, when they are large and bright green. The fruits mature in late summer. Then, in the fall, just as the leaves begin to drop, vines can be pulled down—while they are still somewhat green and flexible—and used in wreaths or cut into foot-long twigs for grilling. If there's a hunter in your family, have him or her bring home some vines while out in the woods in the fall. The bright yellow and red leaves are unmistakable.

The English had embraced all sorts of pickling and preserving ideas from Asia when Charleston was settled. In India, the seeds of grapes are often ground into chutneys, but the seeds of our native slip-skin varieties are far too bitter for the American palate. If you do not live in the Lowcountry, try any slip-skin variety available in your area. Concords are delicious in these recipes, but they are sweeter than scuppernongs, so you may want to add a bit of lemon peel and juice and/or reduce the sugar if you're using Concords.

Preserved Grapevine Leaves

Gather grapevine leaves in early summer when they are still tender, then preserve them in brine according to this recipe.

    50 to 75 **freshly picked grape leaves**
        ½ **cup pure salt**
        2 **quarts water**

Wash the leaves well and stack them in piles of 10 leaves per pile. Roll each little pile of leaves into a cigar shape. Add the salt to the water in a wide nonreactive pot and bring to a boil. Add the rolls of leaves to the brine, turn off the heat, and, using tongs, place the rolls into a sterilized wide-mouth pint jar, packing it tightly. Pour the brine in to fill the jar ¼ inch from the rim. Seal the jar and store in a cool, dark place. No need to process these heavily brined grape leaves. They will last about a year.

When you're ready to use the leaves, remove a roll of leaves, unroll it, and place in a bowl of warm water for easy handling. Rinse each leaf well before using. If the leaves are too tough, simmer them for 10 minutes in water. After opening, store the jar in the refrigerator. Use for Stuffed Grape Leaves, page 54.

SPICED GRAPES

The recipe for spiced grapes that appears in *Charleston Receipts* is found throughout the South in cookbooks that antedate the Lowcountry classic. The tradition of serving spiced fruits with meats goes back to medieval England, with its spiced barberries. Without the cranberries of northern bogs, it is far more likely that early Charleston settlers served local grapes with their fall harvest feasts of venison and wild fowl. I make spiced grapes in much smaller batches than called for in the older recipes, reducing the sugar and spice and adding some onion and lemon juice and zest.

MAKES ABOUT 1 PINT

2 pounds slip-skin grapes (Concords, muscadines, catawbas, or scuppernongs)
1 teaspoon *Quatre-Épices* (page 32)
¾ cup white or cider vinegar
1 medium onion, chopped (about ¾ cup)
½ pound (about 1 cup) sugar
grated zest and juice of 1 lemon

Remove any stems from the grapes, then pulp them by squeezing them with the stem end pointed down into a large saucepan. The pulp of the fruit will pop out. Set the skins aside.

Add the spices and vinegar to the pot and cook over medium heat until the seeds loosen, about 5 or 10 minutes.

Pass the mixture through a colander to remove the seeds, then return the vinegar and pulp mixture to the pot. Add the skins and the remaining ingredients, bring to a boil, and continue to cook until thick. Put the spiced grapes in a sterilized jar and seal. Process in a boiling water bath for 10 minutes.

GRAPE PRESERVES

Many cookbooks tell us that grapes do not have enough pectin to jell, but this is simply not true of the native slip-skin varieties. If you follow a few simple guidelines, jelly making is both easy and a sure success. Don't try to make big batches of jelly, and be sure to include the skins (where the pectin is) or at least one fourth of the volume in green, unripe fruit. There is really no mystique to jelly making at all; what's required is just a bit of patience. The jelly test is described in innumerable cookbooks—and none of them can replace experience. Quite simply, the jelling point is reached when the jelly spills off a spoon in a sheet rather than drops. Or test your kitchen thermometer to see at exactly what temperature water boils, then take the jelly to exactly 8 degrees over that temperature. If you remove your fruit from the heat before it has jelled, don't despair: you can always reduce it for a sauce or serve it over pancakes and waffles. If you cook it too long, so that it is rubbery, you can add some bourbon or scotch to it or melt it either alone or with a little wine and seasonings and use it as a glaze or in a quick stove-top chutney.

This is a two-day recipe, but it's quite easy to make.

GRAPE JELLY

MAKES ABOUT 1 PINT

---

4 cups (about 1½ pounds) slip-skin grapes, at least ¼ of them unripe
¼ cup water
sugar

Stem and crush the grapes, add to the water in a large nonreactive pot, bring to a boil, and simmer for 15 minutes. Strain all of the juice out of the mixture and allow to sit in a cool place overnight.

The next day, strain the juice again to remove the tartrate crystals that should have settled out during the night, clinging to the bottom and sides of the container. Measure the juice and add half the volume of juice in sugar. In a heavy kettle, boil rapidly until the jelly sheets from a cold metal spoon or until the mixture registers 220° on a candy thermometer. Pour the jelly into hot sterilized jars and seal. Process for 5 minutes in a boiling water bath.

GRAPE JAM

Jam includes the tart skins of grapes and is far more flavorful than clear jelly. Remove the skins from the grapes (page 306), and, if desired, run them through a grinder or chop them in a blender or processor (I leave mine whole).

Cook the skins of the grapes very gently for 15 to 20 minutes, adding the slightest amount of water necessary to keep them from sticking to the pot.

In another pot over high heat cook the pulp until the seeds loosen, then push it through a colander to remove the seeds. Add the pulp to the skins and measure. Add three quarters of the quantity in sugar and cook the entire mixture rapidly for about 10 minutes. Continue cooking until the jelling point (220°) is reached, stirring often to prevent sticking. Pour into hot sterilized jars and seal. Process in a boiling water bath for 10 minutes.

HARD SAUCE

So many holdovers from English colonial days are apparent in Lowcountry cooking. Sweets of all sorts are still called puddings, and they are offered with the traditional hard sauce as accompaniment, especially during the holidays from Thanksgiving to New Year's. A condiment for desserts, hard sauce is a Lowcountry staple. The recipe in *Charleston Receipts* of 1950 makes a point of calling for *real* butter.

Beat equal weights of butter and sugar together until the mixture is very light and fluffy. Add an egg white for every cup of butter and continue beating. Then add, a little at a time, whatever flavoring strikes your fancy or complements your dessert—a couple of tablespoons of bourbon or rum, grated lemon zest or nutmeg, or crushed mint leaves. Hard sauce is served cold (i.e., hard) to melt on the warm puddings and cobblers it tops.

MAYONNAISE

I use two mayonnaise formulas at home. Sarah Rutledge's version of 1847, "to be eaten with cold meat or fowl," calls for mustard, a common ingredient in modern recipes; it is otherwise true to the Mediterranean classic. Use the finest, fruitiest extra-virgin olive oil and serve the unctuous sauce on tomato aspic (page 212) and sandwiches. The second recipe, made with a whole egg in a blender, goes into composed dishes such as pimiento cheese (page 43).

CLASSIC MAYONNAISE

The Carolina Housewife tells us that the sauce "should look perfectly smooth. . . . With shrimp or oysters, a little red pepper rubbed in is an improvement."

MAKES ¾ CUP

  1 large egg yolk
 ½ teaspoon salt
     dash of cayenne pepper
2½ teaspoons fresh lemon juice or white vinegar
½ to ¾ cup extra-virgin olive oil

Make sure all ingredients and equipment are at room temperature. Use a large heavy mixing bowl or put a wet towel under a mixing bowl in the sink so that it doesn't move around while you are making the sauce: you will need both hands.

Place the egg yolk in the mixing bowl and whisk until it is light in color. Add the salt, cayenne, and ½ teaspoon of the lemon juice or vinegar and beat in well. Beat in the oil *very slowly,* by droplets at first, then letting it barely trickle from a measuring cup with a spout. The sauce will thicken as the oil is emulsified. Mayonnaise made with 1 large yolk should take ¾ cup of oil, but if the sauce starts to look oily, stop immediately. Whisk in the remaining lemon juice or vinegar. Store in a tightly capped container in the refrigerator. Use within 1 week.

BLENDER MAYONNAISE

If you have a hand-held blender, such as the one made by Braun ("blender on a stick"), you needn't slowly drip the oil in—just put all the ingredients (in this order: the egg, the lemon juice, the oil, then the seasonings) into the mixing bowl, blending constantly until all of the oil is emulsified.

MAKES A LITTLE MORE THAN A CUP

½ teaspoon dry mustard *or* 1 teaspoon prepared
¼ teaspoon salt
1 large egg
1 cup peanut oil
1 tablespoon fresh lemon juice

Put the mustard, salt, and egg in a blender and blend for about 20 seconds. Add the oil very slowly, in droplets, and blend until all of the oil has been bound with the egg mixture and the mayonnaise is thick and creamy. Add the lemon juice and blend briefly to incorporate.

Note: I make several variations on this simple mayonnaise by varying the type of oil that I use. When I have used a jar of my sun-dried tomatoes (page 324), I use that intensely orange-colored oil to make a mayonnaise that I use on avocados and crab cakes. I also make a basil oil by filling a jar of olive oil with fresh basil stalks and leaving them in the oil for several weeks. Mayonnaise made with this greenish, pungent oil is the best dressing for a tomato sandwich.

OKRA PICKLES

Okra pickles are my favorite. All across the South the recipes are just about the same. This recipe looks simple, but in fact the pickles are time-consuming to prepare because you must tightly pack the wide-mouthed jars so that the stem ends alternate up and down (both to fill the jar and to keep the okra from floating to the top). The beauty of this recipe is that the quantity of liquid just fills each jar so that the okra pods sit in no more than they can absorb. Let them rest for two months to ripen, then chill them well before you serve them.

I live on the edge of Ansonborough in the downtown historic district of Charleston. The horse- and mule-drawn carriages full of tourists pass my door each day, and I hear the tour guides saying as they point to my building that the first suburb in America begins here. A dubious distinction, perhaps, but my friends and neighbors call these pickles of mine "Ansonborough Gold." One of my favorite ways to enjoy them is in a glass of chilled Russian vodka.

If you do not grow your own okra, try to find very fresh hand-picked okra, all the same finger length for pickling. Each pound of okra will yield two pints of pickles. Multiply or divide the recipe if you like; you won't have any problems.

MAKES 6 PINTS

---

      3 **pounds small young okra pods, all about the same size**
    12 **garlic cloves, peeled**
6 to 12 **fresh hot peppers (see *Note*)**
      1 **tablespoon mustard seeds (½ teaspoon per jar)**
      3 **cups water**
   ¼ **cup pure salt**
      6 **cups white vinegar**

Wash the okra and trim the ends of the stems down to, but not including any of, the pod. Pack the okra tightly in the jars, alternating stems up and down, then divide the garlic, peppers, and mustard among the jars.

Bring the water, salt, and vinegar to a boil, then pour it over the okra to within ½ inch of the rims. Place a lid and ring on each jar, lower them into the canning kettle, and process for 10 minutes at a full boil.

(continued)

Remove the jars from the water, set aside to cool, and check to be sure each lid has sealed, refrigerating any that do not. Finish tightening any loose screw bands and store the pickles for 2 months before eating.

Note: Use one or two per jar to taste. I use one ripe Thai pepper, which is very hot, per jar. If you are not sure how much to use, put one in some of the jars and two in others; you will then know what to do next year.

PEACHES

Spaniards had brought figs, pomegranates, and peaches to the region a hundred years before Carolina was founded by the English. Naturalized and well established, these and other exotica were taken for granted by Charlestonians from the beginning, even though peaches won't grow on the coast. The nearest orchard to the "Holy City" is about 60 miles inland, but as soon as the first clingstones begin to ripen, trucks full of half-bushel baskets appear along the Ocean Highway and in suburban parking lots for the rest of the summer.

I wait until the first freestones appear (they are easier to work with— and often more delicious), then buy myself a half-bushel basket or two and forfeit one July day to the kitchen. It's a labor of love to cook peaches in the heat of summer when you'd rather be having them out of hand, in ice cream, or in daiquiris, but it is well worth the effort. One day of cooking peaches, then I'm free to enjoy them fresh for the rest of their season— and I have a pantry full of delicacies for the fall and winter.

Boiling a fresh peach in spiced vinegar and sugar may not seem to be an entirely sane project. But spiced peaches appear not only in all the old Carolina cookbooks but also in the 18th- and 19th-century English and even French cookbooks, which led the way for Lowcountry cooks. Elizabeth David suggests serving them alongside ham or turkey, and indeed no taste so conjures up childhood Thanksgivings and Christmases for me as these sweet pickled globes served here in lieu of the New Englander's cranberry sauce.

Go ahead and buy a half-bushel of tree-ripened peaches from a reliable source. It will weigh about 22 pounds, and the count will be from 75 to 100 peaches. The dozen hardest ones can be spiced. Another dozen or so can be dried as leather (see page 276). Children especially love these homemade "fruit rollups." Another 2 dozen can go for ice cream or daiquiris. And the remaining peck will give you 10 pints of my exotic chutney. Remove the kernels inside the pits, and you can make a quart of ratifia (noyau) as well.

Spiced Peaches

I make one big jar (1.5-liter clamp-lid jar, such as LeParfait brand) of spiced peaches to serve during the holiday season at one of our big family meals.

> 3 pounds (8 to 14 small to medium) perfectly ripe, but firm peaches,
>   with no blemishes
>   whole cloves
> 1 cup white vinegar
> 1 pound (2⅓ cups) sugar
> 1 cinnamon stick
>   a 2-inch piece of crystallized ginger

Drop the peaches in boiling water and allow them to boil for about a minute. Plunge them into cold water, peel them, and stick a clove into each peach.

Bring the remaining ingredients to a boil, add peaches, and cook uncovered over a low boil until they are tender, but still whole, about 20 minutes.

Pack the peaches and liquid in a sterilized jar and store in a cool, dark, dry pantry until the holiday season.

Serve with turkey or country ham, using some of the juice to make candied yams (page 208).

FRESH PEACH AND COCONUT CHUTNEY

This recipe calls for about a peck of ripe fresh peaches, minus the three or four you eat out of hand over the sink as you are peeling and stoning them. Most chutney recipes call for firm fruit, but here the desired chunkiness is provided by the coconuts, and the intense flavor of ripe fruit is a foil for the spiciness.

Peel the peaches like tomatoes, by dropping them into boiling water for a few seconds to loosen the skins.

MAKES 5 QUARTS

10 pounds peaches, peeled and pitted
10 (about 4 pounds) onions, peeled and chopped
 3 coconuts, about 2½ pounds meat, removed from the shell, pared,
      and diced into ½- to ¾-inch cubes (page 245)
6½ pounds sugar (about 15 cups)
10 jalapeño peppers, fresh or pickled, seeded and chopped
 ½ pound (about 8 inches) fresh ginger, peeled and grated
 2 quarts white vinegar
      fresh mint sprigs (optional)

Sterilize 5 quart canning jars and lids and have ready for use.

Crush the peaches in your hands, but do not chop them into small pieces.

Boil all of the ingredients, except the mint, together in a preserving kettle until the onions are transparent and the desired consistency is reached. (I like it to be watery so that I can use it as a poaching liquid, but you can cook it longer so that it thickens.) Pack in sterilized jars. Stick a fresh sprig of mint in each jar, if desired, before sealing and process jars in a boiling water bath for 10 minutes.

Let the chutney sit for a few weeks before using. You can simmer shrimp in it, bake a pork roast in it, or use it as a condiment. It is especially tasty with fresh field peas and rice and as a sauce for grilled fish (page 73).

PEANUT SALAD DRESSING

Salad dressings made with egg whites are new to the Lowcountry, brought on by the health crazes of recent years. The peanuts and peppers in this one give it a Lowcountry flavor. Toss it over any sort of salad greens or over blanched asparagus or green beans.

MAKES ENOUGH TO DRESS 3 POUNDS GREEN BEANS (TO FEED 8)
AS A SALAD ASIDE A SOUP OR STEW

2 large egg whites
  juice of 2 small lemons (¼ cup)
1 teaspoon hot red pepper flakes
¾ cup peanut oil or other lightly flavored oil
½ cup dry-roasted, salted peanuts
  salt and freshly ground black pepper to taste

Beat the egg whites, lemon juice, red pepper, and oil together until the dressing is uniformly creamy. Chop the peanuts roughly but evenly in a food processor, working in a series of quick bursts so as not to render the nuts oily. Add the nuts to the dressing and mix in. Season with salt and pepper.

PEAR CHIPS

Charlestonians still refer to their preserves of chopped pears or pumpkins as "chips." Chips appear with biscuits and sour cream or alongside grilled fowl, and, as the Junior League suggests in *Charleston Receipts,* they are "delicious on ice cream."

If you're using very hard pears, poach them first in water until tender, then use the cooking water to make the sugar syrup.

MAKES 5 PINTS

1 quart water or pineapple juice
4 cups sugar
4 pounds pears, peeled, seeded, and uniformly "chipped" (chopped)
2 unpeeled lemons, seeded and thinly sliced

Make a syrup by boiling the water and sugar together in a heavy-bottomed nonreactive pot for 5 minutes. Add the pears and lemons and cook at a low boil until the pears are transparent and the syrup thickens, anywhere from 30 minutes to over an hour, depending on the pears. Pack in sterilized jars and seal. Process for 10 minutes in a boiling water bath or store in the refrigerator.

PEAR RELISH

Our local pears are too hard to eat out of hand, but they are delicious cooked. They're usually put into relishes such as this one, to be served alongside vegetables and meats.

MAKES ABOUT 9 PINTS

1 peck pears, peeled, seeded, and chopped
5 medium to large onions, peeled and quartered
6 medium bell peppers, 3 red and 3 green, seeded
2 fresh red cayenne peppers *or* 1 whole dried
1 tablespoon mustard seeds
1 tablespoon whole cloves
3 cinnamon sticks
1 tablespoon ground turmeric
3 cups sugar
1 quart white vinegar
1 tablespoon pure salt

Run the first 7 ingredients through a meat grinder set with the coarse disk, then add them to the remaining ingredients in a nonreactive pot. Boil for about an hour, then pour into sterilized jars and seal. Process for 20 minutes in a boiling water bath.

GOLDEN PEAR CHUTNEY

Lowcountry cooking is full of ideas that seem foreign to outsiders. This sweet and spicy chutney is the perfect foil for salty country ham. Ground together, the two form a paste for memorable appetizers.

MAKES ABOUT 5 PINTS

3 pounds hard, underripe pears, peeled, seeded, and chopped (about 6 cups)
3 cups light or dark brown sugar
3 cups apple cider vinegar
1 tablespoon mustard seeds
2 teaspoons cayenne pepper
¼ pound crystallized ginger, chopped (about ⅔ cup)
1 teaspoon ground cinnamon
½ teaspoon *Quatre-Épices* (page 32)
1 cup dark raisins
1 cup light raisins
2 cups chopped onion
1 lemon, peeled and thinly sliced

Cook the pears in water to cover until they are medium-soft. Drain, saving the water, then make a syrup of the water in which the pears were cooked and the brown sugar by boiling in a large nonreactive pot until thick, about 20 to 30 minutes. While the syrup is boiling, add the remaining ingredients to the pears, then mix everything together and cook for about 30 minutes or until the raisins are softened, the onions are transparent, and the chutney has a good thick consistency. Transfer to sterilized jars and seal; process in a boiling water bath for 10 minutes.

PEPPERS

There are a half-dozen excellent books dedicated solely to the capsicums—and a dizzying assortment of species in the genus, from the benign bells and bananas to fiery chilies, birds, and bonnets. Native to tropical America, peppers were readily assimilated into the cuisines of the warmer climes, adding relish to the rice-based diet of Southeast Asia and spice to West African greens. Columbus took the plants to the Iberian peninsula, and they quickly gained favor across Europe and Asia as well. Hungarian and Indian cuisine were forever transformed.

By the time the Lowcountry was settled, hot pepper was considered an invariable ingredient in turtle dishes, which had been imported to England from the West Indies. West African slaves and Sephardic Jews in the Caribbean would have already been familiar with the hot peppers endemic to the islands where many came prior to their arrival in Carolina.

No Lowcountry pantry is without a jar of pickled peppers, and kitchen gardens have long boasted numerous peppers, both hot and mild. Wildly promiscuous, new varieties appear yearly in gardens where they are allowed to crossbreed. The following recipes are typical of the Lowcountry's ways with peppers.

HOT PICKLED PEPPERS

Bunky Chinnis of Ravenel, South Carolina, south of Charleston, grows jalapeños, banana peppers, and cayennes in his summer gardens, then puts them away as they mature. This is my version of his pickling recipe, which you can divide in half without fear of failure.

MAKES 4 QUARTS

———

mixed hot peppers
long slices of carrot (optional)
1 garlic clove, peeled, per jar

FOR THE PICKLE:

    1½ quarts white vinegar

    3 cups water

    ½ cup pure salt

    1 large *or* 2 medium onions, peeled and chopped (1½ cups)

    2 tablespoons (⅛ cup) mustard seeds (if you like them very hot; if
        not, use ⅛ cup celery seeds)

Pack 4 sterilized quart jars, or an equivalent, with mixed hot peppers. (Wear rubber gloves while working with the peppers.) Add some long slices of carrots to the jar for color and diversity if you wish. Add the garlic. Mix the ingredients for the pickle and boil in a nonreactive pot for 30 minutes, covered.

After 30 minutes, pour the boiling liquid over the peppers in the jar. Seal and process in a boiling water bath for 10 minutes.

SWEET PEPPER RELISH

Make this sweet pepper relish in midsummer, when bell peppers are red and sweet and sweet onions such as Wadmalaws and Vidalias are available (see page 29 for sources). Use it with spicy pâtés and with sausages such as Oyster Sausage.

MAKES 2 PINTS

———

    4 large red bell peppers, seeded, ribbed, and roughly chopped (about
        4 cups)

    4 medium sweet onions, peeled and roughly chopped (about 3 cups)

    1 quart boiling water

    2 tablespoons (⅛ cup) pure salt

    ½ cup sugar

    ½ cup white vinegar

Put the peppers and onions in a large nonreactive mixing bowl or pot and cover with the boiling water. Allow to sit until the water has cooled, about 30 minutes, then drain into a large colander. Sprinkle the salt over the vegetables and allow them to drain thoroughly for several hours. Proceeding in batches, put the drained vegetables into a food processor and process in quick bursts to finely mince them. Add the vegetables to the sugar and vinegar in a nonreactive pot and boil for 5 minutes. Put into sterilized jars and seal, processing in a boiling water bath for 10 minutes, or storing the relish in the refrigerator if not processed.

ROASTED RED PEPPER PUREE

My mother rarely ate bell peppers—green or ripe red—unless they were peeled. I vividly remember the day she discovered how easy they were to peel—and the added flavor—when they were roasted first. I use roasted peppers in pimiento cheese (page 43), Italian style as a salad, and in this delicious puree for fried bean or crab cakes.

> 3 or 4 ripe red bell peppers
> 2 scallions, white part and a little of the green, chopped
> ¾ cup dry white wine
> 6 Italian flat-leaf parsley sprigs, finely minced
> salt and freshly ground black pepper to taste

First, roast the peppers by placing them in a very hot oven or by applying direct heat to them, preferably an open flame such as a charcoal grill or the gas flame on your stove top, or you may place them under the broiler of your oven. Roast them until the skin blisters and turns black, turning them with tongs as the skin chars. Burn only the skin—not the flesh—of the peppers. Place them in a paper bag and fold down the top for a few minutes so that the charred skins steam away from the flesh. After about 10 minutes, when the peppers have cooled somewhat, remove them from the bag and place them on a cutting board. Peel away the skins, then seed them by pulling the stem end away from the pod. The seeds will usually pull out from the pepper with the stem.

Add the scallions to the white wine in a heavy-bottomed saucepan and reduce by one half. Add the parsley and roasted, peeled, and seeded peppers and puree the mixture until evenly smooth. Season to taste with salt and pepper. Use immediately.

PLUM SAUCE

Use this sauce with game dishes and as a foil for hot and spicy grilled items.

MAKES ABOUT 2 CUPS

1½ cups pitted ripe plums
½ cup mulberry wine (page 289) or port

Simmer the fruit and the wine together in a saucepan for a few minutes, until it begins to thicken, strain well, and cool to room temperature before serving.

TOMATOES

Years ago in my research I found written evidence of tomatoes growing in Lowcountry gardens long before any mention of them in the other of the original thirteen colonies. The final word on the path of the tomato has not yet been written, but several culinary historians are working on the history of "love apples," as they were once called. One bright sunny day in June, when the first tomato crop in the Lowcountry was at its height, I received in the mail a copy of a page from William Salmon's *Botanologia. The English Herbal: or, The History of Plants*, published in London in 1710. Karen Hess, the American culinary historian, had sent me her wonderful find: not only an entire chapter on love apples, but the following:

> They grow naturally in hot Countries, as in Ethiopia, Barbary, Egypt, Syria, Spain, Italy, and other hot Countries: Some report they were first brought to us from Peru; and I have seen them grow in Carolina, which is the SouthEast part of Florida. . . .

Carolina was then, of course, the *northeastern* part of Florida, but I have little doubt that tomatoes were growing here then. The Spanish and Portuguese, who had been not only explorers, but slave traders as well, had taken to the tomato early on. Sephardic Jews who had settled in the

Caribbean later moved to Charleston, possibly bringing the tomato with them. And Hess herself, a stickler for documentation and historical accuracy, has lent credence to Helen Mendes's claim in *The African Heritage Cookbook* that the slaves had long been cooking with tomatoes in West Africa: "If so, it would have been due to the Portuguese, who came to West Africa in the fifteenth century and had early and enthusiastically taken to the tomato."

Whenever the tomato arrived in the Lowcountry, it was being grown for food in 1764 by Henry Laurens in his Charleston garden—overlooking the Cooper River—nearly 20 years before Thomas Jefferson, who has been credited with single-handedly importing them, mentions them. And by 1770, when Harriott Pinckney Horry (1748–1830) wrote down her recipes at her plantation north of Charleston, tomatoes were firmly established in the gardens of the area; her recipe "To Keep Tomatoos [*sic*] for Winter Use" has been called the earliest reference to tomatoes in American cookbooks. Harriott's cooking surely influenced her young cousin Sarah Rutledge (born 1782), whose *Carolina Housewife* of 1847 is a classic of Lowcountry cuisine. Five pages of tomato recipes include the following, titled "To Keep Tomatoes the Whole Year." If you think that sun-dried tomatoes are a trendy new Italian fad, think again: here they are, nearly 150 years ago— and in the Lowcountry! I've tried sun-drying tomatoes in humid Charleston: it takes three dry, hot sunny days or the tomatoes begin to mold or mildew. Cooking some of the water out of the tomatoes first is a brilliant local touch, and I prepare a batch of these every year, drying the little cakes in a low oven.

SUN-DRIED TOMATOES FROM THE CAROLINA HOUSEWIFE

TO KEEP TOMATOES
THE WHOLE YEAR

Take the tomatoes, when perfectly ripe, and scald them in hot water, in order to take off the skin easily. When skinned, boil them well in a little sugar or salt, but no water. Then spread them in cakes about an inch thick, and place the cakes in the sun. They will, in three or four days, be sufficiently dried to pack away in bags, which should hang in a dry place.

The Carolina Housewife, 1847

To use the recipe today, simply sprinkle salt to taste over the stewing tomatoes (I once used an entire bushel, which produced a quart jar of patties—enough for a year.). When the water separates out, pour the tomatoes through a colander, saving the liquid for soup—a little reheated with leftover Frogmore Stew and garnished with fresh basil or cilantro is a treat—or to make red rice. Return the tomatoes to the pan and cook very slowly, stirring occasionally to keep them from sticking, until they are virtually free of water and may be shaped into patties.

Place the patties on greased baking sheets and bake in a very slow oven (140–160°) until the patties are dry and leathery but still pliable. It may take 6 to 8 hours, or it may take much longer, depending on your oven. Warming ovens are perfect. Place the patties in a wide-mouth jar, cover with your favorite olive oil, and use as you would tomato paste or sun-dried tomatoes (see recipe for Pasta with Country Ham and Sun-Dried Tomatoes, page 136). When your jar is empty, use the oil to flavor homemade mayonnaise.

PICCALILLI, OR
GREEN TOMATO RELISH

Many of us in the Lowcountry grow our own tomatoes or live near tomato farms. Choose rock-hard, unblemished, very round fruits with no sign of red for this delicious relish, a favorite local embellishment for rice dishes, roast meats, and vegetables.

MAKES 6 PINTS

FOR THE VEGETABLES:

    5 pounds green tomatoes, cored and ground or finely minced
    1 pound (2 green and 1 red) bell peppers, ground or finely minced
    1 pound (about 3 average) onions, ground or finely minced
1 or 2 fresh hot peppers, such as jalapeño (optional)
    ½ cup pure salt

FOR THE PICKLING SOLUTION:

    4½ cups white vinegar
    1½ cups sugar
    2 tablespoons (⅛ cup) mustard seeds
    1 tablespoon celery seeds

Grind and mix all the vegetables together and sprinkle with the salt. Allow to sit for 3 or 4 hours, then drain well in a colander, squeezing all the excess moisture out of the mixture.

Simmer the pickling ingredients for 15 minutes, add the vegetable mixture, bring to a boil, and add to sterilized jars. Seal. Process in a boiling water bath for 10 minutes.

PORT-SCENTED TOMATO CATSUP

Tomato catsup should taste like tomatoes and spice, mellowed and blended like a fine wine. Traditionally, catsups were added to other sauces and dishes to season and finish them, not served as the sauce itself. *The Carolina Housewife* of 1847 includes recipes for catsups made from walnuts and mushrooms as well as tomato, wisely recommending that the cook add "the best port wine" to each bottle of tomato catsup. Port adds an intriguing roundness of flavor that the commercial brands try, unsuccessfully, to achieve with sugar. Be sure to let the catsup age for at least a month before using.

The traditional way of making catsup on top of the stove is tricky business, because you must stir the pot constantly to prevent the thickening sauce from burning; the slightest bit of burn will flavor the whole pot. It can take as much as an hour; I'm not that patient. I finish the sauce in a slow oven, stirring occasionally. You could also use a slow cooker for this last stage. This recipe takes longer, but the cooking is mostly unattended.

MAKES A LITTLE MORE THAN 6 PINTS

——

1 peck (8 quarts) ripe, meaty tomatoes
  a handful of fresh herbs such as basil, thyme, oregano, parsley, and
     marjoram
1 large celery rib
1 large onion, peeled and quartered; each quarter stuck with a clove
2 bay leaves
1 tablespoon whole allspice
1 teaspoon cayenne pepper
1 teaspoon sugar
1 teaspoon mustard seeds
2 cups white wine vinegar
3 cups port (despite Sarah, don't use "the best")

Wash the tomatoes and quarter them, and, without stirring, simmer them in a large, heavy-bottomed pot on top of the stove until the water separates out to the top of the pot (about 45 minutes). Preheat the oven to 350°. Carefully pour off this liquid (save for use in a soup or to cook rice). Pour the pulp into a large roasting pan and add the remaining ingredients except the port, stirring well to mix it all together. Cover and bake until all the flavors have mingled (about 1 hour). Pour through a large sieve, pressing all the last bits of juice and flavor through. Puree, if necessary, the sauce for an even consistency. Lower the oven to 300° and return the sauce to the roasting pan. Cook, uncovered, until very thick, stirring occasionally. It will take anywhere from one to several hours, depending on how watery the mixture is.

In the meantime, sterilize 7 pint jars and lids. When the catsup is very, very thick, remove from the oven. Add the port and stir in well, then ladle the catsup into the clean jars, leaving ½ inch headroom. Wipe the rims clean, add the lids and screw bands, and process in a boiling water bath for 20 minutes.

WATERMELON RIND PRESERVES

The early Greek settlers in Charleston brought with them a tradition of pickling melon rinds. I have adapted this recipe from several Lowcountry sources, reducing the sugar content called for in *Charleston Receipts* and removing the spices before bottling so that the preserves do not turn a dark brown. Note that it takes two days to make these pickles.

MAKES ABOUT 6 PINTS, DEPENDING ON THE SIZE OF THE MELON

FOR THE WATERMELON RIND:
> rind of 1 large watermelon
> 2 cups pickling lime
> 2 gallons water

(continued)

FOR THE PICKLING SOLUTION:

   1 ounce stick cinnamon
   1 ounce whole cloves
   1 quart white vinegar
   4 pounds sugar

Pare all of the green and all of the red from the melon rind, then cut into 1-inch squares. This is quite a job, so invite a friend over to help you and split the pickles. Put them in a nonreactive container with enough lime water to cover, using the proportions above (1 cup lime per gallon of water). Allow to soak overnight.

Drain the lime water off the rind squares, but don't rinse them. Cover with water and cook in a preserving kettle over medium heat for 2 hours. Drain again.

Tie the spices in a piece of cheesecloth and add to the vinegar and sugar. Bring to a boil in the preserving kettle, then add the rind and cook over low heat for an hour. Remove the spices. Pour into hot sterilized jars and seal. Process in a boiling water bath for 10 minutes.

SELECT BIBLIOGRAPHY

Ball, Anne S. *Pinopolis: History of a Pine-land Village*. Moncks Corner, SC: Office Supply & Equipment Co., 1983.

Barry, John M. *Natural Vegetation of South Carolina*. Columbia: University of South Carolina Press, 1980.

Bartram, John. "Diary of a Journey Through the Carolinas, Georgia, and Florida from July 1, 1765, to April 10, 1766," *Transactions of the American Philosophical Society*, New Series, XXXIII, Part 1. Philadelphia, 1942.

Berry, Mrs. Willie S. "*Don't Forget the Parsley*. . . ." Orangeburg, SC: Orangeburg-Calhoun Technical College Foundation, Inc., 1982.

Bowes, Frederick P. *The Culture of Early Charleston*. Chapel Hill: University of North Carolina Press, 1942.

Brewster, Lawrence Fay. *Summer Migrations and Resorts of South Carolina Low-Country Planters*. Durham, NC: Duke University Press, 1947.

Bridenbaugh, Carl. *Cities in Revolt: Urban Life in America, 1743–1776*. New York: Oxford University Press, 1955.

Bronz, Ruth Adams. *Miss Ruby's American Cooking*. New York: Harper & Row, 1989.

Burn, Billie. *Stirrin' the Pots on Daufuskie*. Daufuskie Island, SC: Burn Books, 1985.

Butler, Jon. *The Huguenots in America*. Cambridge, MA: Harvard University Press, 1984.

Caroll, B. R., ed. *Historical Collections of South Carolina*. New York: Harper, 1836.

Clark, Thomas D., ed. *South Carolina: The Grand Tour 1780–1865*. Columbia: University of South Carolina Press, 1973.

Colquitt, Harriet Ross. *The Savannah Cook Book*. Charleston: Walker, Evans, & Cogswell Co., 1933.

David, Elizabeth. *English Bread and Yeast Cookery*. New York: Viking, 1980.

David, Elizabeth. *French Country Cooking*. Middlesex, Great Britain: Penguin Books, 1958.

Davidson, Alan. *North Atlantic Seafood*. New York: Viking, 1979.

Davis, Richard Beale. *Intellectual Life in the Colonial South 1585–1763*. 3 vols. Knoxville: University of Tennessee Press, 1978.

Doar, David. *Rice and Rice Planting in the South Carolina Low Country*. Charleston: The Charleston Museum, 1936.

Dods, Mistress Margaret (Christine Isabel Johnstone). *The Cook and Housewife's Manual*. Edinburgh, 1826.

Dull, Mrs. S. R. *Southern Cooking*. Atlanta: Cherokee Publishing Co., 1989.

Edgar, Walter B., ed. *The Letterbook of Robert Pringle*. Columbia: University of South Carolina Press, 1972.

Egergton, John. *Southern Food*. New York: Alfred A. Knopf, Inc., 1987.

Elliott, William E. *Carolina Sports by Land and Water*. Charleston: Burges & James, 1846.

Fishburne, Anne Sinkler, ed. *Old Receipts from Old St. Johns*. Pinopolis, SC: N.p., n.d.

————. *Belvidere: A Plantation Memory.* Columbia: University of South Carolina Press, 1949.

Fraser, Walter J., Jr. *Charleston! Charleston!* Columbia: University of South Carolina Press, 1989.

Graydon, Nell. *From My House to Your House.* Greenwood, SC: Drinkard Printing Co., Inc., 1968.

Greek Ladies Philoptochos Society. *Popular Greek Recipes.* Charleston: 1958.

Grigson, Jane. *The Art of Charcuterie.* New York: Alfred A. Knopf, Inc., 1968.

Grosvenor, Verta. *Vibration Cooking.* Garden City, NY: Doubleday & Co., 1970.

Harrigan, Elizabeth Ravenel, ed. *Charleston Recollections and Receipts: Rose P. Ravenel's Cookbook.* Columbia: University of South Carolina Press, 1983.

Hedrick, U. P., ed. *Sturtevant's Edible Plants of the World.* New York: Dover, 1919.

Hess, John L., and Karen Hess. *The Taste of America.* New York: Grossman Publishers, 1977.

Hess, Karen. "The American Loaf: A Historical View," *The Journal of Gastronomy,* Volume 3, Number 4, Winter 1987/1988.
————. *The Carolina Rice Kitchen: The African Connection.* Columbia: University of South Carolina Press, 1992.

————, ed. *Martha Washington's Booke of Cookery.* New York: Columbia University Press, 1981.

Heyward, D. C. *Seed from Madagascar.* Chapel Hill: University of North Carolina Press, 1937.

Hirsch, Arthur H. *The Huguenots of Colonial South Carolina.* Hamden and London, CT: Archon Books, 1962.

Holmes, Francis S., ed. *The Southern Farmer and Market Gardener.* Charleston: N.p., 1852.

Hooker, Richard J., ed. *A Colonial Plantation Cookbook: The Receipt Book of Harriott Pinckney Horry, 1770.* Columbia: University of South Carolina Press, 1984.

Huguenin, Mary V., and Anne M. Stoney, eds. *Charleston Receipts.* Charleston: Walker, Evans, & Cogswell Co., 1950.

Hupping, Carol, and the staff of the Rodale Food Center. *Stocking Up III.* Emmaus, PA: Rodale Press, 1986.

Irving, John B. *A Day on the Cooper River.* Charleston: R. L. Bryan, 1842.

Iseley, N. Jane, and Harlan Greene. *Charleston: City of Memory.* Greensboro, NC: Legacy Publications, 1987.

Iseley, N. Jane, and William P. Baldwin, Jr. *Plantations of the Low Country.* Greensboro, North Carolina: Legacy Publications, 1985.

Jones-Jackson, Patricia. *When Roots Die.* Athens: University of Georgia Press, 1987.

Joyner, Charles. *Down by the Riverside: A South Carolina Slave Community.* Chicago: University of Illinois Press, 1984.

Kovacik, Charles F., and John J. Winberry. *South Carolina: The Making of a Landscape.* Columbia: University of South Carolina Press, 1989.

Lawson, John. *A New Voyage to Carolina, 1712.* Edited and with an Introduction by Hugh Talmage Lefler. Chapel Hill: University of North Carolina Press, 1967.

Leiding, Harriette Kershaw. *Historic Houses of South Carolina.* Philadelphia: J. B. Lippincott Co., 1921.

————. *Charleston, Historic and Romantic.* Philadelphia: J. B. Lippincott Co., 1931.

Lenôtre, Gaston. *Lenôtre's Ice Cream and Candies.* Hyman, Philip and Mary

Hyman, translators. Hauppauge, NY: Barron's Educational Series, Inc., 1979.

Leslie, Eliza. *Directions for Cookery in Its Various Branches.* Philadelphia: Carey & Hart, 1837.

Littlefield, Daniel C. *Rice and Slaves: Ethnicity and the Slave Trade in Colonial South Carolina.* Baton Rouge: Louisiana State University Press, 1981.

Lumpkin, Julie, and Nancy Coleman Wooten, eds. *The Southeastern Wildlife Cookbook.* Columbia: University of South Carolina Press, 1989.

Maynard, Gloria Mann, Meredith Maynard Chase, and Holly Maynard Jenkins. *Caterin' to Charleston.* Charleston: Merritt Publishing Co., 1981.

McClane, A. J. *The Encyclopedia of Fish Cookery.* New York: Henry Holt and Co., 1977.

McCulloch-Williams, Martha. *Dishes and Beverages of the Old South.* Knoxville: University of Tennessee Press, 1988.

McGee, Harold. *On Food and Cooking.* New York: Charles Scribner's Sons, 1984.

McNeill, F. Marian. *The Scots Kitchen.* Glasgow: Blackie & Son, 1929.

Mendelson, Anne. "Regional Cooking." *The Journal of Gastronomy,* Volume 4, Number 3, Autumn 1988.

Moise, Ethel M. *Cook Book of the Family Favorites.* Sumter, SC: N.p., 1974.

Montagné, Prosper. *Larousse Gastronomique.* New York: Crown Publishers, Inc., 1961.

Morton, Dr. Julia F. *Folk Remedies of the Low Country.* Miami: E. A. Seeman, Publisher, 1974.

Neal, Bill. *Biscuits, Spoonbread, and Sweet Potato Pie.* New York: Alfred A. Knopf, Inc., 1990.

Neal, William F. *Bill Neal's Southern Cooking.* Chapel Hill: University of North Carolina Press, 1985.

Neuffer, Claude and Irene. *Correct Mispronunciations of Some South Carolina Names.* Columbia: University of South Carolina Press, 1983.

Orangeburg's Choice Recipes. Orangeburg, South Carolina: Walter D. Berry, 1948.

Ortiz, Elisabeth Lambert. *The Complete Book of Caribbean Cooking.* New York: M. Evans & Co., Inc., 1973.

The Pee Dee Pepper Pot. Darlington, SC: Trinity Methodist Church, 1948.

Pickney, Elise. *Thomas and Elizabeth Lamboll: Early Charleston Gardeners.* Charleston: The Charleston Museum, 1969.

Randolph, Mary. *The Virginia House-Wife.* With Historical Notes and Commentaries by Karen Hess. Columbia: University of South Carolina Press, 1984.

Ravenel, Rose P. *Charleston Recollections and Receipts,* ed. Elizabeth Ravenel Harrigan. Columbia: University of South Carolina Press, 1983.

Recipe Book of Eliza Lucas Pinckney 1756. Charleston: Charleston Lithographing Co., 1936.

Rhett, Blanche S. *Two Hundred Years of Charleston Cooking.* Columbia: University of South Carolina Press, 1930.

Rogers, George C., Jr., *Charleston in the Age of the Pinckneys.* Columbia: University of South Carolina Press, 1980.

————, ed. *The Papers of Henry Laurens, Volume Four.* Columbia: University of South Carolina Press, 1974.

Rosen, Robert N. *A Short History of Charleston.* San Francisco: Lexikos, 1982.

Rutledge, Sarah. *The Carolina Housewife.* Charleston: W. R. Babcock & Co., 1847.

Savage, Henry, Jr. *River of the Carolinas: The Santee.* New York: Rinehart & Co., 1956.

Scaravelli, Paola, and Jon Cohen. *Mediterranean Harvest.* New York: E. P. Dutton, 1986.

Schneider, Elizabeth. *Uncommon Fruits and Vegetables: A Commonsense Guide.* New York: Harper & Row, 1986.

Stoney, Mrs. Samuel G., ed. *Carolina Rice Cook Book.* Charleston: Carolina Rice Kitchen Association, 1901.

Stoney, Samuel Gaillard. *Plantations of the Carolina Low Country.* Charleston: Carolina Art Association, 1938.

———. *This is Charleston.* Charleston: Carolina Art Association, 1976.

Taylor, Rosser H. *Ante-Bellum South Carolina: A Social and Cultural History.* Chapel Hill: University of North Carolina Press, 1942.

Thornton, P. *The Southern Gardener and Receipt Book.* Columbia, SC: N.p., 1840.

Turner, Lorenzo D. *Africanisms in the Gullah Dialect.* Chicago: University of Chicago Press, 1945.

Van Doren, Mark, ed. *The Travels of William Bartram.* Toronto: Macy-Masius, 1928.

Vick, Oscar N., III. *Gullah Cooking.* Charleston: N.p., 1989.

Vlach, John Michael. *Charleston Blacksmith.* Athens: University of Georgia Press, 1981.

Waring, Mary Joseph. *The Centennial Receipt Book.* Charleston (?): N.p., 1876.

Way, William. *History of the New England Society of Charleston, S.C. for One Hundred Years, 1819–1919.* Charleston: New England Society, 1920.

Whitelaw, Robert N. S., and Alice F. Levkoff. *Charleston Come Hell or High Water: A History in Photographs.* Columbia, SC: R. L. Bryan, 1975.

Wilson, Robert, M.D., D.D. *Half-Forgotten By-Ways of the Old South.* Columbia, SC: The State Company, 1928.

Wolfert, Paula. *The Cooking of South-West France.* Garden City, New York: The Dial Press, 1983.

———. *Couscous and Other Good Food From Morocco.* New York: Harper & Row, 1973.

Wongrey, Jon. *Southern Fish and Seafood Cookbook.* Orangeburg, SC: Sandlapper Publishing, Inc., 1975.

———. *Southern Wildfowl and Wild Game Cookbook.* Orangeburg, SC: Sandlapper Publishing, Inc., 1976.

Workers of the Writers' Project of the Work Projects Administration in the State of South Carolina. *South Carolina: A Guide to the Palmetto State.* New York: Oxford University Press, 1941.

Zukin, Jane. *Dairy-Free Cookbook.* Rocklin, CA: Prima Publishing, 1991.

TEXTUAL ACKNOWLEDGMENTS

We have made a concerted effort to obtain permission to quote from copyrighted works. Grateful acknowledgment is made to the following for permission to reprint previously published material:

Carolina Art Association: Excerpt from *This is Charleston* by Samuel G. Stoney. Copyright © 1976 by Carolina Art Association. Reprinted by permission.

E. P. Dutton: Recipe from *Mediterranean Harvest* by Paola Scaravelli and Jon Cohen. Copyright © 1986 by Paola Scaravelli and Jon Cohen. Used by permission of the publisher, Dutton, an imprint of New American Library, a division of Penguin Books USA Inc.

Harlan Greene: Excerpts from *Charleston: City of Memory* by Harlan Greene. Copyright © 1987 by Legacy Publications. Reprinted by permission.

Verta Grosvenor: Excerpts from *Vibration Cooking, or The Travel Notes of a Geechee Girl* by Verta Grosvenor. Copyright © 1970 by Verta Grosvenor. Reprinted by permission.

Houghton-Mifflin Co.: Excerpt from *The Prince of Tides* by Pat Conroy. Copyright © 1986 by Pat Conroy. Reprinted by permission.

Junior League of Charleston, Inc.: Excerpts from *Charleston Receipts*. Copyright © 1950 by Junior League of Charleston, Inc. Reprinted by permission.

Alfred A. Knopf, Inc.: Excerpt from *Southern Food* by John Egerton. Copyright © 1987 by John Egerton. Excerpt from *Biscuits, Spoonbread, and Sweet Potato Pie* by Bill Neal. Copyright © 1990 by Bill Neal. Reprinted by permission.

Lexikos: Excerpts from *A Short History of Charleston* by Robert Rosen. Copyright © 1982 by Robert Rosen. Reprinted by permission.

Anne Mendelson: Excerpt from "Regional Cooking" by Anne Mendelson. *The Journal of Gastronomy*, Volume 4, Number 3. Copyright © 1988 by The American Institute of Wine & Food. Reprinted by permission.

Orangeburg-Calhoun Technical College Foundation, Inc.: Recipe from *"Don't Forget the Parsley. . . ."* by Mrs. Willie S. Berry. Copyright © 1982 by Orangeburg-Calhoun Technical College Foundation, Inc. Reprinted by permission.

University of Georgia Press: Excerpt from *Charleston Blacksmith* by John Michael Vlach. Copyright © 1981 by University of Georgia Press. Reprinted by permission.

University of South Carolina Press: Excerpts from *A Colonial Plantation Cookbook*, edited by Richard J. Hooker. Copyright © 1984 by University of South Carolina. Excerpts from *The Carolina Housewife* by Sarah Rutledge. Copyright © 1979 by Anna Wells Rutledge. Excerpts from *Two Hundred Years of Charleston Cooking*, gathered by Blanche S. Rhett. Copyright © 1976 by University of South Carolina. Excerpts from *Charleston! Charleston!* by Walter J. Fraser, Jr. Copyright © 1989 by Walter J. Fraser, Jr. Excerpts from

INDEX